Tracking Classical Monsters in Popular Culture

Also published by Bloomsbury

Classics on Screen, Alastair Blanshard and Kim Shahabudin
Mythical Monsters in Classical Literature, Paul Murgatroyd
Fellini's Eternal Rome: Paganism and Christianity in the Films of
Federico Fellini, Alessandro Carrera
Frankenstein and its Classics: The Modern Prometheus from Antiquity to Science
Fiction, Jesse Weiner, Benjamin Eldon Stevens and Brett M. Rogers
Once and Future Antiquities in Science Fiction and Fantasy,
Brett M. Rogers and Benjamin Eldon Stevens

Tracking Classical Monsters in Popular Culture

Liz Gloyn

BLOOMSBURY ACADEMIC
LONDON • NEW YORK • OXFORD • NEW DELHI • SYDNEY

BLOOMSBURY ACADEMIC
Bloomsbury Publishing Plc
50 Bedford Square, London, WC1B 3DP, UK
1385 Broadway, New York, NY 10018, USA

BLOOMSBURY, BLOOMSBURY ACADEMIC and the Diana logo are trademarks
of Bloomsbury Publishing Plc

First published in Great Britain 2020

Cover design: Terry Woodley
Cover image: Harrison Birtwistle's *The Minotaur* at the Royal Opera House Covent Garden in London
(photo by Robbie Jack/Corbis via Getty Images)

A catalogue record for this book is available from the British Library.

Library of Congress Cataloging-in-Publication Data
Names: Gloyn, Liz, author.
Title: Tracking classical monsters in popular culture / Liz Gloyn.
Description: London, UK ; New York, NY : Bloomsbury Academic, 2019. | Includes bibliographical
references, filmography, and index. | Summary: "What is it about ancient monsters that popular culture
still finds so enthralling? Why do the monsters of antiquity continue to stride across the modern world?
In this book, the first in-depth study of how post-classical societies use the creatures from ancient myth,
Liz Gloyn reveals the trends behind how we have used monsters since the 1950s to the present day, and
considers why they have remained such a powerful presence in our shared cultural imagination. She
presents a new model for interpreting the extraordinary vitality that classical monsters have shown, and
their enormous adaptability in finding places to dwell in popular culture without sacrificing their
connection to the ancient world. Her argument takes her readers through a comprehensive tour of
monsters on film and television, from the much-loved creations of Ray Harryhausen in Clash of the Titans
to the monster of the week in Hercules: The Legendary Journeys, before looking in detail at the afterlives
of the Medusa and the Minotaur. She develops a broad theory of the ancient monster and its life after
antiquity, investigating its relation to gender, genre and space to offer a bold and novel exploration of
what keeps drawing us back to these mythical beasts. From the siren to the centaur, all monster lovers
will find something to enjoy in this stimulating and accessible book" – Provided by publisher.
Identifiers: LCCN 2019014053 | ISBN 9781784539344 (hardback) | ISBN 9781350109612 (paperback) |
ISBN 9781350114333 (pdf) | ISBN 9781350114340 (epub)
Subjects: LCSH: Monsters in mass media. | Mythology, Classical, in literature. | Popular culture.
Classification: LCC P96.M6 G56 2019 | DDC 398/.45—dc23
LC record available at https://lccn.loc.gov/2019014053

ISBN: HB: 978-1-7845-3934-4
           PB: 978-1-3501-0961-2
           ePDF: 978-1-3501-1433-3
           eBook: 978-1-3501-1434-0

Typeset by RefineCatch Limited, Bungay, Suffolk
Printed and bound in Great Britain

To find out more about our authors and books visit www.bloomsbury.com
and sign up for our newsletters.

In solidarity with the academic precariat

Contents

Figures

Acknowledgements

Although this book is about monsters, I'm delighted to thank some real heroes who have helped me while I was writing it.

I realised this book needed writing as I worked on my paper for Penny Goodman and Steve Green's 2011 conference on the legacy of Ray Harryhausen and the classical world. Attendees at the conferences on Swords, Sorcery, Sandals and Space (2013), From I, Claudius to Private Eyes (2014), Diversity in Speculative Fiction (2014), Our Mythical Childhood: Chasing Mythical Beasts (2016), the Celtic Classics Conference (2016), Transnational Monstrosity in Popular Culture (2017), Nine Worlds (2017) and the departmental research seminar at the University of Liverpool all gave thoughtful feedback on earlier versions of this research.

Monsters seem to inspire generosity. Alexis Christensen, Catherine Edwards, Jon Greenaway, Clara Shaw Hardy, Stuart McKie, Aven McMaster, Farah Mendlesohn, Carly Silver, Diana Spencer and Jeff Veitch advised me on formative reading. Sam Ridley's MA dissertation on the monstrous in Senecan tragedy neatly coincided with my initial grappling with the foundations of monster theory. Anna Reeve kindly loaned me a book (and showed great patience until I eventually returned it). Toph Marshall and Will Duffy shared their work on classical reception in *Dungeons & Dragons*. Hannah Cornwell pointed me to the case study that opens the book, and Natalie Collins led me to the one which closes it. Bitch Media kept me on point in my readings of popular culture, and several articles published by them feature in the bibliography.

Writers of books are members of many different communities, and I am no exception. My colleagues in the Department of Classics at Royal Holloway, University of London, have been unendingly supportive as I've worked to get this book done, not least in facilitating a sabbatical at the start of the research process. In particular, Siobhan Chomse, Zena Kamash and Efi Spentzou have offered unreserved camaraderie. Nick Lowe has embraced the project with his trademark boundless enthusiasm, including enabling my consumption of vast quantities of *Hercules* and *Xena*. I thank everyone who has engaged with me on Twitter as this book has been progressing – you are too numerous to name, and you are all splendid. David Bullen, Jane Draycott, Howard Hardiman, Naomi Gutierrez, Nyasha Junior, Tony Keen, Helen Lovatt, Miriam Moules, Sharleen

Schier and Lucy Shipley, as well as Bloomsbury Academic's two anonymous readers, gave up their time to read and comment on various drafts. Special mention goes to Catherine Baker and Emma Bridges, who not only read the full thing in draft but looked at new and revised sections afterwards! Amelia Dowler, Tony Keen, Ellie Mackin Roberts and Clare Vernon have listened to my triumphs and tribulations in equal measure. Their company in the British Library has made this book much richer than it would otherwise have been.

Alex Wright first convinced me that I could and should write this book, and championed it tirelessly during his time at I.B. Tauris. Alice Wright has shepherded the project through the production process at Bloomsbury Academic, along with Lily Mac Mahon, Rachel Singleton, Roza I. M. El-Eini and Merv Honeywood. The staff of the British Library, the Institute of Classical Studies and the Essex Library Service, along with Debbie Phillips of Royal Holloway, have helped me access volumes on a range of increasingly esoteric subjects.

Emily Anastasi, Emma Bowen, Chelsea Hawkins, Afsha Khan, Nikki Turner and Chanelle Witchell provided fantastic childcare along with the rest of the staff at Kids Inc. Nurseries. Nicoleta Baltac, Leanne Mundell, Nina Nikolova and Lilia Sarpe made sure this book was written in a clean, if not always tidy, house. Without their labour, this book could not have happened.

Having monsters in the home is no laughing matter. My parents, Erica and Bill, have given me time and space to wrangle them, and have encouraged me in this as in everything else. Geoff has borne the invasion of a cluster of mythical beasts with remarkable aplomb, although we will both be glad to see them leave before they completely run down the drinks cupboard. Rufus has never known a world without this book; the contract for it was signed before he was born. He has been very patient with me when I have needed to look after 'mummy's monsters'. I promise them I will try to leave it a bit longer before I write another book.

Finally, a note on this book's dedication. Since I returned to the UK after completing my PhD in the USA, I have seen higher education in this country move towards a system which relies more and more on casualised fractional contracts while permanent jobs become fewer and fewer. I am watching fantastic, talented, insightful colleagues a year or two out of their PhDs being asked to demonstrate to hiring committees that they are internationally recognised experts in their research fields in order to obtain a ten-month teaching contract. In a marketised education system, early career academics find their time, labour and goodwill exploited, while they are told the experience is somehow good for them. These scholars and teachers battle the monsters of precarious employment every day. They are the only heroes I have time for.

Introduction

When we tell the stories of myth, we usually tell the stories of heroes.

I am tired of heroes.

I am fed up of entitled men who stride through the world as if it owes them something, bringing destruction and carnage in their wake.

Does that put me next in line for the chop? Then take me to the monsters.

***

This book belongs to a strand of classics known as 'classical reception studies', which asks what happens to the cultures of classical Greece and Rome in the post-classical world.[1] I take as my focus Anglo-American popular culture from the 1950s to the present, with a particular interest in what has been produced on film, on television and in literature. I am also interested in monsters.

Stories from ancient myth have proved remarkably resilient in the two millennia since they were originally created. Children's books retelling the familiar stories are still published, films drawing on the old tales continue to be made, computer games inspired by ancient myth attract large followings and attain cult status. One of the central theories of classical reception is that every reception can be influenced by every previous reception – so, for example, every time someone retells the story of Perseus and Medusa, that new version exists in relationship with all of the previous versions, from Ovid's story in the *Metamorphoses* to the version in *Clash of the Titans* and everything in between. Each retelling brings out elements of the story that often tell us more about the culture in which it is retold – the receiving culture – than they do about the ancient world, although reworkings can cast new light on texts we thought were familiar.

But there's a catch (there's always a catch). Academic studies of classical reception and myth have tended to look at the hero: how does the hero get represented? What's at stake in how the hero's actions are shaped? Does it matter whether he (and it's always *he*) falls in love? How is his story (and it's always *his* story) repurposed to meet the needs of the receiving culture? What does ancient heroism mean in the modern world?[2]

I am not interested in these questions.

Instead, I am going to look at the monsters in these myths, the ones who get pushed down under the heroes' feet, but who (against the odds) have themselves survived over the ages. Classics as a discipline has started to look at the monsters who appear in ancient sources and to debate their meaning there, but no one has yet looked properly at the ways in which these classical monsters have crept and slithered into the modern world.

This gap needs filling because classical monsters are *everywhere*. As I have been writing this book, I have been genuinely astonished – not to mention rather overwhelmed – by the number of examples that friends and colleagues have passed on to me. To ignore the fact that classical monsters reproduce in popular culture at a frankly astounding rate means missing a trick about how modern audiences understand the ancient world and its relation to the present.

A cynical part of me wonders whether some of this silence is down to the fact that popular culture, where classical monsters are most likely to appear, is often seen as somehow lesser because of its appeal to a mass audience. Classical reception studies has generally been amenable towards examining representations of the ancient world in Hollywood cinema, with a growing interest in television, but has been slower to pick up on other fields, such as videogames, historical fiction, cartoons and so on, in part due to anxieties about whether such subjects are worthy of academic study.[3] The cultural snobbery that leads to the dismissal of this material as somehow worthless because of its target audience or its recent date of production is becoming less and less tenable in a cultural context where a lifelong love of classics can now start from a video game, a film or a children's book.[4] By popular culture, I mean things produced with a mass audience in mind.

For one person to attempt to survey *all* of popular culture would be a massive endeavour, if not a life's work. My case study selections inevitably draw on areas in which I have more analytical expertise and, yes, the things that I like. I like watching film, watching television and reading books. I am less keen on playing video or role-playing games. As such, my selection of material leans towards examples in genres and media that I prefer. I can't claim objectivity in this selection. I am embedded in the culture from which I am selecting my examples, and it would be wrong to claim that my preferences have not affected my choice of evidence. To quote Nisbet, 'we might as well acknowledge not just the impossibility but also the undesirability of maintaining (a pretence of) academic distance from material of this kind'.[5] That said, while I note my own investment in certain kinds of popular culture, that is not the same as vetoing the possibility of critical analysis. You can enjoy something and offer robust critique at the same time.

Equally, it is impossible for this book to survey the full global range of cultures and their engagement with classical monsters. The boundaries I set here again arise from my own limitations: the material I am working with comes almost exclusively from American and British cultural contexts, not least because each culture has its own sociopolitical milieu which affects what it thinks classical monsters should do. I hope that others who are more familiar with the way in which different cultures work will take this book as an inspiration to go hunting for classical monsters around the world.

All of this rather assumes a shared definition of a 'classical monster', and of what we, as humans, find monstrous. There are some characteristics which most monsters seem to share – they are, for instance, abnormally large, they perform hideous acts of violence, they break down barriers in our understanding of the world, they demonstrate physical hybridity, they resist or reject human control.[6] One could hypothesise an agreed list, a canonical spotters' guide, but creating consensus would be far from straightforward – would we, for instance, count Medea as a monster? Do the Titans get included, as the chaotic adversaries of the Olympian gods? I will explore the models of monsters and how they come about in more detail in my first chapter, but here I offer a working definition of the classical monster to be getting on with.

Here, I am guided in part by the way that popular culture has embraced heroic narratives of monster conquest, and in part by the idea of the monster as hybrid. Many humans in ancient myth behave in monstrous ways; however, humans acting inhumanly are not, in the context of this book, monsters. Equally, immortals behaving badly do not fall into my remit; the Titans and the pre-Olympian gods, who arguably stand in positions of chaotic monstrosity in various creation myths, do not appear. In between these two extremes fall the mortal monsters, the ones who tend to suffer most severely at the hands of heroes, and who either cross the boundary between human and animal in their hybrid physical form, or whose physical enormity transgresses the expectations of a normal beast's body.

Again, any discussion of this kind will be selective rather than exhaustive (although, as will become clear, I see this as a positive aspect of this study's approach). Not all of your favourite classical monsters will appear, sometimes because they have not yet made popular culture their home, and sometimes because I have not had the space to do them justice – a more detailed analysis of the centaur and the siren will have, alas, to wait.[7] The case of the cyclops, too, is a perplexing one, complicated from the beginning by Polyphemus and his unfortunate encounter with Odysseus in the ninth book of the *Odyssey*. While Odysseus' narrative presents the cyclops as hostile, brutal and generally deserving of his violent blinding, it is impossible to ignore the fact that Odysseus and his men break the rules of hospitality first by ransacking Polyphemus' cave, killing his flock and eating his cheeses. A cynical reader – more accurately, *this* cynical reader – sees frantic attempts at justifying and excusing the narrator's own unacceptable behaviour in the framing of Polyphemus as a monster. Regardless of how we may interpret the original narrative, Odysseus' version has taken hold. Popular culture now generally sees cyclopes as unredeemed monsters, and treats them accordingly (although not always with the same spelling). I tread the line, as much as is possible, between ancient ambiguity and modern certainty where Polyphemus is concerned.

What does this book hold for the intrepid reader? The first two chapters offer an orientation, scoping out the lie of the land, and an argument for why the old maps are not good enough for tracking classical monsters. Chapter 1 explores various paradigms for understanding monsters and the assumptions that underpin them, and offers a new way of conceptualising the classical monster that takes into account some peculiar features of its behaviour that the standard models do not explain. Chapter 2 continues to outline the particular habits of the classical monster by asking where it dwells, both in terms of physical location and genre, and how location affects the way we respond to monstrous inhabitants. The chapter closes with a consideration of how living on screen can fundamentally alter a monster's existence.

Chapters 3 and 4 offer an overview of classical monsters in Anglo-American cinema, starting with the sword-and-sandal genre popular in the 1950s, and moving up to the present day. Chapter 3 spends some time with the influential oeuvre of Ray Harryhausen, including *Jason and the Argonauts* (1963) and *Clash of the Titans* (1981), and finishes in the dry spell for classical cinema in the 1990s, relieved only by Disney's *Hercules* (1997). Chapter 4 picks up after the rejuvenation of the form following the *Gladiator* phenomenon. It examines two major strands of engagement with classical monsters: those who appear in what we might call the modern hero epic like *Wrath of the Titans* (2012) and *Hercules* (2014); and those who appear elsewhere in contemporary cinema outside classically framed narratives, such as *O Brother, Where Art Thou?* (2000) and *Pan's Labyrinth* (2006), doing different but no less significant cultural work.

Chapters 5 and 6 take us into the world of television, where a different set of production requirements, narrative drives and financial restraints provide an alternative environment for the classical monster to flourish. Chapter 5 offers an extended discussion of *Hercules: The Legendary Journeys*, in which monster-slaying is initially positioned and instrumentalised as central to the hero's character. Over the course of six series, classical monsters develop their own distinctive presences within the show's thematic interests. Chapter 6 looks at two further programmes, *Xena: Warrior Princess* and *Doctor Who*, where monsters appear less frequently but still function in ways which represent a particular strategy for monster-handling in television, specifically the genre of telefantasy.

The book ends with two chapters, each focused on an individual case study. Moving on from tracking trends in particular media, these chapters look at a group of receptions around a particular monster to see what common reference points offer opportunities for creative clustering, and what we might conclude from the most productive nodes of individual narratives. Chapter 7 looks at Medusa (because how can we not?), while Chapter 8 turns to the Minotaur, using a range of literary and visual evidence. I selected these monsters because they appear to be the most popular classical monsters for popular culture to revisit – certainly, most of the examples I've been shown over the course of writing this book have been of Medusa. By charting out some of the patterns in the receptions of specific monsters, these chapters offer some insight into what precisely about these creatures still speaks to popular culture.

By looking at monsters in their various haunts, we gain a better understanding of what popular culture makes of antiquity, and how the continued dialogue between the past and the present flourishes in all areas of society. The classical monster finds space to reincarnate itself in mass media, each time growing into the form allowed by the space provided, but also retaining the distinctive qualities that mark it out as somehow ancient. In this book, I aim to map out some of the territory in which classical monsters now dwell, and to understand some of the factors behind their surprisingly long afterlife. This project will, by necessity, remain incomplete – there will always be another example, either dug up from the archives or presented fresh from the press. That is the attraction of monsters – their ability to continually grow new heads. With that in mind, let us begin.

What Makes a Monster?

A white car drives through a wood. A centaur gallops alongside, through trees set back a little from the road. As the car passes over dusty mountains, Medusa looks up from the snakes in her hands to mark its passing. In the pouring rain, the car's wheels turn and the Minotaur throws back his head to beat his chest. A siren raises her head from a pond, splashing her tail. A Pegasus emerges from fog, beating its wings; the car turns on its headlights in the gathering gloom. 'In a world of hybrids,' says a voice, 'some follow – others lead.'

This is a summary of the 2017 television advert for the Mitsubishi Outlander PHEV, a plug-in hybrid SUV.[1] The message of the advert is clear – all forms of hybridity are subservient to the PHEV's plug-in hybrid technology and low CO_2 emissions. Yet this commercial derives its power from its deployment of classical monsters. It expects its audience to recognise them, to know they are hybrids, to understand them as the system within which the PHEV demands precedence. Why do ancient monsters still wield this kind of influence in contemporary culture, to the extent that a car commercial feels they are mainstream enough to present without comment?

To begin answering this question, I want to explore some existing ways of understanding monsters, and outline my own model for how we might treat monsters found in classical reception. At present, monster studies does not seem to take into account the ancient monster transferred into the modern world. Monster studies itself is a comparatively new field of academic research, arguably established when Jeffrey Cohen's influential Monster Theses were published in 1997.[2] The work that builds on the Monster Theses leaves the monsters under consideration within their own chronological timeline. Let us take the vampire as an example. Scholars may look at Bram Stoker's *Dracula* in the context of when it was written, and see in Dracula a figure who represents the fears of the Victorian era around migration, uncontrolled sexual appetites, the rise of technology and so on. They could look at him in the 1958 Hammer Horror film, where the vampire is imagined as a historical character in a historical setting.

They may also turn to the *Twilight* saga and see the vampire living in the early twenty-first century, embodying the theme of sexual danger under the strong influence of Stephanie Meyer's Mormonism. The vampire endures but becomes the inhabitant of the time period where it lives. Similarly, the underlying concept of the zombie continues, but adapts to the social and temporal circumstances in which it finds itself.

By contrast, the Minotaur, Medusa, the Chimera and other classical monsters have remained remarkably consistent over time. While individual manifestations have changed, their fundamental form has not radically altered. They have not needed to reinvent and reshape themselves on their journey through time. Monster studies does not talk about monsters who not only existed as monstrous in their original culture but are still used as monstrous. The closest the field gets is examinations of monsters like the wendigo, who belongs to the folklore tradition of Algonquian culture but still has a living community who engage with it today.

There is plenty to be said about monsters in ancient literature.[3] But the fact that those monsters have travelled from their lairs in Greece and Italy into our cinemas and living rooms remains unacknowledged. When classical monsters are discussed, it is with the assumption that they don't overstep their temporal boundaries. That is, monster studies assumes that classical monsters only really exist in the classical period. They might be acknowledged in conversations about medieval bestiaries, if they're lucky, but in the main, what happens in Greece and Rome is thought to stay in Greece and Rome.

Consumers of popular culture know differently. Classical monsters see no reason not to follow their heroes out of ancient myth. This chapter explains what happens when they do, and why it matters. Given this goal, it might feel as if we already know what we are looking for – we can spot a classical monster when we see one. However, it will be useful to establish a distinction between monsters, those which we associate with particular heroes and mythic narratives, and the monstrous more generally – that is, between specific creatures and the abstract belief which infuses them. These ideas can be separated out from each other and, where classical monsters in popular culture are concerned, it's particularly important to do so – what operates in the production of monsters does not necessarily apply for the rest of their lives. In what follows, there may be some merging of these two spheres, but hopefully with productive overlaps.

There are various ways of thinking about the monstrous in general and the behaviour of individual monsters specifically. I want to take a turn through these various modes and consider how helpful, or otherwise, they are for exploring the classical monsters who sojourn with us now.

Catalogues and cryptozoology

The most familiar mode of handling monsters is to catalogue them, one by one. Anyone with experience of role-playing games will know the sort of thing I mean – great handbooks, stuffed with various monsters that a games master can unleash upon unwary players, full of stats and special abilities, ordered alphabetically or according to category. The contents of the Dungeons & Dragons (D&D) *Monster Manual* (2014), for instance, begins with the Aarakocra, progressing through Bullywugs, Gargoyles and Pixies until it ends with Yugoloths and Zombies.[4] The tendency to assume that all one needs to do with monsters is count and identify them arises from the medieval bestiary tradition, where lavishly illustrated books described a range of fantastic and commonplace creatures. These books provided not only physical descriptions, but also a note of the animals' habits, often with moralising commentary – for instance, the beaver supposedly gnaws off its own testicles when cornered, which symbolises man's need to cut off his vices. The popularity of Pokémon highlights a continuing belief that monsters must be hunted down and categorised, whether they are caught in their native Japan or after their journey into the West.[5] The sheer amount of knowledge about Pokémon behaviour required to participate in what at first glance looks like a simple children's game 'is that of quasi-scientific classification, along the lines of Linnean taxonomy'.[6] The act of cataloguing is important, but should not be the end point of engaging with monsters.[7]

A parallel temptation is to rationalise the monster. This model, sometimes called 'cryptozoology', applies particularly to the monsters who come out of pre-scientific historical periods. The logic runs that the ancients were clearly scared of *something*; however, it cannot have been an actual monster, since in our enlightened state of scientific understanding, we know that (for instance) giants and harpies and griffins do not actually exist. The solution is to recover the archaeology, to see what reality lies under the fictional scaly skin. There are classical antecedents. In one Greek papyrus fragment, an illustrator has added pictures alongside an otherwise straightforward tale Hercules is telling of his adventures (Fig. 1.1). In contrast to the heroic deeds that Hercules recounts, the illustrator playfully tells a different story – instead of wrestling the Nemean lion, Hercules grapples what is obviously a statue on a plinth; rather than stalking the Stymphalian birds, Hercules

Fig. 1.1 Photo of *P.Oxy.* XXII 2331. Courtesy of the Egypt Exploration Society and the University of Oxford Imaging Papyri Project.

seems to be surprised by a flock while fishing. The great tales we read from the mouth of the hero are undercut by the light-hearted illustrations, showing that even in antiquity not everybody took tales of monsters seriously.[8]

The cryptozoologists take this rationalising approach still further, and seek to uncover what precisely lies behind the monsters of our ancestors' minds. Was it the shared cultural memory of the sabre-tooth tiger that took on new shapes as we left caves behind? Did the discovery of dinosaur fossils necessitate the invention of griffins in order to adequately explain them?[9] Do we fear the Kraken because we did not understand the giant squid? This methodological approach is related to the broader method of euhemerism, which sees myths and legends as grounded in actual historical events which can somehow be recovered, with some attempts more convincing than others. Whatever one might think about this method in principle, in reality any attempt to apply it to monsters from the classical era must inevitably suffer from the sparseness of evidence. Personally, I fear that trying to work out what might have generated the Minotaur, or where Medusa came from, runs the risk of relying on wild assumption. Instead, I want to ask how these monsters behave now that they've made it to modernity.

Basic monster theory

One way of approaching this question is to move away from specific monsters and instead consider the monstrous, particularly through the lens of monster theory. Cohen's influential chapter outlined seven cornerstone principles for understanding the cultural creation of monsters:[10]

1. The monster's body is a cultural body – monsters are culturally specific, constructed in a particular moment.
2. The monster always escapes – whenever you think the monster is dead, it comes back, to be read in new cultural contexts and respond to new fears.
3. The monster is the harbinger of category crisis – you can't categorise a monster. It refuses to accept binaries and disturbs familiar boundaries between human and animal, male and female, and so on.
4. The monster dwells at the gates of difference – monsters tend to reflect fears of 'the other'. That can be the fear of a different gender, sexual orientation, nationality, ethnicity or anything that isn't included in the dominant identity of a culture.
5. The monster polices the borders of the possible – it patrols the behavioural limits both between and inside social units that we cannot cross if society is to continue.
6. Fear of the monster is really a kind of desire – the horror of the monster creates a space in which to express forbidden longings, allowing the wish-fulfilment of dreams that cannot be (acceptably) dreamed. The inevitable destruction of the monster absolves us from enjoying the guilty pleasures they give us.
7. The monster stands at the threshold – as monsters return from our attempts at banishment, they tell us what it is to be human. We define ourselves against their monstrosity, and ask whether they remain as monstrous as they once were.

Cohen's premises underpin a considerable body of work across academic disciplines studying monsters in specific contexts; from the medieval period to media studies, there's always a monster to look at. Whether or not there was *actually* a monster (did the Hydra really exist?) is beside the point – what matters is how a given culture responds to its sense of the monstrous. Mittman summarises this point nicely by arguing that 'the monster is known through its *effect*, its impact'.[11] The feeling of horror and discomfort we feel when seeing a monster comes from the monstrous qualities Cohen identifies in the Monster Theses – the transgression of normally fixed boundaries, things that question our understanding of how the world works, anything that unsettles our complacent confidence in the settled order of the universe.[12] Rather than looking at individual monsters, monster theory looks at their abstract underpinnings.

For those interested in antiquity, monster theory offers a helpful set of principles for considering how ancient ideas of the monstrous might be at work in a particular situation, such as why a Roman prosecutor might compare the man he is accusing to a centaur.[13] However, instances of classical reception respond less well when one tries to apply monster theory to them. The problems which arise aren't immediately obvious; you could argue that the monster's eternal escape and rebirth mean that the constant reappearances of the Minotaur from his labyrinth are always fresh inventions of the society that generates them. This explanation works, up to a point – but then we run into the problem of what Mittman calls the monster's 'effect'. Most of the classical monsters we encounter in popular culture do not generate the sort of stomach-churning horror associated with the monstrous in the abstract.

If you examined the sort of texts from popular culture that monster theory is applied to, you would be forgiven for wondering why this book exists at all. The modern monsters who receive all the attention are the serial killers, the murderous alien races, the mysterious zombie-generating illnesses – or, in more traditional fare, the sparkly vampires and the strapping werewolves.[14] A casual observer might easily think that the Minotaur, Medusa, the centaur, the cyclops and all the other familiar figures from classical myth had quietly faded away, living only in new translations of ancient texts and fresh photographs of vases and frescos.

And yet. Alongside a goodly number of ancient world movies, particularly those with a hero pitted against at least one monster, myth permeates all types of contemporary literature. Canongate Press recently commissioned a series of short novels retelling a whole range of mythic narratives, ancient Greek tales among them. For the younger reader, classical fragments are sprinkled throughout the Harry Potter volumes, while the Percy Jackson books assume Greek mythological figures continue to live in the modern world. Individual classical monsters are not trapped inside their particular myth, although they can be found in such retellings. They often appear in narratives which have no association with their origin stories. Any computer game in which the player is asked to battle against clouds of regenerating harpies and hydras, like the floating clouds of Medusa Heads in the *Castlevania* series, illustrates the continued threat of classical monsters even when they are not occupying their traditional spaces.

So, classical monsters turn up in popular culture, in places that monster theory seems to think they have no right and no ability to be. I think this illustrates some of the limitations with the idea of the 'monstrous' and the assumption that it must lead to terror: the Sphinx has not lost her teeth and settled down into an old age of snoozing on the sofa. Despite being transplanted from their cultures of origin, and often relocated into entirely unrelated stories, classical monsters have an instantly recognisable presence in popular culture. Monster studies has so far been oblivious to their presence, which suggests that there may be something else going on here. To work out what that might be, we first need to look at some historical trends in the forms our monsters have taken.

Historical trends

One of the complicating factors for classical monsters in the modern world is that they have lived through a significant sea change in how the nature of monsters is understood. The concept of 'monster' was originally tied up in its name – the etymology of *monstrare*, to show or demonstrate, and *monere*, to warn, reflected a widespread belief that a monster was monstrous in its external appearance. The sight of a monster was meant to function as an omen – literally, in the classical period, for monsters and *monstra* were seen as signs of divine will. For instance, when the boats of Aeneas and his men turn into sea nymphs after they have been set on fire by the native Latins, Virgil calls the sight a *mirabile monstrum*, an amazing portent (*Aeneid* 9.120). In Cicero's dialogue *On Divination*, his brother Quintus refers to the birth of a hermaphrodite as a deadly monster (*fatale monstrum*), which meant the Romans had to consult the Sibylline books to find out the correct way to respond (*On Divination* 1.98).[15] The poet Horace even goes as far as using the same phrase to refer to the Egyptian queen Cleopatra as a danger which must be overcome (*Odes* 1.37.21).

The sense that monsters communicated divine will continued into the medieval period, where monsters were generated by spiritual dangers and conquered by spiritual virtues – Grendel in *Beowulf* and the monsters of the medieval romances are destroyed, at least in part, by the holiness of their adversaries. Similarly, the bestiary tradition moralised about the appearances and behaviours of animals to provide exhortation to the ideal Christian character. In the medieval chronicles, an unnatural or monstrous birth could be read as the sign that war was on its way, similarly to how Quintus Cicero frames intersex babies. Monsters in the medieval period could also be interpreted as wonders of nature – stories of monstrous races far out at the edges of the map, such as the *cynocephali* or dog-headed people, ran alongside stories of dragons and phoenixes to illustrate the richness of a world outside the everyday. Such a construction of otherness contributed to the politics of burgeoning empire and the idea of race as a discriminatory category: the European West began to identify itself as 'normal', positioning inhabitants of other countries with different skin shades as fundamentally unlike the people in the self-proclaimed centre.

Although what individual cultures found monstrous shifted over time, their beasts remained externally and obviously identifiable. A hangover of the immovability of a monstrous exterior appears in icons made in the Eastern Orthodox Church of Saint Christopher, a *cynocephalus* who met the Christ child, was baptised and received human shape. Despite his inner conversion, some makers of icons continued to paint him with a dog's head. The prioritisation of external appearances went more or less uninterrupted up to the nineteenth century, although explanations for monstrosity drew on science rather than religion. The question was not whether something that looked monstrous was a monster, but how it had become so – a conversation that became even more charged in the context of Charles Darwin's evolutionary theories.

When Mary Shelley's *Frankenstein* was published in 1818, it marked a radical shift in how the link between monstrosity and external appearance was understood, by proposing that the two could be uncoupled. Frankenstein is so overcome by his creature's ghastly form, sewn together from corpses, that he runs away from it, yet despite his appearance the Creature's initial disposition is friendly. As we discover from the Creature's later narration, at first he is a true innocent. He burns himself on a campfire because he does not know fire is hot, for instance, and has to learn by experimentation that wet wood does not provide good fuel. Despite his harmless intentions, the hostile reactions he experiences in response to his appearance eventually drive him to behave like the monster people believe him to be. It is ultimately nurture, not nature, that makes Shelley's Creature monstrous. By contrast, the actions of Frankenstein himself remain deeply ambivalent. Although the mix of epistolary and first-person narrative nudges readers to assume Frankenstein's perspective, his blind pursuit of scientific discovery without considering its ethical implications and his decision to abandon his creation are far from laudable. Shelley's strong suggestions that the respectable scientist is a body snatcher, along with his other questionable personality traits, mean that Frankenstein's self-presentation as the narrative's tragic hero can never be wholly convincing.

Frankenstein breaks the link between a monstrous exterior and a monstrous interior, beginning a fascination with monstrosity's inward manifestations rather than the specific monstrous creatures of earlier eras. Later Victorian novels explore the same idea, with similarly powerful results. Robert Louis Stevenson's *The Strange Case of Dr. Jekyll and Mr. Hyde* (1886) presented a literally two-faced protagonist, allowing the monster in Dr. Jekyll out, and leading to the question of what had been under the good doctor's skin before he came up with his serum. In *The Picture of Dorian Gray* (1890), Oscar Wilde gives a wicked body beautiful a hideous hidden portrait, which records all the vices that are undetectable on the attractive visage of Mr. Gray himself. Without the portrait, Dorian's monstrosity is visually imperceptible.

Both of these examples reflect an interest in what this era saw as an otherwise invisible *human* monstrosity. What is shocking about Dorian and Mr. Hyde is their immoral behaviour. Both men ruin women. Although homosexuality is never explicitly mentioned, the fact that Dorian rents a sordid room by the docks which he only visits in disguise under an assumed name is sufficient indication that his monstrosities are multiple. Dorian's sexuality is an open secret in the text – always plausibly deniable, but clearly on display when you know the signs to look for.[16] The monstrous is now inside us. A newly scientific world makes empirical belief in the Sphinx more or less impossible, but an increasing interest in the hidden workings of the mind will soon allow Freud to give it new life through psychoanalysis.

The next major shift in the monstrous, sixty or so years later, took place alongside the development of the atomic bomb and the Cold War. The detonation of bombs on Hiroshima and Nagasaki meant suddenly we were living in a world where the most monstrous thing imaginable had already happened. The threat of nuclear holocaust gave popular culture, and science fiction (SF) in particular, a new set of fears and anxieties to work with, and the scope to explore full social dystopia. The monsters created by nuclear radiation, emblematic of American monster movies in the 1950s, stood in for a range of other terrors, not least anxiety over communism.[17] While nuclear winter provided a temporary return to the exterior, obvious monster, the human monsters who allowed radioactive monsters to be created or released provided a parallel track of hidden monstrosity. Paranoia about 'Reds under the bed' neatly illustrates the link between the uncertain global political climate and an increased worry over monsters lurking in plain sight.

More recently, contemporary concepts of monstrosity manifest in four interlinked kinds of monsters: the psychopath or the terrorist, who is undiscoverable until it is too late; the corrupt government agency, which infiltrates every aspect of life and against which there is little or no recourse; the invisible virus that cannot be seen as it worms under our skins; and nature itself, violently responding to humanity's outrages against it.[18] These monsters all express fears about the breakdown of the social contract, but also of what cannot be seen, cannot be faced, cannot be proactively countered. They may come into existence because of humanity's own foolishness, or they may be symptoms of a civilisation turning on itself. Yet initially they all merge into society. The serial killer looks like everybody else, until we peep into his basement; the sinister governmental body blends in with the rest; the surface on which the virus rests seems innocuous; nature, our mother, appears passive until goaded to revenge. The monsters which have been generated by the modern world can no longer be identified by sight – unlike classical monsters.

Society's discomfort over these undetectable manifestations of monstrosity has resulted in attempts to work out *how* to spot monsters. The figure of the terrorist, for instance, is frequently associated with people who have brown or black skin, while White terrorists are not labelled as such in media reports of mass shootings or similar attacks. Skin colour can thus become a proxy for detecting monstrosity, but it's highly ineffective; a social attempt to recouple appearance and monstrousness fails, but perpetuates systems of violence which allow, for instance, White North American police to escape prosecution after shooting Black men who do not pose a threat to them.[19] A parallel othering manifests in seeing those with mechanical augmentation as somehow monstrous. The fearsome potential of the Terminator's visible endoskeleton exposes the breakdown of the barrier between the human and the machine, and our perhaps inevitable journey towards becoming cyborgs.[20] In both these cases, external visual markers are treated as if they still signal a relationship to the monstrous, but the breakdown of the internal/external connection means it has become increasingly hard to detect any of the numerous manifestations of the monstrous until it's too late.

Equally, in the late twentieth and early twenty-first centuries, depictions of monsters show not just sympathy for the devil, but a desire to become the devil.[21] Vampires particularly express this modern longing at work, given the obvious parallels between vampiric transformation and sex. In Stephenie Meyer's *Twilight* saga, Bella Swann, the series' protagonist, not only desires the vampire Edward Cullen, but by the end of the novels has become a vampire herself in order to survive. Anne Rice's *Vampire Chronicles* include many characters who beg to be turned into vampires, often without knowing what they're asking for; their transformations are sometimes successful, but sometimes immortality cannot save them from their personal tragedies. Neither the Greeks nor the Romans show any inclination to *become* the monstrous.[22] Given the Greek preference for the rational and the ordered, nothing could be more unappealing than to become the irrational, chaotic other. While the Romans were certainly fascinated by monsters, both as clowns and as exhibitions, they instead identify with the figure of the gladiator, who 'concentrated the extremes of beauty and violation, power and powerlessness, control and abandon'.[23]

For the LBGT+ community, explicit reclamation of the monstrous has become an important act of recuperation. Hollywood cinema has a long-standing tradition of coding its villains and monsters as homosexual, meaning that a queer viewer who takes pleasure in watching a figure they identify with must also watch that figure suffer and be vanquished.[24] However, in the final years of the twentieth century, the queer-coded monster started to come out of its closet. Its grand champion has been Lady Gaga, who has positioned herself as Mother Monster to her fanbase of queer Little Monsters, explicitly reaching out to young people in contemporary America who feel marginalised and othered by their sexuality.[25] The queer aspect of the monstrous seems, in the main, to have passed classical monsters by, although wider cultural trends mean that they offer the potential for this kind of reclamation.

Classical monsters, then, have flouted the evolutionary drift of the monstrous. Their hybridity, their visual obviousness, their ability to be instantly picked out of a line-up, marks them out as creations of earlier civilisations. It is this unusual nature of the obvious monster which enables the 'spotter's guide' approach to monsters I mentioned. That said, it is hardly surprising that monster theorists concentrate on the monster generated by modern concepts of the monstrous to the exclusion of the ancient monster still roaming our cultural landscape. But in order to think a little more about why this omission exists, it is worth digging deeper into some theoretical explanations of the cultural and psychological processes which help the theoretical monstrous create individual monsters.

Anthropology

Mary Douglas' groundbreaking *Purity and Danger* (1966) is the core text for an anthropological reading of the monstrous. Douglas' main contribution to monster studies, building on how her subject cultures conceptualised cleanliness and pollution, was the idea that things became monstrous because they broke out of safe categories and so became unnatural.[26] Her analysis classified monsters as impure because they disrupted social rules and norms. There are various ways that an object or creature might do this – it might straddle the boundaries between settled categories (both human and animal); it might be categorically contradictory (both alive and dead); it might be incomplete or lack a fixed form, creating uncertainty about what it actually is or should be.[27]

This notion of the im/pure leads to the concept of the taboo, and ways to reinforce appropriate social behaviours and prevent pollution. This idea underpins Cohen's fifth Monster Thesis, that the monster patrols the border of the possible. In anthropological terms, the borders in question are those surrounding exogamy and endogamy, or marrying in and marrying out, as well as the borders that create a zone of heteronormative expectations. As a strategy to avoid the incest taboo, women become commodities to be exchanged between kin groups and reinforce homosocial relations. To make sure that social cohesion doesn't break down completely, balance is created by taboos on marrying *too* far out – into other social groups, ethnicities and cultures. These taboos are policed by the monsters created both when you marry too close to and too far from your kin group, or when you cross outside procreative marriage into homosexual or transsexual activity.

Stephen Prince used the idea of taboo to construct the beginnings of a social theory for understanding the horror film.[28] He sees monsters as helping to demarcate blurred borders of the social world, reinforcing systems of order which define what it is to be human. They become a mechanism to reinforce cultural distinctions between clean/unclean, accepted/prohibited that support and protect human communities. They also become 'the manifestation of the internal contradictions that every social order, based upon a classifying operation, must generate' – that is, they reveal the fault lines of the artificial categories that humans impose on their surroundings in order to control them.[29] Yet Prince's focus on the horror film does not consider how the monstrous might manifest outside horror, nor does it account for monsters who travel beyond their origin culture after their creation.

The psychoanalytic tradition also picks up on ideas of pollution and ritual cleansing in order to articulate the development of an individual's sense of self. It is this tradition, which forms the substrate of monster theory, to which we now turn.

Psychoanalysis

Psychoanalytic theory's relationship with the monstrous goes back to Freud's short essay from 1919 on the uncanny, or the *unheimlich*.[30] Freud unpicks the linguistic roots of *unheimlich*, literally translated into English as 'unhomely'. By closely examining the semantic uses of the word in various contexts, he argues that what is unfamiliar is, in fact, deeply familiar. He claims that there are two possible sources of the discomfort felt around *unheimlich* objects. First, the *unheimlich* may resurrect in me the memory of some repressed infantile trauma, such as the fear of castration at the hands of the father. Second, some event reminds me of a primitive mode of thought which I have since outgrown as a civilised human being, but the resonance with that mode of thought gives me pause. For example, if I think that I haven't heard from Julia for a while and shortly afterwards I receive an email from her, I may be tempted to say this is uncanny, particularly if such coincidences occur several times in quick succession. My reaction stems from a hardwired primitive belief in the power of thought itself – that is, humans can bring about events simply by thinking about what they wish to happen. Because I am a modern, civilised human being, I do not fall prey to such primitive superstition, but the echo of the superannuated mode of thought generates a sensation of uncanniness.

An obvious problem with Freud's approach is his belief that 'primitive' cultures exist and that modernity (as embodied by early twentieth-century Europe in general and Vienna in particular) is unsurpassed by any other cultural moment. This view is underpinned by Freud's racist and colonialist assumptions, which see Western civilisation at the top of a developmental curve, and take a positivist approach to the innate superiority of modernity. It also assumes that anyone not living in Western Europe cannot be 'civilised', suggesting non-European people are still susceptible to this kind of superstition. Even Freud seemed to recognise the problems underpinning this conception of *unheimlich* when he acknowledged that it was much more easily dispelled than the first type.

He describes the sense of the uncanny created by repression as 'more resistant', and as creating a more compelling sensation both in real life and in literature.[31] It is this kind of *unheimlich* feeling with which monster studies concerns itself. Indeed, Freud's case that repression creates the uncanny is one of the central planks of Cohen's Monster Theses. Freud argues that an uncanny feeling occurs when 'repressed childhood complexes are revived by some impression'.[32] As a consequence, in order to use the uncanny as Freud understands it, one must also accept that everything we find uncanny springs from something the psyche has hidden away, always and forever entangled with the fear of the father and the desire for the mother. We also must subscribe to Freud's construction of a purely heterosexual 'normal' trajectory of desire, reinforcing a compulsory heterosexuality in us as we experience the uncanny.

The second core psychoanalytic text for monster studies is Kristeva's 1980 *Powers of Horror*, which introduces the concept of abjection. Kristeva argues that the very development of consciousness means that as the human brain comes into existence, there is a primal repression of all the animal instincts and breakdowns of the self that must be tidied away in order to become a human. The material repressed in this manner is the abject, which challenges our sense of identity as independent beings. The ultimate example of the abject, she suggests, is the corpse, where the boundary between the human and the non-human literally decomposes before our eyes. The child-mother-other triangle of traditional psychoanalysis exists on top of this fundamental repression. The abject circles back into our awareness through reminders of primal repression, but can never be truly spoken about because the subject of the abject was repressed before we could speak (and had to be repressed as a condition of our speech).

As a result, the abject and its symbolic reminders must be handled through ceremonial exclusion (such as dietary restrictions) – it is impure and must be thrust away. It can't be done away with entirely, since it remains necessary to our existence as humans, but must be acknowledged without being seen. Ritual allows us to fit the abject into the new, 'rational' order of the mind and into the realm of language and the law, although the abject is precisely that which stands outside these realms. Excrement and menstrual blood are abject, representing on the one hand the danger that comes to the self from outside, and on the other the dangers posed by relationships inside kin groups, the fear of incest, the roles of sexual difference, and the need for these to be managed by taboo and cultural insistence on purity.

Both Freud and Kristeva rely on a system of repression, whether at the primal or the secondary level, and suggest that these repressions are fundamentally concerned with sexual activity, sexual identity and sexual fear. Later monster theorists question this reductive approach, arguing that it is possible to be scared of something not related to sex. Judith Halberstam, for instance, brings out the fullness of the monstrous body in Gothic literature, working with multiple planes of fear along the axes of class, race and nationality as well as gender and sex.[33] By understanding that the monster responds to a wide range of monstrous factors at work in the unconscious, we can get past the Freudian obsession with heteronormative sexually driven infantile trauma. We also allow the notion of the monstrous itself to encompass many different, often muddied, kinds of terror, resisting what Halberstam defines as a search for purity and clarity. We can thus see the wider picture of fright.[34]

So, psychoanalysis gives us a credible mechanism for explaining how abstract and subconscious conceptions of the monstrous generate concrete monsters, particularly the revised model proposed by Halberstam. Debbie Felton has applied this approach to classical monsters, and argues that behind the monsters of Greece lies fear of 'the potential of chaos to overcome order, or irrationality to prevail over reason; the potential victory of nature against the encroaching civilizations of mankind; the little-understood nature of the female in contrast to the male.'[35] This proposition seems sensible enough, given how much the Greeks contrasted themselves to barbarians, and it doesn't require infantile sexual trauma in order to work – all that's needed is a cultural desire to conform to 'normality'. The fear of becoming that barbarian 'other' and falling out of respectable social categories generates the monster, which gains its power from the fear associated with that collapse into confusion.

Yet, even if we accept that we now have a plausible explanation for how psychological conceptions of the monstrous generate monsters in a particular time and place, and that this model works for ancient monsters, the monsters of classical reception still pose a problem – for they are most definitely *out* of their time and place. My catalogue of trends in monstrosity has already shown that there has been a slow but sure disconnection between how monsters look and how they act, and that contemporary Western culture in particular has a paranoid fear of being crept up on and taken unawares. But these were not the fears of the ancient Greeks, nor do we fear what they did.

So, the puzzle stands thus. In turning to reception, we shift from abstract notions of the monstrous to the particular instances of the classical monster. If a monster is generated by the fears and repression that lie in the hidden subconscious of a particular society, what continually draws contemporary popular culture back to the monsters generated by classical culture?

Foucault

At this point, I want to take refuge (perhaps unexpectedly) in Foucault. His impact on monster studies has, as far as I can tell, been quite limited – not least because the work that seems most relevant wasn't published until 2003. Under the general title *Abnormal*, this book presents a series of lectures Foucault gave at the Collège de France in the 1974–5 academic year. Although there is some overlap with his published work, these lectures were not (as far as I am aware) available before their collection and publication, and so were not in circulation when monster studies was first taking shape. Foucault might be surprised that I turn to this particular work, as he is mainly interested in why psychoanalysis' claims of incest and repression were received so placidly by bourgeois families. He therefore focuses on the constructions of power via interactions between the legal, medical and psychoanalytic domains, and how ideas of normal and abnormal were used to manage interactions between these domains.

I want to look more closely at the first part of these lectures, where Foucault lays out two theories of power and control. The first is control via repression; the second is control via quarantine.[36] Foucault illustrates these models by looking at how two different communities handled potentially fatal diseases. The model of control via repression is exemplified by the exclusion of leprosy from communities in the seventeenth century. Lepers were marked as monstrous by the ugliness and deformity of their bodies. They were pushed out of towns into non-civilised spaces, were not allowed to enter urban areas, and had to observe a set of formalised behaviours if they did come within the city walls to enable citizens to know they were coming and avoid them.

Foucault contrasts this repressive control with the system of *quadrillage* practiced during the eighteenth century in French plague-ridden towns. Rather than dumping infected people outside the city boundaries and trying to pretend they didn't exist, *quadrillage* functioned by dividing up a settlement into districts, quarters and streets. Guards, overseers and other watchers were assigned to monitor these subdivisions of space and keep a catalogue of who was infected and who was not. The surveillance of who went where, and who interacted with whom when, was intended to keep the progress of the plague closely monitored, but also gave the city total control over its citizens. Nobody was excluded. Instead, everybody was firmly fixed in their place, sick and well alike, and their status was constantly reviewed.

Foucault summarises the difference between these two systems as 'passing from a technology of power that drives out, excludes, banishes, marginalizes, and represses, to a fundamentally positive power that fashions, observes, knows, and multiplies itself on the basis of its own effects'.[37] I would argue that this move from a negative to a positive model of control is precisely what has happened as far as the classical monster in modern culture is concerned – or, at least, this is what *society* thinks it has done with the classical monster. The original mechanism of monster generation, the technology of exclusion and banishment as a response to the subconscious monstrous, brought these specific monsters into the myths of their originating cultures. As such, they formed part of the literature and material culture that we have inherited.

Consequently, these myths lose an element of their vitality – as Brian Attebery puts it, 'we know of these things only through written texts, which are to living myths as fossil footprints are to dinosaurs'.[38] Attebery sees classical myths as dislocated from their original meanings, and so available for appropriation and reinterpretation. By contrast, stories taken from Aboriginal or Native American oral traditions are still connected to living religious practices and must be treated with respect.[39]

Monsters come into being through a negative, repressive model of control, a response to humanity's fear of the monstrous. Once they exist at a distance from that mechanism, society responds by attempting to manage them using a positive model of control. The replication of monsters through constant literary retellings, the resettling of mythical beasts in medieval bestiaries, even brightly illustrated children's picture books of classical myth, all seek to pin monsters down, to shape them, to observe them and explain their habits. Such a gallery allows us to peruse past cultural responses to the monstrous, and lets us reassure ourselves how out of date these concepts are. The act of sight keeps the monster under surveillance, while flourishing kinds of classical reception keep reproducing it. Each time a myth is retold, the positive model of control believes it has come a little bit closer to restraining the threat. Once they have manifested, monsters can be domesticated.

And, to an extent, popular culture has tamed the classical monster, particularly in those mediums which involve sight – *where* you encounter the classical monster makes a big difference to the effect that this particular monster has on you. But, while the positive model of control tells a reassuring story about how we have brought the classical monster to heel in the safe temple of shared cultural history that is Graeco-Roman antiquity, let us remind ourselves of Cohen's second Monster Thesis – the monster always escapes. As the model of control has changed, the monsters have also evolved.

Feminist monsters

Despite the assumptions of contemporary society and classical reception that classical monsters can be contained, they find ways of creeping out from their pens and back into the shadows. The method I want to use to explain their continued breakouts means abandoning a psychoanalytical view of monsters and taking a fresh tack, moving away from the monstrous as a concept and navigating into thinking about actual monsters who exist. I am going to weave the work of Donna Haraway and Rosi Braidotti together into a modern monstrous web for my classical beasts to inhabit.

Haraway is interested in the promise monsters offer us of ways to access the worlds of today and the future, new ways of thinking in which the monstrous suggests how we might coexist with the world rather than colonising it. To this end, she borrows the idea of the inappropriate/d other from Trinh Minh-ha. For her, 'to be inappropriate/d is to be neither modern nor postmodern, but to insist on the *a*modern'.[40] That is, being inappropriate/d means rejecting narratives of historical progress, of beginnings, endings and changes of direction. We may think we know what has happened to the classical monster and how it has been pushed out of the narrative; the classical monster believes it has never stopped being relevant.

Haraway's model of the monstrous dovetails neatly with some of the key tenets of classical reception theory, most importantly the idea that meaning is generated at the point of reception. To put it another way, what an item of classical culture *means* is not defined until it is looked at by somebody. The monsters of classical reception respond poorly to Foucauldian attempts to control them because their identities as reception and as monsters mean they doubly resist and reject the desire to categorise and to solidify knowledge.

Another way to understand the monster's response to attempts at control is to turn to the idea of the rhizome, through the work of Rosi Braidotti. Braidotti argues that the feminist subject of knowledge is 'an intensive, multiple subject, functioning in a net of inter-connections … rhizomatic (that is to say non-unitary, non-linear, web-like), embodied and therefore perfectly artificial'.[41] The individual subject according to feminism is best pictured not as a single, fixed article, but as a constantly shifting and redeveloping entity – not understood as the 'disempowered reflection' of a dominant masculine subject who boldly stands at the centre of the world, but as an agent in constant flux, always renegotiating her self on her own terms.[42] Classical monsters fit this description perfectly. They adapt their form and operation according to the environment where they find themselves. They are the ultimate modern subject, always becoming again with each new incarnation. Their root-like shape means that one tendril, one manifestation, may come under the scrutiny of a positive system of power, but other tendrils continue unseen, and find other places to escape into our society.

The appropriate response to such monsters is not to try and pin down every tendril – that method belongs to the desire for control. To use Haraway's phrasing, we require an approach that 'does not map where differences appear, but rather maps where the *effects* of difference appear'.[43] This may sound like a fine distinction, but it has significant implications – what is needed is not another set of classifications and lists, but a closer consideration of how specific instances of classical monsters in the modern world come together to create a picture of that monster, its various and shifting components, and the purposes to which it is put. Trying to limit the tale to a single cause, a single repressed fear, a single set of social controls, attempts to explain the unexplainable, namely the psychological monstrous.

So, my goal in this book is not to impose a modern system of regulation upon the classical monster, as tempting as that may be. I do not aspire to comprehensiveness or universality in what will follow, because neither are possible. Instead, I will outline the major features and landmarks on my map – not least because the relationship between monsters and their homes is particularly intimate. I also want to note that by adopting this cartographic approach, I know I will leave some areas undiscovered. There will always be room for more detail inside my outlines. In this, to return to Haraway, my classical monsters are profoundly amodern – they never end. My interpretations of these monsters' behaviour are provisional, offered in the knowledge that tendrils of monstrosity will find new places to manifest, and that my analysis may be insufficient to deal with those forms yet to come.

Given the importance of the relationship between monsters and their place, the next step in this mapping process is to consider the terrain that we will cover. The place where we encounter the monster, as I have hinted, makes a great difference to how that monster presents itself – and, I would argue, to how successfully a given tendril can be pinned down. The classical monster, I think, becomes much less monstrous if you can see it as well as it can see you.

Classical Monsters and Where to Find Them

Where one might encounter monsters depends as much on our expectations of dangerous places as it does on where monsters prefer to lurk. The ancient Greeks and Romans had a fundamentally different understanding of how space operates to us, and so expected to encounter monsters in different places. Moving beyond questions of physical place, monsters also occupy different kinds of media in distinctive ways. A classical monster's behaviour changes depending on whether it appears in a film, on television, in a comic, in a video game, in a role-playing game or in a book – these cultural caverns come in a range of sizes and so allow monsters varying degrees of room to stretch. The question of 'where' covers more than simply the monster's street address.

Let us begin with some truisms about where monsters reside, which have become accepted because they have some truth in them. The first assumption is that monsters dwell far away, on the edges of the map – hence the delight cartographers of the early modern period took in filling oceans with sea monsters and other glorious creations. They are often understood to occupy their own particular region – Asma describes this as the monster zone.[1] This zone tends to be extremely remote. In his study of 1950s monster movies, Booker notes that rampaging monsters 'tended to live in remote Third-World places that kept them away from civilisation, until they were released by human interference, such as nuclear testing'.[2] Carroll gives a similar list of otherwise unknown places to monster-hunt – lost continents, outer space, under the sea or earth.[3] These places are entirely geographically separate from human civilisation. When monsters come out, they become hostile by leaving their own sphere and entering that of the human, regardless of their subsequent actions.

Such divisions of the world into 'civilised' and 'remote' territories are not politically neutral. Cartography has historically been a tool of racialisation, in which European nations have positioned themselves as superior to indigenous people from the sixteenth century onwards. The appropriation of 'empty land' from the Indigenous people of Australia and the creation of reserves for the

Indigenous communities of the United States and Canada are two particularly good examples.[4] With the rise of the colonial powers, narratives of exploration became tools for justifying the domination of distant areas by presenting them as wild and uncontrolled, framing the inhabitants of those lands as monsters to be overcome rather than representatives of autonomous societies with whom to negotiate. These racialising uses and abuses of space were deployed long after classical monsters came into existence. As their homeland is Greece, the so-called cradle of Western civilisation, they sit at the heart of later white colonialism, domestic monsters exported to foreign lands under the guise of progress.

The idea of a distant monster zone has led to a model of monster encounter best called the 'attack narrative', which arguably goes back to Grendel's attack on King Hrothgar's mead-hall. Carroll sketched out a set of possible structures for the horror film revolving around four elements – onset, discovery, confirmation and confrontation.[5] This is the most complex form of plot he outlines, or, rather, the maximum number of 'movements' his model allows a horror movie to contain. A movie can concentrate on fewer movements or even a single one. What's relevant to our discussion is the importance of the 'onset' and 'discovery' movements, when a monster leaves its original location and travels to human territory, to be found there after playing an appropriate amount of havoc. Carroll thus suggests that monsters are always invaders, whether they come from the Arctic or outer space. They live Elsewhere, and have no business being Here.

A parallel paradigm of monstrous encounters involves the traveller who actively searches out the monster zone. In these stories, tales of the monster lure a traveller to the wild edges of the map, where they encounter the monster in its natural habitat. They may kill the monster there, or (as in those 1950s monster movies) do something spectacularly arrogant or dim that gives the monster a way to leave the monster zone and enter human territory. Either way, the traveller must reassert the boundary by thrusting the monster out of the place where it has no business. This negative method of control seeks to drive or hunt out the monster to make sure it never has the chance to come close to humanity.

Both the attack narrative and the travel narrative run into a problem when faced with classical monsters, although some adapt to these patterns. The *Odyssey's* adventure section looks just like a thrilling travel narrative, with Odysseus running the gauntlet of various fabulous beings, monstrous and divine – or so he tells his hosts, as he is wrapped up safe and warm on a Phaeacian dinner couch. Perseus must travel to find Medusa, requisitioning Hermes' winged sandals to get him over the ocean to her cave. But not all classical monsters occupy the edges of the earth.

Hesiod's *Theogony*, a fragment of a poem which recounts the creation of the world, includes a section which gives the genealogies of various monsters (270–336). Strauss Clay has noted that within this catalogue, there is a moment of transition between the kinds of monsters who are described: after starting with the Graiai, the Gorgons and other monsters who live on the edges of the known world, Hesiod changes tack when he brings in the Hydra of Lerna, followed by the Chimera and the Nemean Lion. With these monsters, the chaos of the catalogue 'erupts into the inhabited world, posing a threat to human beings'.[6] That is, the monsters of classical myth have always been right in the middle of the map with us.

Hesiod's view of monsters as living around the corner as well as over the sea highlights an important characteristic of classical monsters – in the ancient world, it is possible to be walking around your local area, round a bend, and without warning encounter a monster. The monster has not come from some out of the way place: its home is the same familiar geographical locale that humans inhabit in their everyday lives. It has not invaded, but shares the space with the humans who find it. It belongs there as much as the trees, the lakes and the non-monstrous fauna. The line between monstrous and non-monstrous animals blurs further when you consider creatures like mountain lions, who threaten human life without being strictly mythological.

The narrative still usually requires that the monster be defeated. Since monsters tend to appear in the narratives of heroes, that's sort of their *raison d'être* (or, perhaps more accurately, their *raison de mourir*). The Hydra is done in by Heracles and Iolaus, following Athena's advice. Although Oedipus defeats the Sphinx through riddling rather than through battle, she throws herself off a cliff when she can riddle no more. The monster's role as antagonist means that eventually the shared space must be cleansed, made fit for purely human habitation – demigods killing off other divine hybrids in an ancient version of an ecological disaster.[7]

One could object that this sense that monsters inhabited the day-to-day landscape was alive and well in myth, but the Greeks felt this idea belonged to the age of heroes, and that the Romans saw it as well behind them. However, the religious practice of both cultures reveals a more complicated understanding of how everyday space was shared. Greek myths frequently featured episodes of nympholepsy, or nymphs snatching away people who caught their fancy. The best known nympholept is probably Hylas, the lover of Hercules, abducted at the spring of Pegae when the Argonauts stopped there. But nympholepsy as an experience was not confined to literature and myth. There are shrines at Vari in

Attica, Pharsalos in Thessaly and Kafizin at Cyprus which all contain inscriptions suggesting they were set up by nympholepts.[8] That is, people who genuinely thought they had been snatched by nymphs turned the location of their abduction into a religious shrine to commemorate their experience and honour the nymphs responsible. The three shrines are all based in caves, which maps on to the literary tradition of nymph encounters happening only in rural areas. Yet, even if these places are secluded, they are still easily reachable from the city – and easy to wander into by accident.

The Romans also saw the natural world as a space where the boundary between the usual and the unusual wobbled. Again, our evidence comes from the world of religion, particularly the groves which were seen as residences of gods. The grove of Diana at Nemi, in the Alban Hills to the south-west of Rome, provides a case in point. The priest there, the *rex nemorensis* or king of the woods, constantly carried a weapon – he had won his office by killing the previous incumbent, and could himself be challenged for a fight to the death at any moment.[9] Diana was associated with other myths where a mortal was punished for straying into her domain. When the hunter Actaeon stumbled upon her bathing with her nymphs, she turned him into a stag and had his own hunting dogs tear him apart.[10] She also sent the Calydonian Boar, a fearsome giant of a beast, to ravage Aetolia as revenge on King Oeneus for neglecting her worship, making the countryside a site of unpredictable terror until it was killed.[11] The sense of the natural world as a permeable space even extended into Roman gardens, supposedly domesticated spaces that showed off human control of nature, but which always retained an element of danger.[12] Sculpture groups, like the *Odyssey*-inspired grouping at Sperlonga featuring the sea-monster Scylla and the cyclops Polyphemus, invited elite Romans to enter this hazardous space of nature and risk encountering the monsters themselves.[13]

The ancient Greeks and Romans had a profound sense that they shared space with the supernatural, and that while spirits were not encountered as a matter of course, the unwary could run into them without warning. This conception of place as communal, populated by humans and non-humans as equal but different inhabitants, feeds into the sense that monsters not only occupy the monster zone but are also your near neighbours. The landscape of the everyday is deceptive. The classical monster may, as Felton observes, avoid urban areas, but that still leaves a lot of the map to choose from.[14]

A classical monster is not relegated to distant and unreachable realms, although some classical monsters prefer that kind of real estate. Their adaptability, or perhaps their decision to bed down in specific locations close to humans, makes them distinct to the monsters usually considered by monster studies. They co-occupy space rather than dwell separately. Carroll offers a compromise by suggesting that monsters are found in 'marginal, hidden, or abandoned sites: graveyards, abandoned towers and castles, sewers, or old houses', yet this doesn't quite fit either.[15] The classical monster that comes closest is the Minotaur – yet, his occupancy of the Labyrinth is forced upon him by Minos, who shuts him up in shame to hide the evidence of his wife Pasiphae's bestiality. It is the human that forces the monster into a place out of the way, and a human that forces others into that space to be devoured, creating the conditions for the monster to come into its own. The Greeks knew that the Minotaur had a full life cycle. An extraordinary red figure vase painting from Etruria, painted around 340 BC, shows Pasiphae with an infant Minotaur on her lap, about to latch onto her breast to feed (Fig. 2.1). Given that the ancients could conceive of a pre-cannibalistic Minotaur, a Minotaur who needed love and care as much as a human baby, one wonders what they might have said about the nature versus nurture debate and Minos' influence in bringing out the beast. The classical monster pays little heed to the maps which modern monster studies painstakingly construct.

Fig. 2.1 Pasiphae breastfeeding the Minotaur, Paris BnF inv. no. 1066. Reproduced with the permission of Bibliothèque nationale de France.

Lurking at the edges

The fourth and fifth of Cohen's Monster Theses, which I outlined in Chapter 1, offer another way of thinking about the monster and space – namely, that the monster dwells at the gates of difference and polices the borders of the possible. To put it another way, the monster likes boundaries and edges, mainly in order to hop from one side of them to the other. Many classical monsters physically embody such borders, since their bodies start as one thing and continue as another, crossing the line between animal species or between human and animal repeatedly as the blood flows through their veins.

The propensity of monsters to favour the border and the threshold, the moments of crossing over and crossing through, means that they can be found wherever there are changes, shifts and alterations. The connection between monsters and boundaries recalls Kristeva's notion of abjection – namely, that abjection happens at the place between 'me' and 'not me', where the boundary of the skin opens and closes for things that once were 'me' to become 'not me'. For Kristeva, the primal repression that allows the foundation for rational human thought requires this pushing away of the reality of the lines between 'me' and 'not me', so that we can psychologically suspend our disbelief in our existential improbability and get on with developing a consciousness. While one may disagree with her premises, it is not necessary to subscribe to her psychoanalytic principles to see the appeal of boundaries to monsters.

In geographical terms, the obvious border is that between the natural and the human, the country and the city. Classical monsters may haunt 'mountains, rocks, caves, cliffs, and other natural places untamed by culture', but the border is inevitably perforated – either by a traveller, seeking out the monster zone, or because the border of a shared space is crossed over more easily than we think.[16] This is another function of the monster's policing of the borders. We reassure ourselves that we know how to accurately distinguish wild areas from cultivated ones. But the ease with which classical heroes fall into the lap of monsters tells a different story – one in which the boundaries are not clearly fixed, and one cannot trust one's intuition about where is safe and where is not. The monster patrols the boundary, sometimes on this side, sometimes on that. The space that was safe yesterday may not be safe today.

The border between the urban and the rural exists in places besides the stark city wall – another tempting fantasy, that promises we know the difference between 'urban' and 'rural', while nature fights to reclaim the cobbled streets. Roman literature offers a clear example of this separation in Horace's *Satire* 1.8, which is spoken by a wooden statue of Priapus set up on the Esquiline in some public gardens reclaimed from the space's previous use as a mass grave for the poor. Into this garden at night come two witches, who proceed to perform all sorts of frightful magic, drawing on the location's deathly past. They are only frightened away when the statue splits itself and lets forth a fart. This poem shows how layers of space and meaning rub against each other, creating air pockets (as it were) into which monsters can slip. The gardens believe that they have suppressed their previous deathly nature, but the tension between ground for growing and ground for sowing is not so easily tidied up. Monsters find cracks to burst out where a new meaning has been papered over the top of an old one.

I first drafted this chapter as the world reacted to the election of Donald Trump as 45th President of the United States. One popular analysis positioned his election as a response to the Obama presidency, to the drive for equality for women, to the increasing public profile of transgender issues, to immigrants and Latinx Americans – in other words, a push back to 'how things used to be', driven by a nostalgia for an era where men were men and women were women, and they were all white. The monstrous realities of American racism, xenophobia and misogyny have not only resisted attempts to write them out of existence, but have appropriated the fresh template that was laid over them. The imposition of a new model, a new way of doing things, never manages to rid itself of the monsters who have been occupying those borders and barriers.

Cohen's second Monster Thesis, that the monster always escapes, warns us that the monster will return to the space which seemed purged of monstrosity.[17] The occupation of borders and boundaries ensures that there is always an exit, and an entrance, nearby. The ability to slip and slide in and out of narratives and genres allows the classical monster to dwell where it wills. Its ubiquity comes from its ability to go *everywhere*, for it can always find shadows and passageways – or fertile ground into which it can send a tendril to take root and bloom.

Genre as place

The classical monster's disregard for place, boundaries and location affects not only the geography of its placement but also the genre in which it appears. This raises an issue from a monster studies perspective – namely, do true monsters only appear in horror? Much scholarly discussion of the monster focuses exclusively on horror texts. In literary terms, Mary Shelley's *Frankenstein* (1818) and Bram Stoker's *Dracula* (1897) are the gothic ancestors of a rich realm of horror writing, including the *oeuvre* of Stephen King. In cinema, key films for discussion include *Alien* (1979) and its sequels, *The Texas Chainsaw Massacre* (1974), *Jaws* (1975), *Carrie* (1976), *The Silence of the Lambs* (1991), *The Hunger* (1983) and *An American Werewolf in London* (1981). In all of these texts, the classical monster is conspicuous by its absence. Does that mean it is not really a monster?

Wood's analysis of horror monsters picks out five key tropes that have been circulating since the 1960s – the monster as psychotic or schizophrenic human; the revenge of Nature; religious disturbance in the form of Satanism, diabolic possession or the Antichrist; the Terrible Child, often connected to the previous type; and cannibalism.[18] This list, dominated by the serial killer, appears to leave no space for classical monsters in horror film. They are much more likely to be found romping in something best labelled the 'heroic epic', such as one of the Percy Jackson films or books, or one of the innumerable films about Hercules.

The reason for this, one might argue, is that classical monsters have been passed down the ages enmeshed in a net of myth. Their entanglement with the narratives of well-respected classical stories may, perhaps, make them appear off-limit to horror. They exist precisely because they encounter a hero, who must overcome them in order to complete his quest, rather than because they create terror in their own right. Sometimes, the hero's success involves the monster's death, as in the case of Perseus beheading Medusa; sometimes, the monster can be conquered in other ways, like Oedipus' answer to the Sphinx's riddle; sometimes, all the hero must do is escape by the skin of his teeth, as when Odysseus sails past Scylla and Charybdis, although six of his nameless sailors sacrifice their lives so that he can continue his voyage. This approach sees the monster as a creature petrified in story-amber, locked into the narrative role that each myth has given it, and deprived of the vitality that living myth or sacred stories have in the process of transmission.[19]

Such an interpretation ignores an important characteristic of ancient myth itself – namely, its constant openness to retelling and fresh interpretation. This versatility goes back to antiquity. The group of poets known as the Alexandrian school, for example, take considerable pride in referring to the most unfamiliar variant of a myth in their poems to show off their esoteric learning and their readers' ability to spot the obscure allusions. As myth has been handed down, it has continued to adapt to suit the times that it finds itself in – hence the frustration I feel when a modern version of a myth is judged in terms of how 'authentic' it is, as if there were only one story from antiquity to follow slavishly.

The so-called 'proper version' is often taken from a popular children's compendium of myth with all the juicy bits taken out, perhaps Bulfinch or Hawthorne, or the pseudo-scholarly account of Robert Graves, rather than from antiquity itself.[20] This belief in fixed stories stands in stark contrast to Ovid's *Metamorphoses*, a compendium of tales which self-consciously revels in the adaptability of myth.

The modern idea that the mythic story must stay within the fixed limits set by white male interpreters of the canon has no power over classical monsters. Myth often travels with them, but they wear its tatters around their shoulders rather than allowing it to tie their hands. When we encounter a classical monster, even though it may be dwelling outside the borders of horror, we still think we are meeting a monster, not just a glorified prop supporting a hero's *amour propre*. The flexibility of myth is precisely what allows the monster to flex away from its companion hero, to find new stories to tell. That these stories do not take place within horror does not, I would argue, make them less *monstrous*.

True, it may make what Mittman calls their *impact* less immediately obvious, especially if we follow Carroll's framework of monstrous force. He argues for a specific form of art-horror, in which the genre of horror organises its narrative elements to create a certain set of responses to the monstrous. He distinguishes art-horror from natural horror, that is, the sort of horror we might feel while seeing footage from Aleppo or Mosul, the uncovering of mass graves of genocide victims, or the election of an American president endorsed by the Ku Klux Klan.[21] He also marks out a difference between the monsters that create art-horror and monsters that live outside the horror genre. His main example comes from fairy tales, under which rubric he also bundles 'myths and odysseys'.[22] The amalgamation is significant, because Carroll's primary distinction is that while in generic horror, humans view monsters as 'abnormal, as disturbances of the natural order', in fairy tales 'monsters are part of the everyday furniture of the universe' – they can be 'accommodated by the metaphysics of the cosmology that produced them' within the borders of the fairy tale world.[23]

This explanation for why the monsters of fairy tale are not art-horror monsters will simply not do for classical myth, for the world of classical myth *is* the human world. While the monsters may have existed during a previous era of gods and demigods, the stories of the nympholepts reveal a conviction that the porous boundary between the earthly and the divine has not been sealed up. Just because something may be an ordinary part of the world's furniture does not mean that it cannot inspire fear and horror. Again, the emphasis on 'horror' as part of the response necessary to monsters is, I think, a red herring. Certainly, horror can sometimes be a useful identifying feature, but the fundamental property of a monster is to make us *think*. Cohen's seventh Monster Thesis, that the monster stands at the threshold, observes that 'monsters ask us how we perceive the world, and how we have misrepresented what we have attempted to place'.[24] We know monsters by their interrogation of us – and sometimes they can ask us frightening questions. The fear that being asked to examine our comfortable preconception can inspire is not restricted to the genre of horror.

Monsters in the basement

A space where many people may encounter classical monsters for the first time, often at a young age, is their own table tops, in the context of role-playing games. While the prevalence of classical content in these games is generally accepted in a vague sort of way, there has been little focused study on how they treat the ancient world. Indeed, I hesitate here, as someone whose knowledge of an exceptionally wide and diverse field comes second and third hand. That said, since the first edition of *Dungeons and Dragons*, created by Gary Gygax, was released in 1974, a survey of D&D bestiaries shows a consistent presence of classical monsters in its game world.[25] While some monsters like the hydra and the Chimera appear in every iteration, others fade in and out, perhaps due to their incompatibility with central game mechanics. Other individual monsters are turned into races – hence a race of medusas and their male counterparts, the maedar, as well as packs of minotaurs. The background provided in the bestiaries, too, changes from handbook to handbook, resulting in a game environment where players are actively encouraged to use their own imaginations in repurposing classical monsters for their adventure narrative.

The use of this aspect of classical heritage alongside myths from other cultures and entirely made-up creatures and deities 'served as a great leveler', in that it created equivalence between historical mythic traditions and imagined ones.[26] This levelling is compounded by the fact that the D&D world locates all its inhabitants in an entirely fictional universe, of which the most significant element for our purposes is its elimination of an equivalent to the ancient Mediterranean.[27] In a game-space in which the Dungeon Master's imagination is essential if the game is to be any fun at all for the other players, classical monsters make versatile gaming pieces, deployed for their function as adversaries rather than their narratives.

That the classical monster inhabits the D&D universe, and the world of 'the game' created wherever a Dungeon Master and Players gather together, may appear an insignificant cultural factoid, yet its inclusion had wide-reaching consequences. The children who grew up playing D&D obsessively, absorbing both the details of classical monsters and the way they responded to the demands that the D&D universe placed on them, grew up to become the creators of mainstream culture in the 1980s and beyond, bringing that understanding of the classical tradition with them. What we can take away from the space of D&D, and tabletop gaming more generally, flags up two important characteristics of the places classical monsters lurk. First, they persevere in the territory they find themselves in; despite the reshaping of their narrative description in every edition of the D&D bestiaries, they continue to be perceived as important inhabitants of the gaming world. Second, classical monsters occupy all forms of popular culture; there are no spaces off limits to them. Equally, no space is less important than any other space. While I concentrate on certain types of reception because that is where my expertise lies, that does not preclude or devalue the other locations in which classical monsters appear.

The message is the medium

There is one further trend about the place and space that monsters occupy that I think is worth commenting on, and that is what happens when a monster gets put on screen. Something about *vision* changes how we conceptualise a classical monster. Words allow space – Homer never tells us what the sirens *look* like, only what they *sound* like. Their monstrosity is rooted somewhere other than their appearance, at least for Odysseus. Yet, when it comes to visual representation, putting the monster into a physical shape is a move towards tying down a tendril. I am reminded of the Ravenous Bugblatter Beast of Traal in Douglas Adams' *The Hitchhiker's Guide to the Galaxy*: 'a mind-bogglingly stupid animal, it assumes that if you can't see it, it can't see you', and so is easily escaped through judicious deployment of the hitchhiker's trusty towel.[28] The sight of a monster becomes a way of fixing it into being.

When this is done on a black or red figure vase, or on a sculpture, the impact of the pinning down is minimal. While a particular image may circulate around a group of viewers, its impact is comparatively limited beyond that circle, particularly in an age before mass media. But something happens as the technology that allows images to be reproduced evolves. Benjamin analysed this change in his essay 'The Work of Art in the Age of Its Technological Reproducibility', which I think helps articulate a further element of how classical monsters are now represented. He argues that as it became possible to reproduce a piece of art, first through printing, then through photography, and finally on film, an important part of the object's aura was lost. The act of reproduction removes the reproduced object from the place that it is inextricably linked to, and from the tradition to which it belongs.[29] That is, the act of reproducing an art work or an item, making it multiple, kills the authenticity which belonged to it when it was unique. Ironically, it is the urge to get close to an object that drives its reproduction in the first place – hundreds, thousands of people can own copies of the *Mona Lisa*, and access a watered-down version of its brilliance, regardless of how far they might be from the Louvre.

Second, Benjamin argues that the main purpose of film is to teach humans how to handle the new realm of technology which governs their lives in unprecedented ways.[30] Film gives office and factory workers a way back to their humanity, after they have spent the day relinquishing it as part of the capitalist machine.[31] Yet Benjamin sees film as something particular, different from painting or photography – the painter or photographer creates a total image, while a film is pieced together through montage to represent the deep reality of something.[32] Its nature allows it to bring out otherwise hidden elements, and, in turn, represent all the *other* cogs in the machinery of capitalism which might otherwise lie outside an individual's sphere of knowledge.

I would argue that Benjamin's observation that a replicated object loses its connection to its unique tradition and meaning also holds true of the classical monster, who has come onto the silver screen in a big way in recent years, in light of the advent of computer-generated imagery (CGI). Initially, screen attempts to do classical monsters had, perhaps, been somewhat optimistic. One thinks of the Nemean Lion in the Steve Reeves *Hercules* (1958), which is no match for the iconic Metro Goldwyn Mayer lion which opens the credits. Things became easier with the rise of stop-motion technology, which enabled Ray Harryhausen to create his iconic creatures, and the increasingly sophisticated development of CGI. These developments have allowed classical monsters to appear on screen with increasing levels of detail and verisimilitude.

But, I think, this desire to be authentic is precisely the problem. At the same time as Benjamin would say technological reproduction takes the classical monster away from the uniqueness that gave it its aura, the increasing power of CGI allows film makers to reproduce monsters in ever more loving detail – every scale on Medusa, every hair of the Chimera's fur can be electronically painted into life. The paradox, I think, is that as the classical monster comes ever more clearly into view, it loses the shadows which let it be monstrous because the cinematic floodlights engulf it.

Haraway has a helpful way of thinking about this effect of light on the monstrous in relation to the patriarchy. She outlines a Western patriarchal narrative which talks about the emergence of the physical body from the first birth (following the first Fall), followed by a second heliotropic birth.[33] This version of history, told from a perspective in which we are always advancing, has a fixed beginning and a definite sense that where we are, right now, is the best place mankind has ever been. The moment at which man really becomes man is the European Enlightenment, the bringing of light through the application of rational thought, the use of the (supposedly infallible and impartial) scientific method, the ever-closer scrutiny and examination of the world around us. Haraway sees this as the moment that creates the heliotropic gaze, a way of looking which turns towards the light of the Enlightenment, and prioritises the Enlightenment's rationalist ideology and the idea that everything can somehow be measured, observed, described, understood through supposedly neutral scientific practices.[34]

The heliotropic gaze matches up with the positive model of power through intense scrutiny outlined by Foucault. Similarly to the system of *quadrillage*, the heliotropic gaze believes that by sufficiently close examination, the world can be thoroughly understood – then made subject to man's authority and put to his use. The light of reason dispels any uncertainty when focused upon an object of study. The ability to look closely at things not only controls them, but also makes us fully rational humans – or, more accurately, fully rational men, for that scrutiny takes as its objects the other, the women, the racialised, and, yes, the monstrous. The glare of that patriarchal heliotropic gaze, the idea that we always look towards the light and that the light is where we ought to look, takes away the darkness in which the monster lurks, and thus takes away a crucial part of the monster itself.

Let me express the same idea using a fitting mythological reference. Whenever classical monsters appear in movies, we, the viewers, become Medusa. Our vision freezes them in place, into living statues on the plinth of the silver screen. By looking at them directly, we pin them down. One rapidly emerging fact about cinema's approach to the classical world in general is that (studios believe) audiences take a very conservative approach to antiquity – they *know* what the ancient world looks like, and get unsettled if they are presented with something else. This expectation accounts for the easy slip-and-slide of factual accuracy that often happens with films set in the Greek world, where soldiers wear Roman army gear; the anachronism doesn't matter, because the army now *looks* like an ancient army.[35] This is the gaze in action – even if the reasons behind these assumptions are inaccurate, the fundamental belief about what we should be looking at persists. In the same way, when a classical monster is put on screen, we *know* what they are supposed to look like. We fix them down with our expectations – and we draw visual and narrative pleasure from taking on the gaze of the camera, controlling the events in front of us.[36]

I will talk more about the consequences of this for classical monsters in the coming chapters, but for now I think it is enough to say that the result of reproducing the monster again and again, on screen after screen in city after city, and in ever increasing detail, is that the spaces it finds in movies and on television are fundamentally different to those spaces it finds in books, even comic books. When we can see the monster, our imaginations are let off the hook. Heliotropic vision chases away the darkness so we view the monster in all its squamosity. Unfortunately, this creates the illusion that we *know* the monster: we are well steeped in the patriarchal narrative that to see is to control. By adopting the position of the camera, by falling for what Haraway calls the 'god trick' of assuming that technology gives us infinite and infallible vision, we think that we are in charge of the story.[37] But, as my alternative rhizomatic model suggests, while one tendril may be pinned down in hostile territory, other roots are stretching out to other, more fertile, soils.

My point, at the end of this theoretical trail, is that in terms of the place where monsters live, not only physical location matters. Thinking about the 'monster zone' on maps and the marginal spaces among human habitation is only one part of the story – monsters are affected by the genre and the medium that they inhabit as much as where they happen to hang their hat(s). The sort of cultural artefact they occupy makes a significant difference to how the monster manifests and the audience's freedom to interpret it. Films, television, books, comics – each domain has its own characteristic soil. With that in mind, I want to spend the next two chapters thinking a bit more closely about the silver screen, to draw out some particularly interesting effects of technological reproduction.

Monsters on Film in the Harryhausen Era

Film is powerful, particularly in the way it tells stories. Yet there is something fascinating and oddly uncomfortable about the way that the classical monster comes to life on the silver screen. They have had plenty of screen time, but often as ancillary props for the hero whose success is the focus of the plot. From the epic films of the mid-twentieth century, in particular those involving the work of Ray Harryhausen, a clear pattern emerges of monsters being shackled to heroes (even if not their own) as set pieces within heroic narratives. They are held fast through the stories they are required to tell, even if they sometimes manage to engage with the cultural fears of their own eras. However, just before the turn of the century, there were some signs that the suffocating cinematic bond between the monster and the hero was beginning to fray.

Film is, in some ways, the perfect location to examine a monster, because it reveals the truth of Cohen's sixth Monster Thesis – 'fear of the monster is really a kind of desire'.[1] Film allows us to look, look and look some more at what is forbidden and what is loathed. The cinema is a peculiarly safe place to encounter the monster – we can come ever closer, seeing its slavering jaws and shuddering at its hybrid transgression, always safe in the knowledge that the film will finish soon, the lights will go up, and we will return to ordinary life. A cinema spectator enjoys the process of identifying with a hero who kills the monster, but also, perhaps, with the monster itself; while not every viewer will experience the same kinds of pleasure in recognition, the enjoyment of being scared by something alien which is then conquered is central to many movie plots. If you wanted to build a cage for a monster, the movie theatre would be a good place to seek inspiration for your design.

Not all classically inspired films house monsters. In historical epic, characterised by movies like *Cleopatra* (1963) and *The Fall of the Roman Empire* (1964), while the characters may possess heroic qualities, their monsters are usually human. We are more likely to find monsters in what we might label mythical epics, in that they retell the *Odyssey*, Hercules' labours, Perseus' rescue of Andromeda and so on. The divide between 'historical' and 'mythical' is somewhat artificial, since these films share a visual style that makes the distinction between the two rather superfluous. The best example is *Pompeii* (2014), which is notionally about a historical episode, but resembles *Clash of the Titans* (2010), and has as its protagonist Kit 'you know nothing, Jon Snow' Harrington, bringing the aura of *Game of Thrones* (2011–19) to the whole production.[2] But, despite overlapping styles, films ostensibly based on history tend to leave classical monsters alone.

There are three waves of films focusing on classical myth. In the first two decades of the twentieth century, alongside historical films cinema-goers could enjoy the legitimised nudity of *Le jugement de Pâris* (*The Judgement of Paris*, 1902), followed by *Island of Calypso: Ulysses and the Giant Polyphemus* (*L'île de Calypso: Ulysse et le géant Polyphème*, 1905), *Le retour d'Ulysse* (*The Return of Ulysses*, 1909), *The Fall of Troy* (*La caduta di Troia*, 1911) and the *Odyssey* (*Odissea*, 1911).[3] The second wave spans the fifties, sixties and seventies, ending with *Clash of the Titans* (1981), and is dominated by the work of Ray Harryhausen. We are currently surfing the third, initiated by the surge of *Gladiator*'s success (2000). You could argue that *Troy* (2004) was the first film to return to myth, although the initial *Percy Jackson* film in 2010 is the first to take myth on its own terms.[4] Many of these films work with the Trojan war cycle, handling the material as if it were historical fiction, and are thus monster-lite. In the words of Solomon, some of 'these films set good standards, yet a truly superb film of ancient Greek myth still waits to be made'.[5] This was true when Solomon was writing in 2000, and remains true now, in that we are still awaiting a great *Odyssey* or *Iliad*. Instead, since 2000, an abundance of films have retold the tales of Hercules, Perseus and a few other Greek heroes. It would be a struggle to call any of these films 'truly superb', more often because of the dialogue and acting than because of their frequent departure from any recognisable version of myth.

Sometimes, it doesn't matter that a movie won't win awards at Cannes. Solomon hits this on the head in his discussion of the sword and sandal or *peplum* genre, a group of films which usually feature a strongman vaguely identified to a USA audience as Hercules who is sent off on an improbable mission with an increasingly tenuous link to the classical world. The most extreme is probably *Hercules Against the Moon Men* (1964). While these films may lack narrative subtlety and realism, 'they do have colourful costumes and imaginative sets and seductive mistresses and burly humor and Mediterranean scenery and bizarre tortures and nineteen-inch biceps and furious battles and likeable heroes and the triumph of good over evil'.[6] Sometimes, this is what you go to the cinema for; if you wanted a nuanced take on the notion of the classical hero, you probably wouldn't have paid to see either version of *Clash of the Titans*. The muscleman inheritance is clearly on show in these new heroic epics, which feature rippling muscles and bulging torsos in glorious enhanced Technicolour. While the actors may no longer be professional bodybuilders, one (Dwayne Johnson) made his name in professional wrestling, and the expectations of personal fitness now placed on male actors are much higher than they used to be.[7]

Films of this type follow narratives of heroes who have particular monsters to fight, and with whom the ancient character is closely aligned. The dominance of the hero epic, particularly the Hercules-style *peplum* or sword-and-sandal number, makes the films of the 1950s and 1960s more interested in the heroic quest against evil than necessarily in monsters themselves. These movies were originally made in Italy, but American producers purchased the rights to distribute them at home, and domestic audiences steeped in the tensions of the Cold War flocked to see them. The narrative of a valiant figure in a 'perpetual, heroic struggle against tyranny' had been well established by Hollywood's earlier Biblical and Roman historiographical films.[8] Equally, the 'Red Scare' created a fear of creeping communism, where your respectable next door neighbour could be a deadly threat to your way of life.[9] The focus on individual struggle and the human bad guy arises as much from the contemporary political climate as from the problems of putting a monster on screen.

Where you do get to see a monster, they tend to be of the less mystical sort. I think particularly of the 1958 *Hercules*, featuring Steve Reeves in his breakout role as the muscle-bound hero – this production was the first of a wave of similar films based (very) loosely on classical myth, and stands in for the whole *peplum* genre.[10] The plot is fairly straightforward: Hercules visits the court of Iolco at the invitation of King Pelias to tutor Prince Iphitus in the ways of war. He is drawn into a dispute over who should rightfully rule the kingdom, and sails to Colchis with the crew of Argo (here, the ship owner) and Prince Jason, son of the murdered king Aeson, to find the golden fleece stolen from Iolco and prove Jason's right to the throne. On the way, Hercules battles various beasts, the crew narrowly escape sudden death on the island of the Amazons, and Pelias' daughter Iole is captivated by the hero's omnipresent chest muscles.

The movie creates a strong division between the threats that Hercules and his companions face, establishing a clear narrative monster zone. The majority of the film focuses on dramatic interpersonal conflict: Pelias is blackmailed by the murderer he hired to kill his brother while Anteia, Queen of the Amazons, is torn between her duty to murder Jason and her passionate love for him. Since one must see Hercules perform deeds of amazing strength in a Hercules film, while in Greece he duly wrestles a lion and the Cretan Bull. Both of these animals are presented as fearsome – the lion actually kills Prince Iphitus, and Pelias demands Hercules fight the Cretan Bull in order to atone for his son's death. However, they are played by 'real' animals, and the scenes are careful confections of shots involving the animal, the animal and a trainer, and Steve Reeves and a more-or-less convincing model. Within the plot, the lion is still sufficiently dangerous to slay Iphitus, and the Bull causes Hercules some problems (not least because he has given up his demigod status in order to win Iole's heart). Indeed, the Bull was played by an American bison which gives it a 'larger than life' look.[11] Nonetheless, despite these monsters' roots in Hercules' twelve labours, the challenges of the Greek mainland remain within the boundaries of the ordinary.

By contrast, two different sorts of monster await the Argonauts in Colchis. When the crew land, they are attacked by a tribe of ghastly monkey men, identified as such in the trailer and whom I can only describe as casually racist in their use of blackface. Asclepius comments they are 'something out of a nightmare', but their unexplained appearance relies on an audience assumption about the barbaric and monstrous nature of inhabitants of distant lands. The second monster is the mythically inevitable dragon who guards the fleece – or, to be more strictly accurate, the pseudo-dinosaur which is napping under the tree and woken when Jason uses it as a stepping stool. Despite Hercules' dominance throughout the rest of the movie, in this scene Jason must tackle the dragon alone. Fabrizio Mioni pluckily dodges and weaves around the set as the beast rears, waves its arms, wiggles its tail and tries to pick him out from behind some rocks. A single spear pierces the dragon's head, allowing Jason to claim the fleece over its prostrate body. The monster is never actually *named*, but that doesn't matter (although the trailer calls it a 'dragon monster'). Hercules proclaims that 'yours was the deed of the king' – Jason has proved both his maturity and his royal credentials through valiant single combat (eerily conducted only to a background hum, which enhances the atmospheric tension). Hercules' most important role in fighting this monster is, ironically, his manly validation of the would-be king who actually conquers it.[12]

By establishing a geographical distinction between monsters found in Greece and those in Colchis, the movie argues that truly terrifying monsters exist only in the monster zone. The 'normal' beasts inhabit territory in Greece which can be easily reached, and is occupied by men who belong to the same social world as Hercules. By contrast, once the expedition lands on Colchis, Hercules and his crew are immediately assailed by monsters who are framed as fantastic, beyond expectation and unknown to the domesticated Greek mainland. The journey into the far reaches of the map, where we expect to find dragons, has given us a dragon. Yet the overall plot is far more concerned with King Pelias' machinations to usurp the throne – the fantastical monsters serve instead to reinforce Hercules' position as hero, defined by his mastery over them.

The impact of Harryhausen

Ray Harryhausen and his *oeuvre* are critical for classical monsters on film. His remarkable grasp of stop-motion animation was built over a career that spanned an apprenticeship on *Mighty Joe Young* (1949) with Willis O'Brien, the mastermind behind *King Kong* (1933), to *Clash of the Titans* (1981).[13] From his first amateur films featuring dinosaurs in his back garden, he was a creator of monsters or, as he preferred to say, 'creatures, always creatures, never monsters'.[14] His classical monsters are neither isolated nor unique – they must be understood as part of a broader body of work which reflects his consistent interests and priorities.[15]

Harryhausen's early career was spent making monster-on-the-rampage movies. *The Beast from 20,000 Fathoms* (1953), *It Came from Beneath the Sea* (1955) and *20 Million Miles to Earth* (1957) all included an exciting beast which caused havoc to the human environment it unexpectedly found itself in. Like many movies of this period, they express anxiety about human use of technology through its role in unleashing monsters on the unsuspecting public. *The Beast from 20,000 Fathoms* featured a rhedosaurus, a sort of dinosaur Harryhausen himself created since the only guidance he got from the screenplay was that 'they wanted a monster'.[16] In an early outline of the film, they had been thinking of using a minotaur. *It Came from Beneath the Sea* featured an octopus (really a 'sixtopus' for reasons of practicality) that destroyed the Golden Gate Bridge in San Francisco. *20 Million Miles to Earth* followed the brief and unfortunate life of the Ymir, which arrived in a crashed spaceship and grew whenever it ate sulphur. Since the crash occurred off the coast of Italy, the Ymir was able to have its final rampage in the Colosseum, which appealed to Harryhausen since 'dramaturgy always demands that the "villain" should die in the most dramatic way possible'.[17]

These films, along with his earlier short film *The Story of King Midas* (1953), point towards an interest in the classical world and the monstrous resources it might provide. This fascination comes to the fore in *The 7th Voyage of Sinbad* (1958), the first feature film where Harryhausen had a producer role and was significantly involved in the overall plot. Among the various wonders put on screen, a servant is transformed into a snakewoman, a magician brings an armed skeleton to life and Sinbad must tackle a Cyclops who threatens his men. The snakewoman owes a lot to the Indian *naga*, but there are also early gestures towards the Medusa myth. The skeleton would later inspire the Children of the Hydra's Teeth in *Jason and the Argonauts*. The Cyclops, a more obviously classical monster, was designed to include a goat's legs and hooves specifically so the audience knew they weren't just looking at a man in a suit (Fig. 3.1).[18] The integration of a classical monster into a film primarily inspired by an Arabic storytelling tradition reinforces my earlier observation that classical monsters are extremely happy to move beyond the bounds of classical mythology, if they see fit.[19]

The Cyclops powerfully signals the transition from the civilised court of the Caliph to the wild island, both as an individual and technically as a whole society. Originally, a 'colony of Cyclops' (*sic*) had been planned for the island around which Sinbad's adventures revolve, but financial constraints led to a more

Fig. 3.1 The Cyclops in *The 7th Voyage of Sinbad* (1958).

pragmatic approach.[20] The script thus sprinkles in liberal references to the Cyclops as a plural entity, even though only one appears on screen at a time. They are rough and non-verbal creatures, bookending the film and locating it in the Monster Zone – the plot opens when Sinbad rescues the wizard Sokurah from one on his way to Baghdad, and the final set-piece battle takes place between a Cyclops that has wandered into the tunnel that leads to Sokurah's lair. The contrast between the primitive lives of the Cyclops and the extraordinary riches of Baghdad reinforces their purpose as a marker of adventure and exoticism.

Despite its transposition into a parallel myth-world, and an aesthetic overhaul, there are still signs that this Cyclops knows his Homer, in particular the episode in book nine of the *Odyssey*, where Odysseus and his men are trapped after invading the cave of the cyclops Polyphemus. As return for their ransacking of his property, he devours the crew, two by two. Odysseus gets him drunk and puts out his eye with a heated spear, escaping by tying himself and his crew under Polyphemus' flock as they go out to graze the next morning. As his boat sails away, Odysseus is unable to resist revealing his identity. Polyphemus curses him as he throws a boulder off-shore and nearly sinks the boat. *The 7th Voyage* features a sequence where Sinbad must rescue one of his men from being roasted on a monstrous spit for dinner, in which the Cyclops is distracted and eventually blinded by a flaming brand that Sinbad waves. At the film's opening, after Sinbad and his crew appear to have got safely out of reach of the Cyclops on the shore, he hurls a huge rock at them and overturns their rowing boat. Homeric narrative history affects the Cyclops' behaviour, even in this new environment.[21]

I can't leave *7th Voyage* without mentioning the sirens, who appear in the film but only aurally. Again, Sinbad is placed within the narrative of the *Odyssey*, potentially a familiarising move to bring the audience closer to the tale. The original scene list included a full sequence of the Isle of Wailing Sirens, with shots of the beasts whom Harryhausen envisioned 'as alluring women with fish tails, but time didn't allow for it'.[22] In the final cut, the sirens remain unseen. When the crew of convicts that Sinbad has recruited revolts and locks their captain and Sokurah in the hold, the wizard portentously reveals that the rebellion is doomed because of the course the rebels have plotted: 'South of Colossa lies an accursèd island inhabited by wailing demons. Their screaming is heard over a hundred leagues. The men hearing it are driven mad. They drive their ships onto the jagged rocks and are devoured by sea serpents.' While the mutineers clutch their ears, shriek in pain and jump from masts in horror, we see waves beating on jagged rocks at the foot of a cliff, coming closer as the ship approaches sure destruction. Aurally, an electronic static gradually increases, giving the sirens an unearthly voice rather than a physical presence – fitting for a monster whose song Homer records but whose appearance he does not describe. Another Homeric touch survives as Sinbad's crew protect themselves by stuffing their ears with cloth – which, as one thoughtfully observes, they can make soundproof with a wax coating. The episode becomes another 'Boys' Own' adventure for Sinbad, yet at the same time reinforces the hierarchy of superiority within the film: the rebellion fails because its leaders cannot offer the knowledge required to evade the dangers posed by the hideous voices of unseen monstrous women.

The next Harryhausen film to feature classical content was *Jason and the Argonauts* (1963), drawing specifically on Greek myth and Jason's quest for the golden fleece. Apollodorus gives us a lengthy account of the story. King Pelias sends Jason on the quest in an attempt to foil a prophecy which declares him the king's murderer. Jason has many exciting adventures on his journey to Colchis, where he is assisted in retrieving the fleece by Medea, the king's daughter, who falls in love with him.[23] Harryhausen and his collaborator Charles Schneer settled on the Jason myth as suitable for cinema since it was a sequence of episodic events that could be organised into a sensible plot, and also provided the opportunity for 'encountering all manner of obstacles and beasts', thus unconsciously adopting the assumption that a monster must be defined by its defeat at a hero's hands.[24] The film features some impressive monsters – Talos, the great bronze guardian of the gods' jewellery box (Fig. 3.2); the harpies which torment the blind seer Phineas (played with panache by Patrick Troughton); the hydra which defends the fleece; and the Children of the Hydra's Teeth, animated skeletons whose memorable extended fight sequence with Jason ends the film. All of these monsters are regulatory – Talos, the hydra and its Children respond to attempted theft, while the harpies are punishments sent by Zeus. The episodic spectacular is augmented by heroic attempts to break the rules.

Jason often refers back to the 1958 *Hercules*, both in having an usurping king's son secretly join the crew, and in the discovery of the fleece itself. Where *Hercules* had the Tyrannosaur-like monster to battle, Harryhausen confronts Jason with a full-blown seven-headed hydra. Jason kills the beast with a sword through the heart, but *Jason* caps *Hercules* by following up with the Children of the Hydra's Teeth. Interestingly, the line where Aeetes, the King of Colchis, calls for the Children of the Hydra's Teeth is the only one that tells us that the beast, now deceased, is actually a hydra – no earlier warnings about a monster guarding the fleece are issued, and for anyone unfamiliar with the story, the appearance of the beast out of the cave must have come as quite a shock. It would also have come

Fig. 3.2 The model of Talos used in *Jason and the Argonauts* (1963).

as a surprise to those who knew the source material, where the original guardian is a dragon. Harryhausen borrowed the hydra from the Hercules cycle after deciding that dragons were now seen as more medieval than classical, and having animated a dragon before.[25] His priority is finding the monster which is the right 'fit' for the classical hero's story, to make its conquest most spectacular and allow him to display his impressive skills in animating it – for that, after all, is the monster's purpose.

Two lengthy sequences featuring Talos and the harpies also provide a spectacular show. Talos is awoken when Hercules steals a brooch pin from the gods' jewellery box, mistaking it for a javelin. The Argonauts attempt to escape the living statue, but it batters the ship with rocks, forcing it back to the shore. Jason uses his crew to distract the statue and removes the plug from its heel, releasing its steaming ichor. As the statue topples, the crew runs. Hylas runs back to collect the dropped brooch pin, only to be squashed as Talos falls on him. The capture of the harpies, by contrast, is the price the seer Phineas sets for telling

Jason and his crew the next step on their quest. Their capture involves an elaborate set-up with a ruined temple, and various establishing shots of them attacking Phineas as he eats. The existence of these monsters as part of the landscapes through which the Argonauts are travelling, just like the Cyclops in *7th Voyage*, signals that Hercules has entered the Monster Zone, and thus augments the fantastic element of his journeys.

After *Jason*, Harryhausen brought elements of classical myth into two further Sinbad films, *The Golden Voyage of Sinbad* (1973) and *Sinbad and the Eye of the Tiger* (1977). *Golden Voyage* nodded toward classical myth in its climactic scene. The two guardians of the Fountain of Destiny, the goal of Sinbad's quest, are a one-eyed centaur and a gryphon. They represent good and evil, paralleling Sinbad and his sorcerer nemesis Koura, whom they battle as part of the climactic sequence. These monsters, inspired by classical mythology, are imbued with symbolic moral power which drives the drama of the finale. Their fight with each other and the two human characters provides a spectacular set-piece, grounded in the display of their abnormality, as well as consummate stop-motion animation.

Sinbad and the Eye of the Tiger, by contrast, has a classical monster given a fascinating modern twist. The beast in question is the Minoton, created by the witch Zenobia to help her chase after Sinbad and stop him undoing the spell which turned her stepson, Prince Kassim, into a baboon. The Minoton is made from bronze, and it is forged on screen, echoing the ancient skill of the craftsman Daedalus – we see the monster literally come into being. It accompanies Zenobia on her journey after her stepson and Sinbad, and ultimately perishes under a huge block that it pulls out of a pyramid on her command.

What makes the Minoton so interesting from a monster studies perspective is the intersection of ancient and modern. One form contemporary monsters take, as I mentioned in Chapter 1, exists at the breakdown of the border between the technological and the biological, where the cyborg comes into being, and computers run amok. The Minoton is a rare example, as far as I am aware, of the technological/biological meeting the human/animal, and creating a monster which questions all these binaries at once. Its uncontrollable bestiality is doubled by its technological imperturbability. Its body, cast from bronze with a mechanical heart of pure gold, brings together and literally embodies several strands of contemporary monstrosity.

That said, as an actual monster, it leaves something to be desired. As Harryhausen himself said, 'Minoton should have been a far more important character and woven more intricately into the story as a terrifying tool of evil.'[26]

The problem arose from the fact that it mainly stood around, occasionally coming to life to perform some feat of strength. Some scenes required so little movement that viewers see a fibreglass suit worn by an actor standing still rather than the animated model.[27] While the creature showed Harryhausen's typical inspiration, it failed to capitalise on the monstrous potential embodied in its parts. Its stillness on screen makes it too easy to pin down and categorise – with more of a moving role, the strange magical uncanniness of stop-motion that Harryhausen felt was so vital for his creatures would have realised the full potential of its multiple hybridities and border transgressions. By keeping the Minoton immobile, the film fails to give its audience the anticipated spectacle of physical monstrosity in action.

There's a strange foretelling, to digress for a moment, of the fate that many of Harryhausen's monsters would eventually meet. The models, now the property of the Ray & Diana Harryhausen Foundation, tour the country for exhibitions and festivals, such as the 'Meet the Creatures' session at the Manchester Animation Festival in November 2016. After a screening of *Clash of the Titans*, attendees were invited to 'meet the stars of the film', Medusa and Calibos. Fans could have their photos taken alongside their favourite monsters, frozen into miniature curios, able to be circumnavigated and viewed from all angles under a convention centre's bright lights or in the safe custody of an exhibition case. There is no stalking off screen for them, no cave to retreat from the cataloguing, analytical, controlling gaze of those in whom they now inspire affection rather than fear. Alas for the Minoton; while Medusa and Calibos inspired viewers with their on-screen personalities, it never even got that far.

Harryhausen's last Hollywood movie was *Clash of the Titans* (1981), a version of the Perseus myth. One of this film's significant contributions to the rhetoric of cinematic monsters is the Kraken. The Kraken originally comes from Norse mythology, but the screenwriter of *Clash* felt that 'as a name for a sea monster, it was too good to miss' – again, the priority is the spectacle, not what the monster might signify.[28] It takes the shape of 'the mutant offspring of a prehistoric reptile that had mated with one of the mighty Titans', modelled on a merman with a fish tail and four prehensile arms that were meant to look like an octopus' tentacles;[29] as the film's major monster, it is thus linked to the sea goddess Thetis, who acts as the main divine antagonist. Harryhausen repeats the trick of using the same monster to bookend the film, although with decided differences between the two episodes. The film opens when King Acrisius throws his daughter Danae and her baby son into the sea to atone for her sin. Zeus decrees that he must be punished for this crime, not least because he is the father of the infant. His chosen punishment is for the Kraken to be released and set loose on the city of Argos to destroy it.

Our encounter with the Kraken at this stage is quite impressionistic. We see its massive body come out of its underwater cave, and its segmented torso leaps through the waves on the way to Argos. Yet, when the actual city is destroyed, we get little sign of the Kraken's involvement. Instead, gigantic waves assail buildings, statues and citizens, giving the impression the city is falling to a tsunami event rather than a Godzilla-like attack. Zeus kills Acrisius by crushing a terracotta statue representing him on Mount Olympus, giving him what looks like a massive heart attack. The Kraken compliantly returns to its lair, where it remains until summoned forth by a dispirited Zeus for the film's finale. However, its presence looms over the plot. After Queen Cassiopeia compares her daughter Andromeda with Thetis, the goddess has the pretext she needs to take revenge on behalf of her son Calibos. She demands Andromeda be sacrificed to the Kraken. When Perseus consults the man-eating Stygian Witches about how to kill the monster, they suggest the head of Medusa will change the Kraken to stone – 'a Titan against a Titan!' as one of them cackles, signalling an inevitable reiteration of monster after monster, and the spectacular parade of Perseus' quest within the film.

The Kraken reappears after Andromeda has been chained to a convenient rock, when it appears that Perseus' quest has been unsuccessful. Its slow release from the cave and gradual approach towards Andromeda aims to ratchet up the tension of the sequence. This time, we see the monster levering itself up behind some cliffs, showing off its multiple arms and torso to fine effect (Fig. 3.3). The viewer has more time to contemplate it, perhaps noting its similarities to the Creature from the Black Lagoon and the implicit sexual threat it thus poses to Andromeda. As the Kraken reaches down to grab the princess, Perseus appears on Pegasus, and after a dramatic aerial battle he holds Medusa's head aloft. The Kraken is transfixed and its petrified body slowly crumbles. The need for one monster to see the other leads to the death of both – Perseus' control of the visual act is thus the embodiment of the heliotropic gaze. After the tantalising opening destruction of Argos, the audience is finally allowed to sate their visual appetite for the Kraken's monstrosity, released once more from beneath the waves for their viewing pleasure. The enticing glimpse offered at the film's beginning is a promise of a postponed fearsome delight. After seeing only brief shots of the monster's body, the audience may enjoy the deferred pleasure not only of seeing the Kraken as a whole, but also watching its destruction.

It is, I think, no coincidence that Andromeda's sacrifice is scheduled for the evening of the longest day, because *Clash* makes some significant links between

Fig. 3.3 The Kraken in *Clash of the Titans* (1981).

monstrosity, twilight, dusk and shadow. All the monsters which Perseus encounters are somehow connected to dark times or spaces. Calibos, the monstrous King of the Marsh and the film's initial antagonist, occupies a torch-lit grove which Perseus and Andromeda's spirit only ever visit at night. Medusa lives under a ruined temple; the flickering braziers which send disturbing shadows up the walls disorientate her prey, but allow Perseus to lure her in close enough with his reflective shield to decapitate her. The colossal scorpions which come from Medusa's blood generate when Calibos takes advantage of Perseus' sound slumber to pierce the bag holding the decapitated head. The monsters of *Clash* literally live in the dark; when they are seen, or when light comes to them, they inevitably perish.[30]

This lack of seeing even manifests in the making of monstrosity. Calibos becomes a monster during the film's plot, a punishment for (among other things) killing all of Zeus' sacred winged horses except the stallion, Pegasus. The transformation takes place before the viewer's eyes, but by proxy. When Zeus places the terracotta statue of Calibos on the arena representing the world, the shot focuses on the statue's shadow as Zeus intones his fate: 'he will become abhorrent to human sight. He'll be shunned and forced to live as an outcast in the swamps and marshes. He'll be transformed into a mortal mockery, a shameful mark of his vile cruelty.' As Zeus passes judgement, the shadow of the statue writhes, and takes the form of the demonic cloven-hoofed half-human who will terrorise Andromeda now she will no longer marry him (Fig. 3.4).

The importance of the visual for the monster is underscored by Harryhausen's own comments on the design of Medusa. He claimed to find her representation as a beautiful woman with snakes for hair profoundly unsatisfying, and so is the first person (as far as I am aware) to represent Medusa with a snake's torso and tail (Fig. 3.5). Medusa is now overwhelmingly likely to be represented with a snake tail on screen and in books. Harryhausen created this shift by choosing to prioritise monstrosity over beauty: 'I felt we needed a striking and yet unconventionally hideously ugly demon.'[31] To this end, he took the bone structure of Medusa's severed head in Cellini's *Perseus with the head of Medusa* and made it ugly; the snake tail felt like 'an obvious progression' from the snakes in her hair.[32] His decision creates a shift in monstrous femininity, again structured by an instinct for cinematic impact – but its influence highlights the control creators hold over monsters on the screen.

Why were Harryhausen's monsters so successful, planting the yardstick for nostalgic animators of the next generation, and inspiring a love of classical mythology in the young audiences who saw the film when it came out and on innumerable damp bank holiday afternoons? (Confession – as a child, I had easy

Fig. 3.4 Calibos (Neil McCarthy) in *Clash of the Titans* (1981).

Fig. 3.5 Medusa in *Clash of the Titans* (1981).

access to both *Jason* and *Clash* on well-worn VHS tapes.) Harryhausen himself had something to say about the change in industry expectations and practices:

> Model animation has been relegated to a reflection, or a starting point for creature computer effects that has reached a high few could have anticipated. However, for all the wonderful achievements of the computer, the process creates creatures that are too realistic and for me that makes them unreal because they have lost one vital element – a dream quality. Fantasy, for me, is realizing strange beings that are so far removed from the 21st century. [...] Fantastical creatures where the unreal quality becomes even more vital. Stop-motion supplies the perfect breath of life for them, offering a look of pure fantasy because their movements are beyond anything we know.[33]

Harryhausen's particular gift for creating monsters that gripped his viewers relied precisely upon stop-motion's failure to create the real. His beasts occupy the geographical boundary between reality and fantasy, drawing vitality from their liminality. The articulation of armatures and padding, of fur and feathers and fabric, in his view worked because it did not attempt to give its audience realism. In bringing his creatures to life, acting as a Pygmalion of his maquettes rather than a statue, he did not seek a Foucauldian control over them, making them hyper-real, fixing them in the world where he gave them temporary life.[34]

His commitment to character design and allowing his creatures personality means that they retain autonomy despite their episodic deployment. Some of their energy comes from the way that these creatures were filmed – painstaking frame-by-frame movements that took weeks and months to complete, requiring complete dedication to the work and constant methodological innovation to keep up with developments in film technology. The slow, almost meditative quality of this labour comes through the accounts Harryhausen gives of his creative activity. It is not an act of pinning down, but an act of setting free. The goal is to communicate the spirit of the beast rather than provide an accurate vision of its appearance. For Harryhausen, unreality makes the monster live.

Some interim monsters

After *Clash*, there was something of a lull in classical movies featuring monsters, which had always been a subset of wider classically inspired cinema, due to a shift in film-making practices concerning the ancient world. The disasters associated with *Cleopatra* (1963) put studios off investing in another big ancient epic project, making *The Fall of the Roman Empire* (1964) the last of that particular genre for a few decades.[35] Ancient world movies either focused on comedy, as in *Carry on Cleo* (1964) and *A Funny Thing Happened on the Way to the Forum* (1966), or were art-house productions primarily interested in human monstrosity – *Fellini Satyricon* (1969) and Michael Cacoyannis's adaptations of Greek tragedy come to mind. Equally, Harryhausen himself observed that when he made *Clash*, heroes were losing ground to anti-heroes; while the *Star Wars* films gave audiences the heroic fix they needed (1977, 1980 and 1983), the *Mad Max* trilogy (1979, 1981 and 1985) pointed in the direction of things to come. The Greek hero, along with his monstrous companions, were on a break.

One unlikely film did handle classical monsters, before *Gladiator* revitalised the ancient world epic in 2000 – Disney's animated version of *Hercules* (1997), which embraced its sword-and-sandal heritage with gusto.[36] On his journey to reclaim the divinity that Hades steals from him, Hercules encounters some truly frightening monsters. Three main episodes of monster encounter each mark a significant stage of Hercules' life story. He meets the river guardian centaur Nessus on his way to establish himself as a hero in Thebes, and there first encounters the beautiful Megara who serves as the plot's main love interest; he battles the Hydra to prove to the Thebans that he truly is a hero; and in the final battle with the Titans, his intervention turns the tide and allows the Olympians to defeat their enemies. Monsters thus signpost significant achievements in the hero's journey.

Other monsters are mentioned. In particular, after the defeat of the Hydra and during the musical number 'Zero to Hero', a montage presents Hercules completing a number of opponents familiar from the labours (the Erymanthian Boar, the Nemean Lion, a single Stymphalian bird, a random sea serpent, and a trio of the Minotaur, Medusa and something that looks like a griffin); the sequence provided 'an opportunity for the otherwise restricted animators to embrace their creative impulses', in this case through setting up Hercules as a monster-conquering brand.[37] Hercules seems to view the conquering of monsters as the epitome of what he should be doing as a hero, so it comes as a shock to him when his father Zeus tells him that he has not yet proven himself a *true* hero. 'But father, I've beaten every single monster I've come up against, I'm the most famous person in all of Greece, I, I'm an action figure!' Hercules stutters, holding out said action figure as proof. He has confused the fighting of monsters with real heroism – which, it turns out, is being willing to die for another.[38] This self-referential awareness of the way in which monsters are used signals that, for *Hercules*, monsters play an important instrumental role but are not the critical element for defining the hero.

That said, the fantasy world of cartoon cel animation, with its freedom from the laws of physics and its vibrant colour palettes, gives the film's monsters the same dream quality that Harryhausen felt stop-motion animation gave his monsters. The influence of caricaturist Gerald Scarfe on the film's aesthetic also adds to this sense of the fantastic.[39] Unusually large bodies are tinted with dark colours and often encountered in shadows, setting a striking contrast to the sunny Greece in which the film is set and providing unambiguous visual pleasure as Hercules wallops them. The best example comes from Hercules' battle with the Hydra, which has been set up as a fixed contest by Hades to kill the hero at the start of his career. After freeing two children (Hades' henchdemons Pain and Panic in disguise) from under a rock, Hercules releases the Hydra from its cave, a symbolic unintended consequence of a seemingly virtuous act. Although the beast initially swallows Hercules, he cuts his way out by decapitation and stands, panting, next to the headless steaming carcass. His jubilation is short-lived – the head regenerates multiple times, and in the following sequence Hercules attempts decapitations in bulk, only for more heads to grow back. Dramatic backgrounds and music raise tension levels, especially when Hercules brings a cliff crashing down on the beast and initially appears to have perished with it.

The extended nature of the battle, made distinctive within the film by the incorporation of CGI techniques, allows the Hydra to become a real threat, and for this to feel like a genuine watershed moment for Hercules as a hero (Fig. 3.6). His previous encounter with the centaur Nessus was defused by Megara refusing to conform to the anticipated damsel in distress stereotype; the Hydra is the make or break moment for Hercules' foray into heroism, hence its overdetermined bodily presence as the keystone villain. The drawn-out fight sequence, the reversal of fortune and the temporary suggestion that he has died along with the Hydra combine to make this monstrous conquest matter. By contrast, the chirpy tune of the 'Zero to Hero' song and the effortless, comic ease with which Hercules dispatches the rest of his monstrous opponents makes them feel less significant – and prepares the viewer for Zeus' puncturing of Hercules' heroism bubble. The cartoon format allows the plot to refocus itself on Hades' dastardly plans to overthrow Zeus by swiftly shifting the monsters from threatening to laughable. They are, as will become clear through the rest of the film's narrative, not where the real threat to humanity lies, but rather Hades' tools – neatly illustrated during 'Zero to Hero' by shots of Hades moving monster pieces around on a chessboard.

Since the earliest days of cinema, and particularly through the era of Ray Harryhausen, classical monsters have been tied to hero narratives. While they might shuffle from one hero's story to another, they have remained props, set pieces, supports for heroic *amour propre*. They are rarely allowed to speak; while some tap into the contemporary monstrous, in general their purpose is purely

Fig. 3.6 Facing down the hydra in Disney's *Hercules* (1997).

spectacular. What Disney's *Hercules* demonstrates is an awareness both of this monstrous deployment strategy and its failings: by the end of the twentieth century, there is something lacking if a hero is defined solely by his conquests. The corollary of this is that a monster lacks something if defined solely by its hero. What *Hercules* offers as a wry response to Harryhausen-esque tropes develops, over the next few decades, into a fully fledged break away from the framework of classical myth. The jump into the new millennium takes us to some monsters who are trapped in the same patterns as their predecessors, but others who escape to fresh territories.

Muscles and Imagination

The Modern Peplum and Beyond

The success of *Gladiator* in 2000 is often seen as a watershed moment for classics and film, which established that classical content was commercially viable on the big screen again. In the new millennium, two kinds of films involving the classical monster emerged. The first, exemplified by *Clash of the Titans* (2010) and *Hercules* (2014), continued the traditions of the *peplum*, seeing the monster in its traditional role as adversary to a particular hero. The second, including *O Brother, Where Art Thou?* (2000) and *Pan's Labyrinth* (2006), are less invested in the monster's defeat and more interested in its nature. The differences between these two modes are stark – a monster in a hero epic finds itself on limited territory, but other genres prove more promising.

Back to the peplum

As well as *Gladiator*, the *Lord of the Rings* (*LotR*) trilogy (2001–3) and *300* (2007) established that heroic epic could once again be a box office triumph. The *LotR* trilogy has been extremely influential in the visual language used for fantastic battle scenes of all sorts; for instance, the final battle between the Greek forces and the multi-armed hell warriors in *Wrath of the Titans* (2012) looks similar to any battle featuring orcs in the trilogy. The trilogy also epitomises the quest-based plot, which focuses on the adventures of a particular individual (usually male) and permits the development of financially attractive multi-film franchises. *300* also contributed to a pool of shared visual language through its portrayal of stylised violence, which drew heavily on the original comic by Frank Miller and Lynn Varley.[1] That kind of imagery has since become part of the standard graphic repertoire for films set in the ancient world, in which battles and conflict are presented as aesthetically awe-inspiring rather than horrific.

Since 2000, a number of modern hero epics or contemporary *pepla* have appeared in cinemas.[2] The films I group in this category include *Percy Jackson and the Olympians: The Lightning Thief* (2010) and its sequel *Percy Jackson: Sea of Monsters* (2013); the remake of *Clash of the Titans* (2010) and its sequel *Wrath of the Titans* (2012); *Immortals* (2011); *Hercules* (2014) starring Dwayne 'The Rock' Johnson; and *The Legend of Hercules* (2014), starring Kellan Lutz. Like earlier movies, these films all follow specific heroes with particular story arcs, although not always ones derived from ancient sources; as the remade *Clash* shows, post-Harryhausen it has become impossible to think of Perseus without his Kraken.[3] These films also draw heavily on pre-existing source material – *Clash* speaks to *Clash*, the Percy Jackson films are adaptations of a successful series of books written by Rick Riordan, and *Hercules* took Steve Moore's comic *Hercules: The Thracian Wars* as its starting point.

These films also have the advantage of being created in the age of CGI. Solomon noted that new electronic techniques allowed filmmakers to have sumptuous sets and locations without the bother of travel, or to have a cast of actual thousands.[4] The way these films follow the *Lord of the Rings* trilogy in using technology to bring the monstrous to life is, I would argue, a critical change in the representation of monsters – by moving towards creation by technology, film makers take the monsters *further away* from their characters. They are disembodied, in that the bodies the audience watch on screen do not, in fact, exist. The act of giving the monster exclusively computer-generated flesh means it is completely removed from the physical world that we humans inhabit. CGI cannot quite deliver the pleasures expected from seeing monstrous flesh in motion. It is impossible to identify with something that is not actually there. There is no one, *à la* more frugal episodes of *Doctor Who*, dressed up in some enthusiastically painted bin bags and household cleaning implements, while the directors hope for the best. There are none of Harryhausen's maquettes or models. The workings are invisible.

This is the equivalent of the medieval practice of putting monsters at the edge of the map, creating an us-and-them between the objects on the screen and the viewers. By giving them form yet keeping them isolated, monsters become credible but are kept at a safe distance. This distancing is in line with the general plot arc of these films, in which a young man must learn what it means to be a man in the world he inhabits. These heroes have simple needs – they must stab things with pointy teeth, not die, and get the girl – which gesture nostalgically towards a simpler time, when men didn't have to worry about the very technologies that enable CGI. These technologies automate workplaces and eradicate blue collar manufacturing jobs, raising uncomfortable questions about what masculinity looks like in the current context of the continued decline of industry and the growth of factories outside the USA and Europe. The heroes in these films are questing after what Courcoux has termed a 'transcendental masculinity' as much as anything else.[5] The setting of the films in an ancient world, apart from the 'feminised' elements of modern technology, insulates this wistful daydream of gender identity in the same way the construction of the monsters through the CGI process pushes them even further away from the viewer.

As an aside, I note that the film industry is starting to kick back against the estranging effects of CGI in its tales of adventure and derring-do. In the hugely successful *Mad Max: Fury Road* (2015), the car chase scenes were performed live by stunt drivers. The main contribution of CGI was to enhance the landscapes, weather and colours of the finished movie. One wonders whether *Fury Road's* feminist leanings, in its focus on Imperator Furiosa rather than Max himself, have anything to do with this move away from the idealised and the imaginary on screen, regardless of the science fiction setting. In a more classical vein, the publicity material for *Ben-Hur* (2016) loudly proclaimed that the chariot-race scene was filmed without CGI, despite what audiences might assume.

Paradoxically (or not), the choice to make a film featuring a classical monster is a retrograde step. It turns against the decoupling of the appearance of monstrosity with actual monstrosity that has been at work since Frankenstein and his Creature. It radically rejects the contemporary monstrous with its fear of terror invisible and undetectable among the everyday, and instead gives us a full-on, properly slavering brute. Yet this, too, is an artefact of nostalgia, a choice to step back from the modern world and its perils. There is something safer about being able to identify what you are supposed to be fighting, regardless of how many teeth and claws it may have. The obvious monster is a refuge from uncertainty.

Alongside the desire to use the monstrous as an escape route from the realities of modern life, these hero movies also insist on the hyperreal, losing the distinction between what is naturally possible and what is artificially constructed.[6] They present the bodies of their protagonists in glorious (enhanced) close-up, bringing their muscles into close focus and demonstrating their physical prowess, creating pleasures of appreciation for some and of identification (wistful or otherwise) for others. By using CGI, they seek to convince you that you are seeing something unarguably real – with the addition of 3D vision, to make you feel as if you are literally in the middle of the action. The hypermasculinity on display is enabled and augmented by the fantastical properties of technology. The audience relish the sight of the embodied star at the peak of his physical prowess, yet the monster who is the target of his violence is clearly computer-generated, depriving viewers of the satisfaction of bodies making contact. Equally, the assumed requirement for monstrous combat leads to an eclectic gathering of monsters from far and wide, but no engagement with their mythic contexts.

Wrath of the Titans (2012) clearly illustrates the problems with assuming that the force of the spectacular battle set piece will overcome an absence of narrative framing. Early in this film, a beast crawls out of a volcanic gully located conveniently close to the small fishing village where Perseus is living with his son. It flies to the village and wreaks havoc. It has two heads, can breathe fire from one mouth and petrol from the other, and has great bat-like wings and a tail with a fanged mouth of its own at its tip (Fig. 4.1). Perseus runs to get his armour out of a hidden underground storage locker. Despite being rather out of shape, he manages to get the beast to set fire to itself, and the sequence ends. From the beast appearing on screen to being despatched takes about four and a half minutes. Perseus then is seen pensively staring through a window, pondering

Fig. 4.1 A poster for *Wrath of the Titans* (2012) featuring the Chimera.

what can be going on in the world of the gods to allow this creature to disturb his domestic arrangements.

If you know your classical myth, you might be able to identify the monster as the Chimera from Hesiod's description of the beast as having a lion's head at the front, a dragon's head at the back and a goat's head somewhere in the middle (although he does not specify which one breathes fire).[7] However, the word 'chimera' is never mentioned in the script, and there is no hint of the wider mythological context in which the beast appears.[8] The Chimera is originally pitted against the hero Bellerophon, who is sent to fight it by Iobates, the King of Lycia. Iobates has received a note from Proitos, King of Tiryns, saying simply, 'Kill Bellerophon.' Proitos is seeking revenge since Stheneboea, his wife, has accused Bellerophon of raping her after the hero spurned her advances. Bellerophon defeats the Chimera with the help of Pegasus.[9] In *Wrath*, Pegasus doesn't turn up until Perseus has defeated the Chimera, despite his pivotal role in the earlier *Clash of the Titans* remake (2010) – and, of course, the Chimera has lost its hero. But the movie gives you no hint of this alternative story as you watch, limiting the Chimera to a device that indicates Perseus is a protective father.

A different picture emerges from the 'Chimera Featurette' on YouTube, a behind-the-scenes video which balances shots from the film with soundbites from the movie's director, writer, lead digital artist and executive producer, plus a voiceover informing us that 'these ferocious creatures are truly the harbingers of doom'.[10] A lot of work clearly went into the conception of the monster. The writer, Dan Mazeau, says, 'it's this weird Frankenstein amalgam of all these different creatures, and then we thought that could be really terrifying'. From the comments of the director, Jonathan Liebesman, the team had taken the time to work out the logistics of the two heads working 'in tandem', one breathing out fuel and the other breathing out a heat haze. However, the result is a fetish of the digital artist. The Chimera becomes the victim of a desire to show off esoteric knowledge about the monsters of a long-dead culture. The viewer's pleasure from the spectacular fight is undermined by the lack of meaningful context in which to situate and understand the monster. Its sole purpose is to be displayed, freak-like, before being killed.

Wrath does exactly the same with the Minotaur, the subject of another YouTube featurette.[11] In order to get into Tartarus to stop the dastardly plan of his grandfather Chronos, Perseus and his companions must find their way through a mechanical labyrinth constructed by Hephaestus. As they reach the end, they encounter a half-man, half-bull who has been stalking them. Perseus defeats it relatively quickly and the team continue onwards. There is no dialogue. Once more, the featurette reveals there was more conceptual framework behind the beast than made it onto the screen. Nick Davis, the VFX supervisor, calls the Minotaur 'a tortured soul of a man with this sort of hideous deformity', while the producer, Basil Iwanyk, says, 'it's the devil, for all intents and purposes'. But Sam Worthington, who plays Perseus, says something that I think inadvertently reveals even more about the movie's underlying attitude to monsters. Worthington comments, 'it'd be like a UFC [Ultimate Fighting Championship] fight, he doesn't know what's coming at him, it's just another big monster' – and that is all it is. Just another big monster.

The film has a critics' rating of 26 per cent on RottenTomatoes.com, and many reviewers comment on the special effects in their critiques. For instance, Liam Lacey in *The Globe and Mail* called the movie 'a series of monster wrestling matches' and noted that 'the monster fights occur at regular 10-minute intervals', specifically finding the Minotaur 'underwhelming'.[12] In the *San Francisco Chronicle*, Mick LaSalle complained that 'this is a movie in which whole sequences consist of nothing but guys fighting stiff computer images'.[13] Ironically, Joe Neumaier complained in the *New York Daily News* that 'comparatively little attention is given to the monsters'.[14] The backstories that the directorial and production team put together get utterly lost in the finished product. Without their broader context and the individuality that Harryhausen gave them, the monsters lose their energy.

Immortals (2011) gives the impression of equally earnest attempts to engage with the underlying mythology of its source material. It also gives us a Minotaur, this time a man in a bull's headpiece, a henchman of King Hyperion who is seeking to bring down the gods by releasing the Titans. The headpiece offers a homage to the bull's head libation vase found in the Little Palace of Knossos on Crete, a location strongly associated with the Minotaur. The Minotaur serves as Hyperion's chief torturer, and as one of his duties he maintains a bull made out of bronze in which he can roast victims to death. This device nods to the theory that the Minotaur was a monster inspired by the Phoenician god Baal-Moloch, supposedly worshipped by human sacrifice carried out in this way. The movie also self-consciously plays with the concept of myth creation. The fight scene between Theseus and a man in the bull-head mask explicitly becomes a battle between the hero and a man-bull hybrid on a commemorative sculpture in the closing sequence. There has, at some level, been a sincere attempt to engage with scholarly ideas about euhemerism and how history transforms into myth.

Unfortunately, one of the film's weaknesses (from a monstrous perspective) is that its narrative trajectory does not see the death of the Minotaur as a climactic episode, but instead focuses on a story of gigantomachy grounded in Hyperion's desire to release the Titans. The Minotaur of *Immortals* is enervated by the decision to demystify monstrosity – we *know* it's only a chap wearing a dramatic headdress, and he is quickly overpowered in a brief and bathetic fight scene (Fig. 4.2). The things that make the monster powerful – its transgression, its casual disregard of normal semantic categories, its otherness – are dismantled, rationalised, and domesticated. A narrative which claims to be the 'real story' behind the myth feels particularly peculiar in a movie where the gods play a significant on-screen role. The boundary into fantasy is already well behind us, so resisting a proper man-bull hybrid feels unnecessarily coy. As Stephen Whitty said in his review for NJ.com, 'it's a movie about myth with no sense of magic'.[15]

That is not to say that movies cannot question the origins and reality of monsters, and the role they play in reinforcing the hero's identity. While looking at monsters on screen may freeze them into a system of control where they are defined by being looked at, it is possible to consider these questions without buying into the heliotropic gaze.[16] I'd argue that *Hercules* (2014), starring Dwayne 'The Rock' Johnson, manages to communicate this alternative view particularly well. The plot of the movie is monster-lite – Hercules and his team of mercenaries

Fig. 4.2 Theseus (Henry Cavill) and the Minotaur (Robert Maillet) in *Immortals* (2011).

are hired by King Cotys of Thrace to train his soldiers, ostensibly to defeat a local warlord. Cotys turns out to be a tyrant who wishes to enslave Greece. The film is primarily about the team working out they are on the wrong side, and deciding what to do about it. A subplot explores Hercules' befuddled memories of killing his wife Megara and their children, and whether his actions arose from Hera's influence or because he is insane.

The opening sequence introduces these self-referential concerns about belief, trust and fact. The audience watches some familiar episodes from Hercules' backstory play out on the screen, including his encounters with the Hydra, the Erymanthian Boar and the Nemean Lion. It becomes clear that these stories are being told by Iolaus, Hercules' nephew, when one of the pirates holding him captive succinctly responds, 'what a load of crap'. Hercules and his companions rescue Iolaus and slaughter the pirates just before the young man meets a sticky end, but the rest of the movie focuses heavily on the significance of image and spin, implying throughout that although these are the tales that get told, the monsters aren't *real*. In one scene, Hercules returns to King Eurystheus from his mission to kill the hydra with a bag full of its heads, and pulls out the heads of soldiers in snake masks – 'no wonder men thought they were serpents', says the king. The 'centaurs' that frighten Cotys' army turn out to be expert cavalry with the light behind them. Hercules' groggy memories of a Cerberus-like dog attacking his family are drug-addled recollections of three savage hounds.

The movie is narratively careful that when we see monsters on the screen, we are always seeing them indirectly, via Iolaus' storytelling or Hercules' confused flashbacks. They never appear on-screen unmediated, with the exception of the horsemen-centaurs who are soon demystified. Nonetheless, while the film explores the same theories of mythologising as *Immortals*, in its final moments *Hercules* does a surprise reverse to reintroduce the prospect that the world contains real gods and monsters. Hercules performs a heroic feat of strength to push over a statue of Hera and crush Cotys, suggesting he might really be the son of Zeus. The closing credits follow up this revelation with the chance that the monsters he faced *were* real after all.

The aesthetic style of the final credit sequence is strikingly different to the rest of the film. The shots show a sketched-out wirework version of CGI that has been given only rough texture and shading around jagged electronic edges, all in an orange tone. This is clearly work in progress rather than the final cinematic product. Using this draft style, the credits show us each of the labours we saw in the opening sequence – not revealing that the monster didn't exist, but uncovering the unsung role that the companions played in helping Hercules take the monster down. Playing into the possibility that all of this supernatural stuff could be genuine, the use of the 'draft' visual language in the credits allows the movie to have its cake and eat it.

The groundwork for this about-face has been laid by the movie's attitude to prophecy and the seer Amphiaraus (Ian McShane, who in my opinion is having far too much fun). Amphiaraus knows the time of his own death, but 'as always, the gods are generous with hints, but cheap on specifics'. At one stage, as burning arrows fall onto a battlefield and the rest of the army hide behind their shields, Amphiaraus stands with arms outstretched – every arrow misses him, and he opens one eye cautiously to discover he has not been pinioned. Before the team go to face Cotys, he announces that he will die – 'tonight, a spear of flame will pierce my heart'. As the team fight their way out of Cotys' dungeons, a warrior throws a spear through a torch, which ignites it. Amphiaraus sees it coming and whispers, 'my time!' Appropriately portentous music plays as he shuts his eyes and opens his arms wide to receive the weapon into his chest ... then Hercules snatches the spear out of the air and kills the warrior who flung it. 'Excuse me, that was my moment, my fate,' says Amphiaraus huffily. 'You're welcome,' says Hercules, continuing on up the staircase. As Amphiaraus is the only character given access to the gods, with information that appears to be accurate if vague, this twist prepares the audience to question whether the expectations the film has set up about the supernatural are to be believed.

Hercules avoids the pitfalls of *Immortals* by presenting monsters as an important factor in hero-image without trivialising them. Since the gods stay off-screen, the movie can keep its internal world consistent. By allowing the narrative to waver between the rational interpretation of monsters and the possibility that maybe, just maybe, these things might exist, it appeals to the wonder of the monstrous without disembowelling it as *Immortals* does. The whole conceptual world of the movie invites us to question whether what we are told is true, just as Hercules must unravel what really happened to his family. The spaces at the edges are left wide enough to allow the monstrous to creep back in to the story, and for Hercules' heroism to retain the aura of the mythic.

Both what might be termed *Hercules'* effective and *Immortals'* ineffective approach to monsters appear together in the first Percy Jackson film, *Percy Jackson & The Olympians: The Lightning Thief* (2010). The Minotaur epitomises the latter when he appears just as the hero Percy, his companion Grover and his mother Sally come close to Camp Halfblood and overturns the car they are travelling in. The Minotaur apparently kills Sally, and Percy, in turn, kills the Minotaur with one of its own horns. This plot development allows the rest of the film to unfold – Sally is not dead but has instead been transported to Hades, requiring a mythic underage road-trip to go and recover her. As in *Immortals*, *The Lightning Thief* gives the Minotaur no backstory, and never refers to the Labyrinth, Pasiphae or Crete. The monster simply appears in a bit of Long Island forest at a plot-critical moment, acting (as it were) as a *monstrum ex machina* to ensure Percy has something to do for the rest of the film.[17]

In this episode, the monster is frightening because it is unexpected, it comes out of nowhere, and it poses a significant threat to Percy's mother. However, nothing marks the situation as one specifically requiring the Minotaur, other than wanting a fairly familiar creature from Greek mythology. By contrast, the episode in the original novel makes it clear that the Minotaur's pursuit is a sign of how seriously Percy is being taken by Hades. In the fight, it is hampered by its poor sight and hearing; the opportunity to fight the Minotaur specifically is seen as a prestige marker, equal to being sent on a quest.[18] When the film removes the monster from its mythic context, the set piece loses its force – the Minotaur becomes a generic baddie, vanquished almost as soon as it is introduced, in line with the episodic use of monsters in the Harryhausen era.

By contrast, the episode involving Medusa incorporates her into the story in a more meaningful way. On their road trip to the underworld, Percy, Grover and their friend Annabeth end up in a garden centre with an unusual range of statues. It is actually the lair of Medusa, who not only explains how she came to be monstrous to Annabeth, conveniently daughter of Athena, but also utters the marvellous line 'I used to date your Daddy' to Percy, son of Poseidon, before shoving a row of statues onto him (Fig. 4.3). This monster gets a full backstory, a personal connection to the protagonists which generates terror based on their own experiences, a location fitting for her monstrosity, and poses a threat that takes more than a couple of minutes to overpower.[19] She has been allowed to find a space in the modern world where one might actually encounter her – haven't you ever wondered where designers get the ideas for all that kitsch garden statuary? As the cinema audience watches along, enjoying that safe distance from the monstrous that lets them see what should never be seen, they know that they have the cinema screen as the safe barrier between them and Medusa's terrible eyes – but those eyes are only truly terrifying because she is not seen as just another opponent but as a fully integrated element within the corner of the hero's world that she has colonised.

The Lightning Thief shows us that when monsters are essentially asked to step into the shoes of the disposable baddies in a James Bond movie, they lose their specific link to the hero and thus their impact. That one film can handle monsters

Fig. 4.3 Medusa (Uma Thurman) in a publicity poster for *Percy Jackson and the Olympians: The Lightning Thief* (2010).

in two such different ways reveals that it's an easy slip to make. If you want your monster to be a credible threat to your hero, it needs a credible reason to be in the story in the first place.

We return to the desire for authenticity on screen that I circled around in the previous chapter. It is possible to misjudge the pleasures of seeing things 'just so'. Modern hero epics exhibit a tension between the advantages of putting monsters on the screen using modern technology, and the pitfalls of a slavish obsession with visual authenticity. When the heliotropic gaze fixes a monster in perfect detail, the Medusa-like vision of the spectator freezes it into narrative stupor. It becomes submissive to its creators, who prod and poke it into position, to serve the narrative purpose envisaged for it, and then to be despatched. The pleasures of seeing the monstrous body are broken by the cost of such tameness. However, CGI does not *inevitably* mean that monsters are separated from their monstrous roots and lose, as Benjamin would put it, the aura that gives them their authenticity. Movies which are willing to loosen the barriers around how an ancient monster *should* look and behave, even when defining the monster in terms of the hero, diffuse the heliotropic gaze and allow the monster to find its own frightening corner. But the temptation of the heroic narrative, in which a monster must always play a role that is fixed in its function if not its opponent, is a difficult lure to resist.

A different approach to monsters

In contrast to what might be most kindly referred to as the literal approach to monsters found in modern heroic epics, some movies take a more imaginative approach. Rather than seeing monsters as umbilically connected to a hero, these films take advantage of their metaphorical potential. Let's begin with the Coen Brothers' *O Brother, Where Art Thou?* (2000), the only serious attempt to engage with the *Odyssey* in the twenty-first century, if we discount the Sci-Fi channel's *Odysseus: Voyage to the Underworld* (2008).[20] *O Brother* transplants the *Odyssey* into the Depression-era 1930s Deep South. The Coens never claim to offer a literal retelling of Homer, but instead engage creatively with their source material. Enough familiar episodes from Homer's epic are recreated to produce some innovative approaches to ancient monsters and bring them into the modern world.

The film cultivates a dream-like quality which plays with perception and belief from the outset. The protagonist, Ulysses Everett McGill, escapes from prison with fellow convicts Pete and Delmar. After a short stop at a farm owned by Pete's relatives where they are betrayed to the officials following them, the trio join a group dressed in white walking down to a river, where a preacher is offering full-body immersion baptism and forgiveness of sins – the film's equivalent of the Lotus Eaters. Pete and Delmar comfort themselves with the promised fresh start, while Ulysses maintains his religious scepticism. The otherworldly aesthetic that this encounter establishes for the movie as a whole preserves the fantastic nature of Odysseus' journey without Ulysses ever leaving Alabama.

The film finds other ways to bring in the monstrous, not least through Big Dan Teague (played with considerable charm by John Goodman), a Bible salesman wearing an eyepatch who parallels the cyclops Polyphemus (Fig. 4.4). Ulysses and Delmar encounter Teague in a restaurant, where he dupes them into providing him with lunch on the understanding he will teach them the secrets of successful Bible salesmanship. Instead, he beats them with a branch and steals their money. The failure of guest-friendship which Odysseus and Polyphemus

Fig. 4.4 Big Dan Teague (John Goodman) in *O Brother, Where Art Thou?* (2000).

share in the *Odyssey* is transformed into Teague's deception of the gullible Ulysses, who remains oblivious to the tree branch until it is forcefully applied to him. His parting line is 'y'all seen the end of Big Dan Teague,' suggesting his monstrosity arises from his faux hospitality, but we meet him again when Ulysses, Pete and Delmar infiltrate a Ku Klux Klan rally to rescue Tommy Johnson, a black friend of theirs who is about to be lynched as the rally's centrepiece.[21] Big Dan is immediately identified by his one-eyed Klansman hood, which he lifts to sniff the air. The rally is an imaginative recreation of Polyphemus' sheep and Odysseus' ram trick – the Klansmen, in white, walk around in highly ritualised patterns and bleat their responses in unison, forming a herd who respond to the commands of the Grand Wizard, while the trio hide under 'sheepskins' by putting on Klansmen's robes.

The deception is not successful as Big Dan identifies them as interlopers, but in the intervening chaos, the *Odyssey* asserts itself. A flag falls towards Big Dan, threatening to pierce his eye and blind him, but he catches it. The Klansmen nod smugly, as if this is going to be where they escape narrative destiny – then, Big Dan is instead crushed under a large burning cross, as Ulysses has been busy cutting its supporting ropes. The toxic organisation Big Dan belongs to kills him. His participation in a contemporary form of horror proves fatal rather than his narrative origins. The film as a whole makes plain that there is no place for this kind of monstrosity, at least not where it can be seen. When the 'reform' candidate challenging the incumbent governor is revealed as the Klan's Grand Wizard, he is run out of town on a rail.

The other episode worth dwelling on is the trio's encounter with the sirens, which offers an example of monstrosity hidden yet present within the normal, with wider implications for the movie. The trio are driving along a road when suddenly Pete shouts that he needs to get out, and his companions follow him down to a stream. Three suggestively soaked-through women are singing and doing some perfunctory laundry, perhaps distantly evoking the Phaeacian princess Nausicaa whom Odysseus encounters in book six of the *Odyssey*. The women sing the song 'Go to Sleep, You Little Baby' continually, never speaking a word, although the voluble Ulysses does his best to effect a formal introduction (Fig. 4.5). The women walk over to the men, embrace them, ply them with large jugs marked XX (presumably some form of potent homebrew as we're in the Prohibition era), and the screen fades to black.

When Delmar wakes, he sees Pete's clothes laid out on the riverbank. After a moment of believing Pete has been murdered, he finds a toad inside Pete's clothes – leading to the magnificent line 'them sigh-reens did this to Pete – they done loved him up an' turned him into a horney-toad!' (perhaps another *Odyssey* bleed-through from Circe, the witch who turns men into pigs).[22] Despite Ulysses' gentle observation that 'I'm not sure that's Pete,' Delmar insists on carrying the toad with them until it is squished by Big Dan. Delmar genuinely believes in the

Fig. 4.5 The sirens in *O Brother, Where Art Thou?* (2000).

power of the sirens to invoke supernatural forces. Ulysses is sure there must be a rational explanation but doesn't aggressively challenge his friend's belief. They later encounter Pete as part of a road gang, have a katabatic encounter with him in a cinema, and rescue him from prison, when they discover that the sirens handed him in for the bounty on his head (and thus turn out to embody monstrous deceptive femininity in another form). So there is a rational explanation, but only after we have shared the horror of seeing Pete the toad squashed with Delmar. That Ulysses and Delmar meet Pete in circumstances that are themselves unworldly means that the viewer is invited to suspend their disbelief and join Delmar in a world where being turned into a horny toad is an all too real risk.

O Brother's non-literal approach to classical monsters does not require them to look as we would expect them to but still captures the essence of the fear they inspire in us. By contrast, *Argo* (2012), directed by and starring Ben Affleck, uses a classical monster to create a subtle but important thematic distinction within the structure of the film. *Argo* dramatises the true story of a secret CIA mission. When the staff of the American embassy in Iran were taken hostage in 1979, six employees escaped and went into hiding at the house of the Canadian ambassador. About three months after the embassy was taken, a CIA operative called Tony Mendez (played by Affleck) went into Iran and brought them out – under the pretence that they were a film crew doing a location scout for a sci-fi movie in production called *Argo*. There are plentiful references to the myth of Jason and the Argonauts, including a homage to the Argo escaping from between the clashing rocks as Mendez drives a minibus safely between two 'waves' of protesting Iranians, but the film also gives its audience an unexpected Minotaur on screen.

You may well ask why. The reason is connected to the cover story for Mendez' mission. In order to get CIA approval to run the operation and make the cover story look plausible, Mendez has to put a solid backstory in place, which means creating a fake production company and team in Hollywood. Mendez gets in touch with John Chambers (John Goodman, again), who was the prosthetics expert behind *Planet of the Apes* and had previously worked with the CIA. Our first encounter with him, and with Hollywood, is a close-up of a scantily clad space-nurse in red latex who breathily mutters, 'my creation ... my creation ...' as she injects a Minotaur strapped to an operating table with a large syringe. The Minotaur bellows in pain, rears against his bonds – and headbutts the space-nurse, leading a weary director to shout, 'cut!' Chambers is summoned on-set and informed that 'he says the Minotaur prosthetic is too tight so he can't act'. Chambers responds, 'if he could act, he wouldn't be playing the Minotaur.'

We never see the Minotaur again, but for the next twenty minutes or so that the film spends in Hollywood, a number of small references point back to our monstrous bull. The office of the agent selling the rights to the *Argo* script is Max Klein Productions – Bullseye Films. When Mendez and Lester (Alan Arkin), the producer who signs on to provide some credibility, have a heart-to-heart about families, Lester comments, 'I was a terrible father. The bullshit business . . . it's like coal-mining, you come home to your wife and kids and you can't, you can't wash it off.' When the camera pans over a mocked-up publicity poster for *Argo*, a distinctly Minotaur-esque face looms in the background behind a couple of space-age gliders and a vaguely Middle Eastern palace complex.

What are we to make of this apparently brief and cursory deployment of the Minotaur? I would argue that *Argo* uses the classical monster to comment on the whole nature of Hollywood as being precisely 'the bullshit business'. The hybrid synthesis between truth and fiction, the artistry of putting together the disparate limbs of a false story, prosthetics which alter reality, are what makes Hollywood Hollywood. The Minotaur offers a glitzy hybrid homage to and shorthand for that crossover of monstrous deal-making, faking the other guy out and putting on a good show. The good-natured monster with an adjustable prosthetic that can be gulled by glamour is a kitten in comparison to the Iranian regime, whose violence looms over the movie. The heart of the plot's monstrosity is the tension about whether the trapped Americans will escape from the lair of murderous politics rather than a dopey and affable man-bull. The film's epic narrative might lead us to expect a different Minotaur, but the parallel between the ancient and modern underlines the idea that the classical monster is comfortably retrograde and straightforward – despite appearing in a space opera. The comic initial presentation of the Minotaur and the light-hearted feel of the Hollywood segment mirror the disbelief of CIA officials that such an outrageous plan is being considered. When Mendez boards a plane and begins his journey towards Iran, the time for this reassuring levity passes, and things become deadly serious.

My final case study, Guillermo del Toro's *Pan's Labyrinth* (*El laberinto del fauno*, 2006), combines several threads of modern monster-ism, both in terms of content and director – del Toro has built up a reputation as perhaps the premier monster-film maker currently active in cinema. His portfolio ranges from *Pan's Labyrinth* and other Spanish-language horror/gothic films to commercial blockbusters like the *Hellboy* films (2004 and 2008), *Pacific Rim* (2013) and *The Shape of Water* (2017). He fits into neither the arthouse nor the Hollywood box;[23] instead, the defining link in his *oeuvre* appears to be monstrosity and fantasy. His preference for working with a particular group of similarly minded actors and technicians undermines the myth of the individual *auteur*, but his is the dominant creative voice.[24] He carefully cultivates the persona of monster expert and uber-fan, including a long-cherished but unrealised project to film H. P. Lovecraft's *At the Mountains of Madness*. His approach to monstrosity is encyclopaedic and diverse. The same film comfortably accommodates elven lore rubbing up against hard-core occult theory. Classical monsters are in good company among the other objects of del Toro's curatorial eclecticism.

Pan's Labyrinth encapsulates del Toro's cheerful blending of monster-lore in its title, combining as it does the Minotaur's home with the pastoral faun. The name 'Pan' only occurs in the title's English translation, but the faun or satyr is a classical monster, a rural nature spirit who embodied uncontrolled masculinity. The film also includes fairy-tale figures such as fairies, a gigantic toad poisoning the roots of a tree, and the Pale Man, who has eyes in his hands and eats children. Del Toro freely acknowledges his debt to Jungian archetypes. These are supposedly revealed through the symbols and myths of various cultures, and help the collective unconscious communicate with the individual consciousness. Del Toro's reference to Jung manifests in several ways, including the design of the Faun's face, which echoes the female reproductive system, and a 'fallopian palette of colours' comprising golds and crimsons to colour the fantasy world (Fig. 4.6).[25] Another possible influence appears in the similarities between the

Fig. 4.6 The Faun (Doug Jones) in *Pan's Labyrinth* (2006).

two monsters of the film, the Faun and Captain Vidal, stepfather of the child protagonist Ofelia. The Captain is an officer in the Spanish army under the Franco dictatorship. He has brought Ofelia and her mother, pregnant with his child, to a remote mill where he is leading a campaign against rebel forces. As Ofelia learns she is the long-lost daughter of the king of the underworld and seeks to complete three tasks set to prove she has not become fully mortal, Vidal tries to hunt down the rebels, exerting his authority on the locals and his wife through soft-spoken brutality.

It is no accident that Ofelia's encounters with the faun occur immediately before or after scenes featuring the Captain. For instance, before Ofelia first ventures into the labyrinth in the forest near the mill compound, led by a stick insect which turns out to be a fairy, we see Vidal calmly shoot two men his soldiers have found in the woods, claiming to be hunting rabbits – then discover a rabbit in their bag. The Captain's compulsive neatness and mechanical control, symbolised by his obsession with the mechanism of his father's cracked pocket watch, contrast strongly to the messiness and mossiness of the Faun and its world, but for all the differences there are enough parallels to make Ofelia's caution towards her supposed guide completely credible. Returning to del Toro's self-confessed Jungian influences, we might think of one as the shadow-self of the other, the repressed characteristics which the conscious self hides away from public view. Whether the Captain is the Faun's shadow-self or vice versa remains to be seen.

The Faun and the fairies are many miles away from Tinkerbell and Mr. Tumnus. The relationship between the Faun and Ofelia never becomes cosy; instead, Ofelia remains ambivalent about the Faun, and the Faun has no hesitation in berating her when she fails to carry out her second task after her mother haemorrhages. After Ofelia tells Mercedes, a local woman working for the soldiers at the mill, that a faun has visited her, Mercedes replies, 'my granny used to say that you should keep away from them', just as the Captain comes around the corner of an outbuilding and calls for her. When Ofelia tells the Faun she has completed her first task, he is eating some unidentifiable red meat that he feeds to a fairy – his link to nature is not just to the vegetal part of the wild kingdom, but also to the bestial. Eventually, he visits Ofelia in her bedroom, invading her space, and echoing an incident from del Toro's own childhood, where he believes he was visited by a faun which lived behind an armoire in his room in his grandmother's house.[26] The Faun's sudden snaps between anger and calm reflect similar switches in the Captain's personality, especially since many of the conflicts Ofelia faces are over obedience – the Faun rages at her when she disobeys his instructions not to eat anything from the kingdom she must enter in her second task, and she volunteers to give up her throne rather than complete what she believes is the third task, the sacrifice of her baby brother. The monstrous figures in her life push her towards roles she does not wish to fulfil, obedient princesses in one form or another – her rebellion is pushing back.

I want to suggest that the Faun offers a general comment on the fate of classical monsters. As Ofelia progresses through her tasks, the Faun becomes younger each time he appears on screen. The first change is quite subtle, but gradually the wrinkles on his face smooth out, his hair becomes fuller and more luscious, and the creaking sounds that accompany his movements sound less decrepit and more like trees moving in the breeze. Ofelia's attention and vision rejuvenate him. Yet, when the Faun chastises her for ignoring his instructions, he reveals an anxiety about the wider consequences of her disobedience. His last words before he vanishes into the darkness of Ofelia's bedroom are telling:

> You cannot return! The moon will be full in three days. Your spirit shall forever remain among humans! You shall age like them, you shall die like them! All memory of you shall fade in time. And we shall vanish along with it. You shall never see us again!

The Faun makes an explicit link between Ofelia's commitment to her task and to the survival of the Underground Realm. The threatened ban on seeing the fantastic is inextricably linked to memory and survival. Here, I think, is a comment on the way that classical monsters survive in the world. Their existence is bound up in human vision and human remembrance. It is precisely because contemporary society honours the classical past that the memory of their ancient creators survives and keeps them alive. Ofelia's willingness to go underground, into the Faun's cavern and the darkness, reflects our psychological willingness as humans to go looking in the shadows for the monsters we have been told are there. Ofelia's guide is her book of fairy tales. Our guides are the compendiums of classical myth that circulate among children and never quite lose their attraction.

Del Toro places the Faun rather than a Minotaur at the centre of his Labyrinth, the monster of record in the film's Spanish title, although it shares a landscape occupied with creatures from a wide range of source material and his own fertile imagination. This choice makes classical monsters a keystone on which all other monstrosity relies. The Underground Realm is only accessible and interpretable through the Faun. Although Ofelia's first encounter with the parallel universe is with a giant bug which turns out to be a fairy, it cannot speak to her and instead leads her to the Faun. The classical becomes an entry point, a gate keeper, although one which has not been domesticated and tamed. The Faun feeds off the contemporary monstrous, augmented by the horrific and incomprehensible realities of the Spanish Civil War. Political horror becomes the darkness through which it can find a new expression.

***

Tracing the emergence of the classical monster through the latter part of the twentieth century and into the twenty-first has brought out some key features of how classical monsters work in contemporary culture. They respond poorly to literal and reverential treatment – they are, after all, not gods but monsters. The fantastic and unreal nature of Ray Harryhausen's stop-motion animation first gave them substantial life on the silver screen, free from the 'man-in-a-suit' problem. The recent return to the swords and sandals film has given them another opportunity to come onto the screen, but the sincerity with which they are often handled and the freezing close-ups of CGI technology petrify them into stilted graphics rather than powerful figures of fear. Embodying the monster so the hero can defeat it becomes the priority, rather than considering what the monster can do.

The monsters who appear to thrive on screen are the ones whose new incarnations do not tie them to a fervently earnest approach to their origins. The Faun in *Pan's Labyrinth* again offers an interesting example. The Faun was played by Doug Jones, who also played the Pale Man and had appeared as a monster in other del Toro films. Jones became the Faun via a latex mask and make-up, not through CGI. One of the reasons the Faun is effective is because there is *something* on screen, visible and real. Animated monsters evade these expectations thanks to generic suspension of disbelief; CGI monsters, however finely detailed, cannot capture that sense of existence, of tangibility, that a physical actor brings. New prosthetic technologies and advances in film cosmetics might have made Harryhausen reconsider his prejudices against the 'man in a suit'.

Classical monsters on film reveal a paradox of monstrosity. By their very nature, monsters linger on the border of real and unreal. They have an ontological ambiguity which arises from their location on knife-edges and thresholds. We know they are there, yet we hope they are not there (or perhaps vice versa). They derive their power from this perhaps-ness – in the case of classical monsters, this manifests in both their insistence that they have a role to play in a modern story, and their inescapable connection with the ancient past. The different approaches that film takes to classical monsters, the tendrils that I have mapped out in this chapter, show that when this tension is not respected, the viewers become Medusa and turn the monster into stone. Where the prerequisites of a monster's role are made fixed and immobile, both by computer technology and by limited box-ticking plot lines, the soil provided for the monster to grow in is poor. The demand for control manifests in directorial strategies rather than in the classification processes I outlined in Chapter 1 – but they exist all the same.

Such attempts at classification are, as I have argued, doomed to failure with classical monsters, partly because of their amodern nature, in that they resist being forced back into antiquity (however constructed), and partly because their rhizomatic nature allows them to appear in multiple places in multiple forms, making any appeals to absolute visual or narrative authenticity collapse as soon as they are made. This tracery of monstrous guest appearances warns us that the classical monster does not like to be taken too seriously. The world of ancient myth, its seed bed, is not where it seeks to dwell; rather, it feeds on other sources of monstrosity, nourishing itself with our fears yet maintaining its classical shape. Does this pattern transfer from the silver screen to the small screen? It is time to turn to the world of television and to see whether the same challenges face the classical monster there.

Monsters and Mythologies in *Hercules: The Legendary Journeys*

Studying classical reception on television presents a challenge, due to the ephemeral nature of television as a product. Until the rise of the DVD and the boxed set in the 1990s, once a programme had aired there were few opportunities to see it again, unless your chosen series was released on VHS or you were organised enough to record something yourself. The sorts of things that have entered the televisual canon of classical 'must watches' also fit a certain pattern, best exemplified by the BBC's 1976 adaptation of *I, Claudius* – scandalous in its time, but using its historical setting to excuse its dancing girls.[1] This does not, at first glance, appear to be fertile ground for monsters.

Indeed, television (and classicists who work on television) seem to prefer historical topics. This emerges in the historical documentary, of the sort fronted by Mary Beard or Bettany Hughes, found on public service broadcasters or the likes of the History Channel. It can be drama set in the ancient world, like HBO's *Rome*, Starz's *Spartacus: Blood and Sand*, or the more light-hearted *Plebs* from ITV2. I suspect that this may be rooted in opinions that television is somehow a less valuable cultural medium than film established in the 1950s and 1960s as film tried to compete with its new competition, rather than the kind of quality television programming now found across a range of terrestrial and digital content providers. The appeal to classical history, a bastion of respectability, justifies the production of a television series or programme which explores that history, using the 'low' medium of television to communicate the 'high' cultural content of antiquity in documentary or dramatic form.[2] ITV2's reality television series *Bromans* reached the pinnacle of combining these two cultural opposites.

Where does this leave classical myth? The tales of monsters, heroes and gods which have provided popular storylines in contemporary cinema have not been retold in the same way on television. Instead, myth has become the preserve of telefantasy, a fan-generated term that refers to a range of cult television which uses fantastic and generic flexibility to explore the self-contained worlds built for the audience's enjoyment.[3] A popular example might be *Buffy the Vampire Slayer*, which turns the story of Pygmalion into a tale of a geek creating a perfect robot girlfriend ('I Was Made to Love You', 5.15);[4] similarly, *My Little Pony: Friendship is Magic* reimagines the Minotaur as Iron Will, an assertiveness coach who is a bit too assertive ('Putting Your Hoof Down', 2.19). Writers select mythic elements to use within individual episodes rather than using a myth as a complete narrative skeleton. As Willis astutely notes, these decontextualised cameos are not weak or superficial, but instead fit into the broader storytelling and interpretative traditions of popular culture.[5]

That said, cinema and television make varying demands on classical material. A film must function as a free-standing narrative; a television series needs to offer a set of episodes that stand together as a group through their story, characters, visual style and general tone, as well as offering sufficient variety to avoid viewer boredom. One-off television 'specials' on a particular subject tend to work better for a single focused historical subject than myth. Despite television's potential to tell larger scale stories, the only projects to take up the challenge have been Tony Robinson's retelling of the *Iliad* and *Odyssey* under the Jackanory brand ('Odysseus: The Greatest Hero of Them All', 1986) and Jim Henson's *The Storyteller: Greek Myths* (1990), a four episode mini-series that retold selected myths in the distinctive visual style of the Jim Henson Creature Shop.

One notable outlier which illustrates the possibilities and limitations of myth is *Hercules: The Legendary Journeys* (1995–1999).[6] In this chapter and the one that follows, I will explore how this series in particular handles classical monsters, how the world it builds is carried over to its spin-off series *Xena: Warrior Princess*, and compare this with the use of classical monsters in a telefantasy set for the most part outside the ancient world, *Doctor Who*. These series offer a sophisticated adaptation of myth without the burden of the thirst for authenticity which troubled classical monsters in my film case studies. What I propose has happened in television is that worries about presenting history 'authentically' cluster around historical drama, where the dormice at the banquet become signs of 'genuine' historical knowledge, playing into expectations of an accurate representation of an unrecoverable past.[7] For viewers, watching myth on television is a conscious decision to put aside realism and not fuss over accuracy.

That said, telefantasy is also serious about credibility. Maintaining socio-cultural verisimilitude is a critical part of telefantasy's agenda, since it must remain generally plausible for its fantastic elements to challenge audience perceptions of reality.[8] Once a rule has been established about how a fantasy world works, it must be applied consistently; for instance, *Doctor Who* confirmed that Time Lords could change gender with the Master and Missy before following through between Doctors Twelve and Thirteen. The carefully balanced tension between maintaining social and cultural realism and using the fantastic to push against convention provides exactly the liminal space in which classical monsters can adapt to the opportunities offered by a new environment. *Hercules: The Legendary Journeys* is thus free to construct a world where monsters reinforce the series' central themes without needing to justify their existence.

Monsters as adversaries

This is the story of a time long ago – a time of myth and legend, when the ancient gods were petty and cruel, and they plagued mankind with suffering. Only one man dared to challenge their power – Hercules. Hercules possessed a strength the world had never seen, a strength surpassed only by the power of his heart. He journeyed the earth, battling the minions of his wicked stepmother Hera, the all-powerful queen of the gods. But wherever there was evil, wherever an innocent would suffer, there would be – Hercules!

Title sequence voiceover, *Hercules: The Legendary Journeys*

Hercules: The Legendary Journeys (1995–1999) has received surprisingly little academic attention, at least from classicists. While this may in part come from pressures classical reception scholars feel to justify their study beyond the ancient world, there are also practical issues. There are one hundred and eleven episodes of *Hercules*, each running to about 45 minutes. That adds up to over eighty hours of television to watch, as opposed to two and a half hours for an average feature film – and that's without the five made-for-television movies shown in 1994, six series of *Xena: Warrior Princess*, fifty episodes of *Young Hercules*, and a 1998 Hercules/Xena animated movie. While DVD technology has made the series available to its fans in boxed set form, giving this amount of material the attention it deserves is a daunting prospect.

Yet it is the sheer wealth of material that makes *Hercules* such an excellent case study, not least because of its world-building. Like most telefantasy, *Hercules* is characterised by what Hills calls hyperdiegesis, or 'the creation of a vast and detailed narrative space, only a fraction of which is ever directly seen or encountered within the text, but which nevertheless appears to operate according to principles of internal logic and extension'.[9] Along with its spin-off companion series *Xena: Warrior Princess* (1995–2001) and *The Young Hercules* (1998–1999), it offers a record of how contemporary society views ancient myth; it develops a consistent world over six seasons, and preserves a detailed picture of cultural attitudes during the period it was produced.[10] Over the course of the series, the way which monsters are handled changes drastically, partly due to the series' own evolving sense of identity, and partly due to a shift in the characterisation of its hero.

Hercules itself is a spin-off of five made-for-television movies commissioned by Universal Television to sell to syndicated television stations in the US as part of a larger 'Action Pack' offering of films, produced by Renaissance Pictures. The five features were *Hercules and the Amazon Women*, *Hercules and the Lost Kingdom*, *Hercules and the Circle of Fire*, *Hercules in the Underworld* and *Hercules in the Maze of the Minotaur*; they established the Hercules 'brand' and visual style as commercially viable, and persuaded television executives to commission a series based on them before they had seen the films' ratings.[11] The films established that Greek myth was there to be adapted rather than slavishly followed; for instance, *Underworld* used the tradition of Deianeira giving Hercules a cloak poisoned by the blood of the dying centaur Nessus, but created a redemptive ending where Hercules returned from the underworld after capturing an escaped Cerberus.

The six seasons all used the same introductory title sequence, which remained identical over the program's lifespan despite its developing personality. This introduction, shown after the start of the programme had set up that week's plot, illustrates *Hercules'* general attitude to monsters. In a sequence lasting about a minute, the audience sees nine monsters, by a conservative count – a hydra, a she-demon, a giant, a water-beast, two centaurs, the Stymphalian bird, the minotaur and an extremely large lizard. The sequence includes several other common series tropes – stock villagers, well-endowed flirty women, fearsomely dressed yet incompetent soldiers, and Kevin Sorbo exercising his muscles in the leading role (Fig. 5.1). Yet the title sequence gives most of its attention to the monsters, the implied object of the superhuman strength the voiceover ascribes to the protagonist, and one subset of his stepmother Hera's minions. The viewer is promised monsters and, at least to begin with, monsters are what the viewer gets.

Hercules divides neatly into three phases: the first and second seasons; the third season and first half of the fourth season; and the second half of the fourth season until the end of the sixth season. Each represents different stages in the show's identity and its handling of monsters. During the first two series, the

Fig. 5.1 Kevin Sorbo as Hercules.

show is finding its feet, establishing its characters and building its world. The first season features major monsters in eight of its thirteen episodes, with a promised monster in a further episode and a spoken dialogue allusion to monsters in another – only three episodes have no monster content. Each of these three episodes has an independent combat set piece that replaces the central monster fight – there's a gang of child-warriors possessed by Ares, the god of war, who also makes a personal appearance ('Ares', 1.5); feats of martial arts as a woman searches for her lost husband ('The March to Freedom', 1.8); and gladiatorial fights to the death ('Gladiator', 1.10).

The second season again has a high monster content, with fourteen of twenty-four episodes containing monsters, one 'monster' catapult, and the final episode featuring a kitten that sounds like a monster in the cave where it is trapped ('The Cave of Echoes', 2.24). The episodes without monsters often feature gods as key protagonists, and sometimes monsters and gods appear in the same episode. Some element of the supernatural appears each week, counterbalanced by Hercules' commitment to humanity. This first phase moves towards more anthropomorphic monsters, which often function like packs of soldiers, facilitating carefully choreographed and visually impressive fight scenes. In thinking about what counts as a monster, I use the label broadly to reach beyond the classical canon and include, for instance, Pyro the fire monster ('The Fire Down Below', 2.9) and the orc-like mesomorphs ('Let the Games Begin', 2.16) who have been created specifically for the programme and do not belong to another mythical tradition. A wide mix of monsters meeting this definition serve a range of purposes in the first two seasons.

A number of episodes feature rent-a-monsters which are snakes, serpents or otherwise snake-like. In 'Pride Comes Before A Brawl' (1.7), Iolaus fights some giant water eels which attack him and a girl as they hide in a river; in 'The Festival of Dionysus' (1.4), Hercules must strangle what I can only describe as a serpentine fanged umbrella which inhabits the Bond villain-like pit into which he has been dropped. As an index of the classical, there may be an echo of the famous statue depicting Laocoön and his children, where the central figure grapples with two snakes sent to kill the priest and his sons for nearly revealing the ruse of the Trojan horse.[12] The prevalence of the snake as adversary may also draw on the influence that Joseph Campbell's concept of the hero's journey has exercised as a storytelling device in Hollywood;[13] according to this narrative template, the conquest of a dragon is a central part of the hero's growth towards independence. The prevalence of these serpentine adversaries also feels like a homage to Hercules' earliest attested adventure: Hera sent a pair of serpents to kill Hercules as a baby in his cradle, but the youthful demi-god strangled them.[14] Classical influences thus shape even the most mundane monsters deemed necessary for an action-adventure format.

Hercules also draws on the adult Hercules' Twelve Labours, which feature a multiplicity of monsters against which the hero proves his humanity by defeating the non-human. According to what became the canonical list of the labours given in Apollodorus' mythical compendium, Hercules battled the Nemean Lion, the Lernean Hydra, the Erymanthean Boar, the Stymphalian Birds, the flesh-eating Horses of Diomedes, Geryon's cattle, and Cerberus, the three-headed dog who guards the underworld. While some of these monsters appear in *Hercules*, the series prioritises the internal consistency of its telefantastic universe over the authenticity trap. This move is driven by an early decision to steer a new course between the bleakness of the original Greek myth and the 'stilted' style of the Italian *peplum* movies. Instead, the producers decided to go for an 'irreverent' style and give Hercules 'a contemporary sense of humour'.[15]

As a result, the Twelve Labours as a fixed set vanish from the series, mainly because Hercules traditionally was assigned them as penance for killing his own children. Such events, along with the rest of the myth's trajectory, 'would scarcely appeal to modern audiences raised on upright heroes and happy endings'.[16] Instead, the series begins with Hera's murder of Deianeira and the three children, establishing the antagonism that drives the conflict each week ('The Wrong Path', 1.1). Yet the series nods to the monsters of the labours, particularly to the Nemean Lion, the Hydra and the Stymphalian birds – or, to be more precise, the Stymphalian bird, whom Hercules kills after it attacks him and a group of refugees he is escorting across the Stymphalian swamp ('The Road to Calydon', 1.3). Having turned a flock of vicious birds into a single pterodactyl-like opponent, subsequent episodes religiously refer to the Bird in the singular.

The Bird is the best represented canonical monster. Iolaus battles a hydra without making the mistake of cutting its head off, referring to a previous battle as the source of his hydra knowledge ('Pride Comes Before A Brawl', 2.7). A double-headed hydra appears in the opening credit sequence, but belongs to the made-for-television movie *Hercules and the Amazon Women*. We later see the battle in a 'clip show' episode as Iolaus retells the story ('The Cave of Echoes', 2.24). Yet the monsters of the Labours appear frequently in dialogue, often to establish Hercules' status as monster slayer; for instance, when Hercules refers to the trouble he's having finishing off his mother Alcmene's wall (a running joke until Alcmene's death), he is asked, 'is it tougher than the Nemean lion?' ('The Warrior Princess', 1.9). The series uses the monsters of the 'authentic' Hercules story to signal fidelity to the ancient sources without constraining what those monsters can do, or bringing in the more grisly parts of the mythic tradition.

Many stories in the first phase of the series revolve around an underlying assumption that monsters are 'just like us', an idea that *Buffy the Vampire Slayer* (1996–2003) would also soon begin to explore. This premise plays out through the cyclops ('Eye of the Beholder', 1.2) and the centaurs ('As Darkness Falls', 1.6; 'Outcast', 2.5; 'Centaur Mentor Journey', 2.23). The general message is that these monsters are just misunderstood: if they do bad things, it is the fault of the humans who treat them badly. The classical monsters retain their monstrosity, to return to Cohen's Monster Theses, by settling down at the gates of difference.[17] The cyclops is particularly straightforward; he has rerouted a stream away from a village and towards Hera's vineyard not because of any loyalty to the queen of the gods, but because her henchman is comparatively kind to him after he has suffered years of abuse from the villagers. Later, one of the villagers calls him a 'freak', only for another villager to stand up in his defence and pointedly call him a 'man'. The truce that Hercules brokers at the end of the episode reinforces the breaking of the tie between appearance and moral character.

The centaurs are more complex, because they offer a way to talk about racism. 'As Darkness Falls' (1.6) follows events in *Hercules in the Underworld*, where the dying centaur Nessus tricked Deianeira into giving Hercules a cloak soaked with his poisonous blood. Hercules attends a wedding which is disrupted by Nessus' twin Nemis, who kidnaps Penelope, the bride, and hopes to persuade her to marry him by killing Hercules. He is assisted by two other centaurs, Craesus and Deric, and Deric's human girlfriend Lyla. We first meet the centaurs complaining about the table they have been given at the wedding; despite working for Penelope's father for ten years, they have been seated between the children and where the animals will be tethered. Later, we learn that Nemis and Penelope used to play together, but her father drove him off when he started getting too 'familiar'. Deric and Lyla decide to leave before the final confrontation with Nemis; Deric explains that 'Nemis wasn't always bad … life, death, wore him down.' Nemis redeems himself at the end of the episode as he holds up a collapsing cave to allow Hercules and Penelope to escape, sacrificing his life for theirs, which leads to Penelope sighing that she knows Nemis' love was true, but she's 'just sorry his love led him so far astray'.

Putting aside the issue of rape apologism for a moment, this line cements the episode's moral that Nemis was a good centaur who went bad because of his life experiences, and that the prejudice centaurs face collectively is unjustified. The link between the centaurs' experience and American racism is made more explicit in season two's 'Outcast', when a mob sets Lyla and Deric's house on fire. Lyla is killed, although Deric and their centaur son Kefor survive. When Hercules runs into Lyla's sister, she explains that a group named the Cretans poisoned the townspeople against them. The Cretans use language charged with racial overtones, such as 'we don't like centaurs or centaur-lovers in this town', 'we don't care for their kind around here' and 'the only good centaur is a dead centaur'. Lyla is called a 'centaur-loving slut' and various references are made to teaching 'filthy centaurs' a lesson. Hercules has to persuade Deric not to kill any Cretans and track down the true culprits. In doing so, he explicitly tells Deric that he can't be blamed for standing up for his rights, and emphasises the importance of following due legal process. Kevin Sorbo felt positive about this episode's themes, saying, 'I thought there was a great message in this episode about [the evils of] racism, and I think it's good that we send such messages …,' so the parallels are deliberate.[18] The episode frames racism as a personal prejudice that can be eradicated through re-education, like much 1990s progressive culture, but ignores the structural factors which perpetuate racism by excluding minorities from participating in social institutions.

'Centaur Mentor Journey' built on this theme, with Sorbo noting, 'Yes, it was a civil rights episode.'[19] Hercules is sent by his dying mentor, the centaur Ceridian, to help Cassius, a young centaur leading a Centaur Power movement protesting against segregation at the town drinking fountain. The ban was imposed by a corrupt town magistrate who wants to frame the centaurs for violence as part of a plan to seize another man's estate. When we first meet the magistrate, he claims that centaurs are only fit to be blacksmiths, fighters and workers. Later, reassuring a crony, he asks, 'if the centaurs start drinking from the same fountain as humans, where will it end? Do we want them playing with our children – our women?' Again, interspecies romance causes problems, not least because of Cassius' own fraught relationship with a human woman. The episode concludes with Hercules leading the centaurs on a peaceful protest march to the water fountain, the magistrate's plans being exposed, and everyone symbolically drinking from the same cup. Again, racism is framed as the result of an individual's moral failings rather than the result of a centuries-long history of one group oppressing another.

The centaurs explore the contemporary American social phenomenon of racism from the safe distance of antiquity, and replace discussions of miscegenation with implied concerns over bestiality. Centaurs are a particularly good space to explore these issues. The ancient Greeks saw them as hypermasculine in their sexuality and violence, situated past the limits of civilisation and defining culture by their defiance of it.[20] Their hybridity allows the series to portray them sympathetically by drawing on their part-human nature, which, in turn, becomes central to their role as a monster created by human animosity (Fig. 5.2). The argument might be made that one reason *Hercules* can offer this sort of content is precisely because it is telefantasy, and went under various forms of disciplinary radar. I would add that the cloak of antiquity, however threadbare, allows an ancient monster to reanimate itself through a modern monstrosity. Nonetheless, it is notable that this interpretation of the centaur racialises the monster, drawing on that practice of othering which emerged out of the colonial Western tradition.[21]

Another contemporary anxiety, the fear of the empowered female, manifests through the language of the monster in 'The Warrior Princess' (1.9). This episode introduces Xena, a warlord who wishes to kill Hercules as part of her plan to conquer Greece. To trap him, Xena seduces Iolaus and creates a confrontation. Hercules is about to walk away but instead a villager challenges him – 'She's a monster! Just like the Nemean Lion and the Stymphalian bird! You didn't walk away from fighting them, and you can't walk away from fighting her!' Hercules agrees and proceeds to rescue Iolaus. At the end of the episode, the companions

Fig. 5.2 A centaur from *Hercules: The Legendary Journeys*.

repair their relationship with some light-hearted banter – Iolaus says, 'If you're going to lecture me, it should be about the kind of woman I'm attracted to,' to which Hercules replies 'Yeah, you'd be better off with a black widow.' The comparison between the monsters Hercules has previously fought and Xena drives him to return to fight her. She is positioned as the monster which follows the Nemean Lion, the Hydra and the Bird, and as a monstrous black widow in her own right.

Signifiers of monstrosity are strongly gendered, and have extra impact because Xena subverts the norms of feminine behaviour. She presents herself to Iolaus as a helpless, hyperfeminine girl who just happens to command an army, but her homicidal urges and expansionist ambitions come through in the climactic battle scene, where she turns on Iolaus after Hercules refuses to kill him. The plot categorises her as a monster to be both desired and feared. Positioning the murderous female as the equivalent of the inhuman monster is the signpost for a gendering of monsters established in the first two episodes of season one. The first monster Hercules must face is a she-demon ('The Wrong Path', 1.1), followed by the cyclops of 'Eye of the Beholder' (1.2). In opposition to the cyclops' inherent reasonableness, the she-demon tricks men into falling in love with her and turns them into stone when they touch her, sending their souls to Hecate. She takes the form of a beautiful girl wearing a large white skirt, from which a serpent's tail creeps. When Hercules steps on the skirt, her serpentine bottom half is revealed, and he must avoid being caught in her coils or being stung. She is eventually turned to stone by her own stinger, the sign of her inherent sexual threat.

The monstering of active female sexuality mirrors broader fears in popular culture about women in control of their own desire. Ancient Greek monsters also operated along a gender binary that opposed chaos and femininity against order and masculinity. This division is articulated particularly clearly in creation myths, such as the conquest of Zeus' rationality over the untrammelled disorder of Gaia.[22] But the way that women who control their own sexual activity are depicted in *Hercules*' first season speaks to a cultural fear about the emancipated woman, which manifests in the series' use of physical and linguistic monstering. This pattern could be seen as part of a wider backlash against various advances in women's rights, particularly in the area of reproductive freedom;[23] the latter was particularly prominent following two record-breaking protest marches in Washington, DC, organised by the National Organization for Women in support of abortion rights during April 1989 and April 1992. As a response, the conquest of feminine coded monsters becomes a way of reinforcing and securing Hercules' masculinity in the series' initial phase.

Feminine sexual agency is not the only way women are monstered; maternity also becomes a locus of monstrosity through the character of Echidna, the mother of all monsters. Her story arc in *Hercules* is one of her rare appearances in popular culture, although she has excellent mythic credentials. She appears in Hesiod's *Theogony* as the mother of, among others, Cerberus and the Lernean Hydra, so has a prior connection to the Hercules myth. When we meet *Hercules*' version of her in 'The Mother of All Monsters' (2.7), she introduces herself as the mother of not only the Hydra, but also the She-demon (now a singular) and the Stymphalian Bird. She plans to send her henchman Demetrius to seduce Alcmene, Hercules' mother; kidnap her as a lure for her son; and kill them both, one for raising a killer and the other for killing her children.

The episode raises some troubling questions about the monstrous, the maternal and the sexual that it never really resolves. The parallels between Echidna and Alcmene are constantly re-emphasised. When Echidna first sees Demetrius, she muses, 'Yes, you'll do nicely' – not just as a lackey, but also as sufficiently attractive to capture Alcmene's interest. Echidna gives female desire an explicit voice, but her musing implies that she and Alcmene have a shared standard of male attractiveness; there is also a queer component in Echidna seducing Alcmene by proxy. Demetrius succeeds in ensnaring Alcmene. Hercules experiences a very particular kind of horror when he comes home and interrupts them in the middle of a passionate embrace. When Alcmene is thrown at Echidna's feet (or tail) after they believe Hercules has been killed, the two have a spirited exchange:

> **Echidna**   Did it hurt when you saw your son die? Did you feel your heart crumble?
>
> **Alcmene**   I'm not going to give you the satisfaction of seeing me cry. Just kill me and get it over with.
>
> **Echidna**   You don't get off so easily after raising a killer.
>
> **Alcmene**   Hercules is no killer.
>
> **Echidna**   Yes he is – he killed my children, he killed them one after another! No mother should have to endure that.
>
> **Alcmene**   Your children were monsters just like you, they murdered and maimed for any god corrupt enough to use them.

Their contest over who is the best mother and who has raised true monsters continues when Hercules has rescued his mother and is about to kill Echidna. Just before he stabs her, Alcmene holds him back:

> We're not monsters! We're not instruments of death and destruction, we're human beings! Besides, now I know how she felt when her children died. She acted the same way I would've.

Alcmene's double-pronged argument is decidedly odd. On the one hand, she and Hercules are different to Echidna; on the other, motherhood creates a bond that she understands. So the viewer is offered a deliberately contradictory juxtaposition of monstrous and non-monstrous, of othering and sympathy – all articulated through the identity of maternity. Western society has traditionally been deeply ambivalent about the sexuality of older women, especially those past childbearing age, as demonstrated by the difficulty until very recently of finding good Hollywood roles for women over the age of 40;[24] that ambivalence becomes the angst on which this monster feeds.

Echidna's monstrosity is further developed in 'Cast a Giant Shadow' (2.10), when Hercules rescues the giant Typhon, who has had one foot stuck in a rock for over a hundred years. He explains that this was because of his wife – 'Hera wanted her to do bad things but she was always happy when I was around.' Only after Hercules and Typhon have developed a rapport is it revealed that Typhon's wife is Echidna and all those children he's looking forward to seeing are the monsters we know Hercules has killed:

Typhon   Tell me what she [Echidna] did. Did she hurt you?

Hercules   Well, at first she wanted to, but then we found a way round that.

Typhon   Sounds like she's changed! In the old days, if I wasn't with her when she blew her stack, people got hurt. Hurt bad.

Hercules   To tell you the truth, that's what I thought was going to happen to me.

Typhon   Were the kids with her? The Hydra, the Stymphalian Bird, the She-demon?

Hercules   Well . . .

Typhon   I hope they weren't getting into trouble again.

Hercules   They . . . do have a reputation as a wild bunch, don't they . . .

Typhon   Only because nobody ever took a look at their good qualities. I bet you never knew the Hydra could knit. Or the Stymphalian Bird was a great dancer. And the She-demon? Oh! You should have heard her sing.

The vision of a knitting hydra aside, Hercules squirms precisely because Typhon is so good-natured and unmonstrous; he and Iolaus consistently struggle with how such a 'sweet, innocent guy' could be married to the monster they know. Once again, we are shown a sympathetic side to the classical monsters which forces us to question the image we have of Hercules as an unproblematic hero, and our assumptions about the monsters we have met. While Weisbrot says this episode 'plays for comedy rather than chills', and Typhon is an undeniably light-hearted character, it reinforces Echidna's case in 'Mother of All Monsters' that Hercules' actions were not as laudable as the series has hitherto presented them.[25] That Typhon can see the loveable side of Echidna also signals that he is not as harmless as the humans think he is.

Hercules manages to negotiate this difficult moment by explaining to Typhon that Hera separated him from his children so that they would fall into a life of crime, and that he had no choice but to kill them. Typhon forgives him, and Hercules reunites him with Echidna. After he has explained about being trapped for the last century, their reconciliation is swift:

Hercules   Hera wanted to keep you and Typhon apart because she knew how angry that would make you.

Echidna   And it did. I've been such a fool, and I've done such horrible things.

Typhon	But I still love ya, Echidna!
Echidna	You do? Then come 'ere, lover-boy!
Typhon	Oh, baby you're the greatest!

The last we see of the two monsters is their passionate embrace as Hercules and Iolaus sidle out of the cave in an embarrassed fashion. The reintroduction of Typhon as a paternal figure means that Echidna's rogue maternity can be contained within the restored nuclear patriarchal family. She is reintegrated into an acceptable social structure as she becomes a spouse rather than a free agent.

The Echidna arc also brings the issue of agency to the fore in this first phase of *Hercules*. The reason that Hercules can justify his actions to Typhon is that 'they didn't give [him] a choice' and that 'Hera had them under her power, there's no way they could do anything good'. Hera is also responsible for trapping Typhon so he could not bring out Echidna's better side. Echidna's redemption comes because the responsibility is explicitly shifted to the goddess who, lest we forget, is only a stepmother. The intruder in the family remains the ultimate source of monstrosity.

Hera is not the only Olympian to weaponise monsters – Ares's hell-hound provides the main monstrous focus in the final three episodes of the first season, for example. Nemis is not absolved of moral responsibility in 'As Darkness Falls', but excuses are made for his behaviour which have the same effect and prevent the same behaviour being expected of other centaurs. A significant part of how monsters are handled arises from who is using them and for what nefarious purpose. There will be an adequate explanation if they are acting independently. More likely, they will be positioned as tools of the episode's central villain. Even the fanged umbrella serpent of 'The Festival of Dionysus' (1.4) only goes for Hercules because it has been trapped in a pit and is, presumably, a bit peckish.

The first phase of *Hercules* sees monsters primarily as a way to define the hero, but also as a space for raising ethical questions about the nature of monsters themselves. The classical monsters draw on multiple contemporary issues, including the backlash against advances in women's economic and reproductive rights, the impact of the 1991 Civil Rights Act which made employment discrimination based on race and gender illegal, and the changing face of America's role in international relations. This last, in particular, arose from the conflict in Bosnia (1992–5), where America found itself acting more as peacekeeper than world's policeman, in a marked contrast to the First Gulf War (1990–1). The need to find a new model of masculinity which relied less on beating things up than on reaching peaceful reconciliation accounts for much of

Hercules' emphasis on the hero as negotiator, with force as a last (spectacular) resort – at least as far as humans are concerned.

Hercules, Phase Two

The second phase of the series, season three and the first half of season four, settles into its trademark playfulness. The clip show 'Les Contemptibles' (3.17), set in revolutionary France, is typically jokey: some bandits are inspired to revolutionary fervour by tales of the ancient Hercules' derring-do. More episodes abandon monsters, balanced to some extent by an interest in anachronistic technology and war machines (such as Daedalus' megalith in 'Doomsday', 3.2). Of the monsters that do appear, the sand sharks which Hercules and an escaped prisoner must negotiate in 'Mercenary' (3.1) come the closest to the serpentine monster-of-the-week that featured in the first phase. They live under the desert and come when they feel vibrations on the sand, leaping out to snatch their prey back underground. The episode offers a homage to the sandworms of *Dune* (1984) as well as the graboids of *Tremors* (1990), exploiting telefantasy's freedom with generic expectations to widen the range of possible stories available in any given format.

In general, the rent-a-monster fades away, as do gangs of anthropomorphic monsters, to be replaced by monsters who sit at the centre of the weekly plot in smaller numbers, but with greater narrative significance. This leads to an emphasis on speaking monsters, such as the infant dragon Braxus in 'The Lady and the Dragon' (3.10). Although the classical *drakōn* features in classical myth, here the inspiration seems taken from Tolkienesque fantasy.[26] Braxus' ability to hold a conversation lets us understand he has been tricked into thinking that Hercules and Iolaus killed his mother, but his speech also comes as a surprise to the heroes. 'What are you talking to it for? It's a dragon!' says Iolaus in exasperation as Hercules tries to reason with Braxus, only to observe, 'a talking dragon. Huh!' when Braxus replies. As well as dispelling the misapprehension that he is a silent brute, Braxus also turns out to be an impressionable child who longs to return to his home in Tarsus.

The treatment of Braxus explores many issues touched on in the episode with the cyclops in season one ('Eye of the Beholder', 1.2), but with a twist. Since Braxus is not an anthropomorphic monster, the case that monsters are 'just like us' becomes much more difficult to accept. After all, Braxus can incinerate anyone who upsets him. Yet the innocence that the episode's warlord villain has abused provides a foil to the monstrous potential that Braxus possesses, and once more poses the question of whether we can judge a monster simply by its appearance. In the case of Arachne ('Web of Desire', 4.4), by the time that Hercules, Iolaus and the pirate captain Nebula encounter her, the answer is a straightforward yes. The story that Hercules tells to explain Arachne's transformation differs entirely from Ovid's version in book six of the *Metamorphoses*, where she is transformed into a spider after daring to challenge the goddess Athena to a weaving contest. According to Hercules, Arachne was originally a very vain and very beautiful queen. She gave birth to a daughter who was even more beautiful and threw her into the sea out of spite. The gods then cursed her, transforming her into a gigantic spider-human hybrid.

'Web of Desire' dwells on the theme of monstrous appearance and what it means for Arachne and those around her. After identifying Arachne as the creature responsible for picking off various shipwrecked sailors who die horribly in the caves where they are sheltering from a raging storm, Hercules observes, 'Arachne moves in the shadows because she's ashamed of her appearance. Light is her enemy.' At the close of the episode, Arachne is defeated when her lair is firebombed, and the plan to light up the cave is explicitly framed as a way to make Arachne uncomfortable. Yet Arachne herself doesn't seem to buy into this rhetoric. When the audience sees her caressing the captured pirate Paxxon, her opening line is 'do you think I'm . . . beautiful?' followed by a seductive pout, and she uses the same line on Iolaus. Rather than hide herself away in shame, Arachne intends to use her captives as hosts for a horde of baby spiders that she will unleash upon unsuspecting humanity. She becomes another monstrous mother, even more so as she is choosing to act in this way of her own free will. As Hercules begins to set fire to her clutch, she explains her understanding of her plan – 'I prefer to think of it as spreading beauty – the world will know true beauty once again.'

The composition of shots concentrates on Arachne's spidery legs and her vampiresque teeth, yet despite Hercules' assertion that her appearance is now hateful, she behaves as if she wants that appearance to take over the world. Her transformation from beauty to monster also implies that her inner and outer selves are now aligned. Perhaps Hercules' assumption that she would be ashamed that her physical appearance matches her moral qualities rests in his own firmly virtuous character and well-developed physique. Whatever story others tell about her, Arachne revels in her monstrosity and seeks to literally infect others with it. She dwells enthusiastically on the boundaries of the possible, both in terms of her physicality and her ambition. She offers a monster who is comfortable with her own darkness, which was there even before her transformation – in some ways, this makes her more dangerous than most of Hercules' adversaries.

Appearance, internal disposition and monstrousness are again key to 'The Green-Eyed Monster' (3.7). The episode takes the myth of Cupid and Psyche as its loose inspiration. Aphrodite does not approve of Cupid's infatuation with the mortal Psyche and orders him to make her fall in love with someone else. Hercules, Cupid's 'favourite uncle', is brought in to make him see sense, but is accidentally hit by one of Cupid's arrows and falls in love with Psyche himself. As Cupid watches Hercules gush, he turns green with envy, quite literally, and is transformed into a flying scaly monster rather reminiscent of the Grinch. Aphrodite's earlier admonishment that jealousy will turn him into a different person stops sounding quite so metaphorical.

There is, inevitably, a back story, in that Cupid is under a curse from Hera that turns him monstrous whenever he feels a pang of unrequited love. If he transforms three times, he will be a monster forever. Hercules is freed from the power of the arrow by remembering the true love he felt for Deianeira, Aphrodite relents, and Psyche is given immortality so that Cupid never has to fear turning into a green-eyed monster again. The happy ending glides over the problems the episodes poses – although Hera's curse makes the metaphorical green-eyed monster real, does it do anything more than bring what was already in Cupid's character to the surface? Cupid is excused from being held accountable by 'true love', with worrying echoes of excuses made by domestic abusers.[27] The need to rescue Cupid from his monstrous self, supposedly imposed by Hera, means that the full implications of that self are not explored – which may be deliberate. Monsters sometimes exist to police the borders of the possible – when Cupid crosses the line of abusive behaviour, the norms of healthy relationships are reinstated by the creation of a world where his monstrous behaviour is no longer possible. Since Psyche rather than Cupid is the one who changes, it is still the female who is presented as the problem which needs to be solved, further absolving Cupid from responsibility.

While some monsters in this second phase grapple with the relationship between external appearance and monstrosity, others are shaped by the series' characteristic light-hearted comedy. In 'The Green-Eyed Monster', one of the reasons Aphrodite is worried about Cupid is that he's started hanging out with a bad crowd – who turn out to be a bunch of frat-boy satyrs, woodland gods with a goat's legs and horns, who think of nothing except toga parties. While Cupid does command the satyrs to watch out for Hercules and they end up fighting him, they are never presented as a credible threat like the bands of monster-warriors found in the first phase of the series. These ancient monsters are mostly harmless and played for laughs. The move to humour rather than horror is both a response to the evolving playfulness of *Hercules*, but also a canny mapping of the satyr's central features – sexual desire and alcoholism – onto a social phenomenon familiar to an American audience. The stereotype of the gormless and inebriated jock communicates the essence of what satyrs are far quicker than any exposition; either you know what a satyr is, or cultural resonance lets you fill in the gaps.

Wit and pathos are mixed in 'Monster Child in the Promised Land' (3.6), the conclusion of the Echidna/Typhon arc. When Hercules and Iolaus receive a message that Echidna and Typhon have had another child, the thief Klepto takes the opportunity to steal baby Obie, intending to hand him over to the local warlord. The warlord has been ordered to steal Obie by Hera, who wishes to turn him evil as she did his siblings. The episode returns to the tensions established in our earlier encounters with the couple, as Echidna is perturbed by this attempt to bring her and her son back into Hera's fold. As she sadly observes, 'when it comes to evil, the mother of all monsters is always in demand.' The episode also defers the revelation of what precisely the baby looks like. Obie is kept bundled up in a blanket until Klepto comes to visit under the pretence that Hercules and Iolaus sent him, when the blanket is removed to dramatic chords. What we actually see is a Muppet-like, small, green walrus with tentacles, which squeaks adorably and engages in toddler-like pranks. Klepto, who begins by viewing Obie as a tiny monstrous bargaining chip, is eventually won over and ends up thinking he's 'a great little guy'.

Monstrous motherhood remains dangerous, although Echidna is over-whelmed with anxiety for her stolen child. When Hera's chief minion appears, she gloats, 'how touching – the mother of all monsters showing her sensitive side' before Echidna attacks her. Obie both reasserts her identity as mother of all monsters – for he, too, is a monster – but also confronts her with her past, and Obie's potential future, as Hera's creature. She relives the trauma of the previous deaths of her children as she sobs, 'I've lost another baby, I know I have.' Her deep emotional turmoil blocks her ability to act. It is perhaps not coincidental that it is Typhon who disciplines Obie when he is about to savage Hercules and prevents him from getting the first taste of blood that would give Hera control over him ('listen to your dad, little guy', says Hercules, optimistically). Monstrous maternity cannot handle the task of preventing monstrosity becoming an instrument of evil – a firm patriarchal hand is still required for that – but Obie's charming childishness challenges the idea that wickedness and monstrosity must go hand in hand.

The patriarchal power to control the monster does not go uninterrogated. In 'Beanstalks and Bad Eggs' (4.1), Hercules and the king of thieves Autolycus climb a beanstalk to discover a human woman and a giant, Leanna and Typhoon, looking after a clutch of Harpy eggs waiting to hatch. (Typhoon will later be revealed to be the brother of Typhon, explaining the family resemblance caused by Glenn Shadix playing both roles.) The episode is a mash-up of 'Jack and the Giant Beanstalk' and *Gremlins* (1984); the Harpies hatch while Hercules and Autolycus are in the cloud castle, and are strongly reminiscent of Gizmo and his fellow mogwai. The similarities extend beyond the visual, since one could interpret *Gremlins* as being about parenthood, and the misdeeds of the misbehaving mogwai express anxieties about the illicit activities of teenagers. In 'Beanstalks', the Harpies are positioned as the children of Leanna and Typhoon, who towards the end of the episode talk about raising 'those kids' well. As Typhoon promises, 'they'll grow up to be *good* harpies, you'll see!'

This promise has been hard-won. When we first meet Typhoon, he is furious to discover a 'Grecian man' with Leanna, and indeed is livid with Leanna herself. This frustration arises from the circumstances of their confinement – Hades has ordained that Leanna must care for the clutch of Harpy eggs until they hatch, in order to save her village from Harpy attack, and Typhoon must protect them from harm. Living together in such close quarters has created resentment, but also affection; as Typhoon confides to Autolycus, he wishes he could tell Leanna how he really feels. The audience is explicitly invited to compare the tender Typhon with his irascible brother, and to see Autolycus' lessons in gentlemanly courtship (taken from the 'rose between one's teeth' school of romance) as an attempt to tame the giant's savagery. This domestication is not simply about whether Typhoon can repair his relationship with Leanna; he needs to bring his raging anger under control to provide the sort of positive masculine influence on the harpies that Typhon offers Obie.

Although Autolycus' lessons in love fail to hit the spot, Typhoon realises he must address his control issues to win Leanna. The episode ends with the happy couple foreseeing a life of domestic harmony and child-rearing. Once again, the implication that the monstrous nature of the man involved in a controlling (and thus potentially abusive) relationship can instantaneously be changed is deeply problematic, but relies on the same trope that monstrosity lies in behaviour rather than in appearance. Typhoon is introduced as a 'real' giant who must overcome his inner rage in order to domesticate himself into the family unit and play the good patriarch. I don't think that the fact that he is partnered with a human woman is coincidental. Whereas Echidna's maternal monstrosity requires the intervention of a benign paternalistic presence, Leanna's mortality means that the episode can focus on Typhoon's need to manage his internal horrors to perform his allotted social role.

This transformation is necessitated by the newly hatched harpies, who are undeniably monstrous both in appearance and behaviour. They are, however, vulnerable – one is eaten by a cloud snake lurking outside the castle before Hercules rescues it via the Heimlich manoeuvre. When they attempt to climb down the beanstalk, one slips and must be saved with the help of a swiftly improvised bungee cord. Leanna and Typhoon's concern with the harpies' safety feels incongruous alongside Hercules and Autolycus' battle to make sure they cannot cause havoc in the human realm. As Hercules notes when refusing to take the unhatched eggs down the beanstalk with Leanna, 'once you have harpies, you can't get rid of them'.[28] The harpies are both threatening and defenceless, a danger yet endangered. Their characterisation as potentially chaotic yet impressionable enough to respond to guidance puts implicit narrative pressure on Typhoon to undertake that responsibility. Their childish monstrosity and monstrous childhood return to the idea that runs all through the second phase – that what makes a monster monstrous is not always as clear cut as it might first appear.

Once *Hercules* has established itself and can begin to really explore the mythic world that it has constructed, the series dispenses with the utilitarian serpents of phase one. Instead, monsters are fully involved in the plot and get corresponding character development. Hercules himself is still characterised through his monster-killing prowess in the opening title sequence, and dialogue references support that presentation, even as the proportion of monsters faced dwindles and their inclusion becomes more about quality rather than quantity. But just as this more reflective phase was beginning to hit its stride, disaster struck. On 3 September 1997, Kevin Sorbo suffered a severe aneurysm in his left arm followed by a series of strokes.

Hercules, Phase Three

After his medical crisis, Kevin Sorbo suffered a permanent ten per cent loss in his vision, problems with his balance, physical weakness, headaches, sensitivity to light, anxiety and panic attacks. Although Sorbo was keen to return to work, the production team had to figure out how the show could continue while taking its star's changed physical abilities into account. Previously, Sorbo had been doing punishing days on set, waking at 4.30 a.m., getting to set at 6.30 a.m., leaving for the gym at 7.30 p.m., and starting all over again after just four-and-a-half hours sleep.[29] When he returned to New Zealand in late November 1997, he was only able to manage an hour on set at a time.[30]

Sorbo gradually worked up to a fuller production schedule, but in the meantime, solutions had to be found. More episodes were promised on a tight deadline, and *Hercules* wouldn't work without – well, Hercules. There was also intense pressure for the series to rack up 100 episodes, which was then the threshold a series needed to pass to make a good syndication deal so it could generate income from reruns.[31] Initially, the writers came up with new episodes or revised existing ones to either take Hercules out of the picture completely, or to minimise the time he spent on screen. The fact the series had already played with episodes like 'Les Contemptibles' (3.17) set outside the series' usual universe made running similar time-hop clip shows like 'Yes, Virginia, There is a Hercules' (4.15) easier. While actors playing various members of the production crew in modern Los Angeles worried what they would do now that Kevin Sorbo had gone missing, Sorbo himself only had to appear on camera for a single shot to deliver one line – the first one since his aneurysm.[32] Other episodes were equally inventive. In 'Porkules' (4.16), possibly drawing on the story of Circe in the *Odyssey*, Hercules is turned into a pig, which required a lot of voiceover but little physical work. 'Memory' episodes also used the conceit of flashbacks to Hercules' youthful escapades with Iolaus and Jason. These were so successful that a second spin-off, *Young Hercules*, was commissioned for the Fox Kids Network.

I linger on Hercules because the need to respond to Sorbo's medical needs resulted in a different approach to monsters. This shift is slightly difficult to track because the division of the seasons does not match up with when episodes were actually filmed. Sorbo's aneurysm occurred while the series was on filming hiatus, but the break in season four occurs between episodes eight and nine, which were first aired in November 1997 and January 1998, respectively. From this point, apart from the flashback episodes and some dialogue references, monsters more or less disappear from the series.

One advantage of returning to Hercules' past adventures was that it allowed the series to have Hercules fighting monsters, just as a younger incarnation of himself (played by Ryan Gosling, in his last role as a children's television actor). It also filled out the backstory of the series, using the rich hinterland of telefantasy to provide narrative material which was in keeping with the overall feel of the series but without putting pressure on the recovering Sorbo. This strategy is neatly illustrated by 'Medea Culpa' (4.11), framed as a series of reminiscences between the adult Hercules, Jason and Iolaus while on a fishing trip. They recall an incident which nearly tore their friendship apart, namely an encounter with a teenage Medea (who, it will come as no surprise to learn, was in the pay of Hera to try and break up the friends so that Hercules could die horribly). Hercules is able both to fight and not fight. Gosling handles the monster whilst Sorbo sits on a log and talks about fish.

This episode offers some insight into the series' sense of how monsters became integral to Hercules' identity. On a visit to the young king Jason, Hercules is told by a little girl (Hera in disguise) that her parents were killed when a ghidra attacked her village. The dialogue that follows is instructive:

> **Hercules**   Looks like I'm going to have to cut my visit short.
>
> **Jason**   Awww, don't be a sore loser, you just got here.
>
> **Iolaus**   No no no no, Hercules fancies himself as a bit of a monster slayer.
>
> **Jason**   A monster?
>
> **Iolaus**   Yeah, a ghidra no less.

The story we are about to see unfold on screen is framed as foundational to our adult characters in more ways than simply not letting sexual jealousy get between them. We are, we are led to believe, seeing the start of the legendary journeys of the series' title. What do we find out about the ghidra? Hercules explicitly labels it one of 'Hera's little pets' when he discovers it is on the loose, suggesting that the enmity between him and Hera has always been at the heart of his monstrous escapades, and confirming Hera's long-standing connection to monsters. The group find a village that has been burned down by the ghidra, although we do not see it. When Iolaus and Hercules eventually corner the beast in its cave lair, again, the dialogue is revealing:

> **Iolaus**   You, er, you ever killed a monster before?
>
> **Hercules**   Yeah, the snake. You remember? Ares' cavern?
>
> [pause]
>
> **Iolaus**   Maybe you should go first.
>
> **Hercules**   What are you, scared?
>
> **Iolaus**   No!
>
> **Hercules**   Me too.

This clarification suggests an earlier monster encounter, but positions this as the first monster that Iolaus and Hercules are going to fight as a team. It is significant that the two teenagers acknowledge their fear response, and that they are allowed to be insecure. There is a distinct contrast between this tentative foray and the more confident escapades of the grown-up Hercules and Iolaus. The monster becomes *more* monstrous because of the youth of the protagonists, and the mysteriousness of the ghidra, a new arrival in the world of Greek myth. It appears to have been inspired by King Ghidorah, sometimes anglicised as Ghidrah, a monster who appeared in a series of films produced by the Japanese film company Toho from 1964 onwards.[33] This marks another characteristic of this third phase, in that it broadens out to use monsters which have obviously non-classical roots but are identified as natural inhabitants of the *Hercules* universe.

The nature of the monster as unseen and unknown is underlined by the exchange between Hercules and Iolaus once they locate the ghidra:

Iolaus   You didn't tell me it has two heads.[34]

Hercules   Slipped my mind.

Iolaus   Anything else you'd care to mention?

Hercules   Yeah. The stinger on that tail is instant death.

Iolaus   Anything else?

Hercules   Yeah. It breathes fire, too.

Iolaus   Anything else?

Hercules   That's about it.

Hercules holds a privileged position as the possessor of monstrous knowledge, whilst Iolaus and the viewer receive a quick primer to prepare them for the ensuing fight. The actual monster itself looks like a giant two-headed crocodile (with stinger tail and fire breath), and the litany of deadly characteristics makes it seem a real threat that the duo need Jason's help to overcome.

The use of backstory to establish Hercules' identity without new monster fights also surfaces in 'Yes, Virginia, There is a Hercules' (4.15). As the show's production team brainstorm ways to handle Kevin Sorbo's mysterious disappearance, one suggestion explicitly references the 'in-filling' technique. The producer's assistant asks, 'what was the first monster he killed?', which allows the episode to show a number of clips of the young Hercules fighting monsters, including the giant snake that 'Medea Culpa' mentioned in passing – as the sequence ends, the assistant rhapsodises, 'it'll be just like *The Wonder Years*, but with giant snakes!', implying that battling a serpent should somehow be seen as a rite of passage akin to negotiating the tensions of a high school prom.[35] I noted that in phase one of the series, the rent-a-monsters tended towards the serpentine.

This inset moment returns to that idea, offering a neat mythic in-joke for those who have been paying attention.

The sudden shift away from monsters is neatly illustrated by the companion episode to 'Porkules', 'One Fowl Day' (4.17), which features two not-really-monsters. The first is made up of Iolaus and Autolycus, chained together by Ares as punishment for turning his crony Discord into a chicken in the previous episode. Ares takes away their capacity for human speech, gets them covered in mud, gives them giant feet and protruding teeth, and generally makes the local populace believe this strange creature is a monster – 'It's an abomination! The only good monster is a dead monster! Let's destroy it before it destroys our minds!' In a stroke of luck for the unfortunate duo, P. T. Barnabus appears and purchases them for his freak show, where Hercules is able to break Ares' chain and free them from the curse.

Just as things are looking up, Autolycus encounters something on the road that turns him into a gibbering wreck. When the audience and Iolaus see it, it turns out to be – a giant chicken. More precisely, it is Discord still in chicken form, but a giant chicken, nonetheless. Iolaus and Autolycus manage to defeat her, but they are aware of the absurdity of the situation:

> **Autolycus** Iolaus, wait 'til Hercules hears that we took on a monster all by ourselves.
>
> **Iolaus** Yeah. You going to tell him it was a chicken?
>
> [pause]
>
> **Iolaus** That'll be our secret.

This, dare I say it, goofy approach to monsters clearly would not have been sustainable in the long term, and the monster as opponent never really recovers in this third phase. Series four flags this up through the plot of the final episode, in which Hera is trapped in the pit of Tartarus after an attempt to depose Zeus and turn him into a mortal. Although this is never explicitly stated, the lack of monsters in Hercules' life thereafter could easily be explained as a direct consequence of Hera's absence. She has been the driving force behind the monstrous threats that Hercules has faced in phases one and two, so within the world of the series it naturally follows that her defeat would lead to a drop in monster attacks.

Series five embraces the move into a heroism without monsters in multiple ways. The first episode, 'Faith' (5.1), sees Hercules and Iolaus receive an invitation from King Gilgamesh of Sumeria to help him fight against his own hostile gods.

The king's name evokes the mythic tradition of the *Epic of Gilgamesh*, but the series does not draw on that potential narrative. Although Iolaus is sceptical about getting involved with a whole other pantheon, Hercules observes 'it's about time we broaden our horizons'. One might have expected this expansion to bring on a legion of exotic foreign monsters, but instead the series focuses on Hercules' relationship with the gods, wherever they may be. Once he has finished in Sumeria, Hercules travels to Eire, Norway and an alternate universe, besides returning occasionally to Greece. The series finale brings in the Four Horsemen of the Apocalypse for good measure. Hercules' motivation moves from fighting monsters to addressing the arbitrary cruelty of the gods, and the potential return of the ultimate force of evil. Much of the series explores what might be called New Age spiritual themes, particularly those episodes set in Eire.

The season appears to be self-aware enough to pre-empt the response that its viewers might have to this change in tone and content. In 'Descent' (5.2), Hercules travels to the gates of the Sumerian underworld to try and save Iolaus, driven by deep guilt about his companion's death at the end of 'Faith'. During the journey, while camping for the evening, the following conversation takes place between Nebula (who, after we first encountered her in 'Web of Desire', turns out to be a Sumerian princess), one of her crew, and Hercules, who is sitting a little way off with his back to the campfire:

Danaeus   So, that's the legendary Hercules, is it?

Nebula   In the flesh.

Danaeus   Gotta say, I'm a little disappointed.

Nebula   Why? Were you expecting him to fly?

Danaeus   I thought he'd be a little more – I don't know, inspiring? I mean, he took down the hydra and the cyclops. I was hoping for some action.

Hercules   Danaeus. If you came looking for a cheap thrill, you're at the wrong place at the wrong time with the wrong guy.

Danaeus   I, I didn't mean . . .

Hercules   I don't care what you meant. I'm not here to entertain you. Just – stay out of my way.

The gay subtext of this encounter, which can be read as Hercules rejecting Danaeus' fannish advances, is reinforced when Danaeus storms away from the campsite and has his soul drained to keep the gatekeeper of the Sumerian underworld alive, but that's another story. This exchange is deeply reflexive. It acknowledges the season's change of tone, and foreshadows the inner conflict that will plague Hercules as he wrestles with his guilt over Iolaus' death and his fundamental doubts over his life's purpose. Despite the expectations of Danaeus, who thinks he knows what Hercules is all about, the reality is an angry and brooding hero who disavows his previous exploits. As viewers, we know that Hercules' presence on the television flatly contradicts his statement: he *is* there to entertain the audience, if not Danaeus. What this moment allows the series to do is reframe the expectations of that entertainment, away from the spectacular, and towards episodes with a greater focus on relationships.

The series universe continues to be populated by monsters who leave their marks in other ways, not least in the opening title sequence. 'Fade Out' (5.20) is based on the magical properties of fossilised cyclopes' eyes, although the brothers they belonged to are long dead. In 'The Academy', Hercules and Jason meet the centaur Chiron's human son, while 'Sky High' (5.12) brings a centaur back to the screen. The episode once again raises issues with racial overtones. Nagus is seeking vengeance for his son who has been killed by Kurth, a local troublemaker. At the same time, he had warned his son about the company he was keeping – 'they only wanted him because a centaur makes a handy partner in crime'. That Nagus' son was in the wrong place with the wrong people at the wrong time becomes a cipher for young African American men caught up in gang violence. Nagus becomes even angrier when Kurth volunteers to help Hercules transport dangerous crystals up a volcano to divert a lava flow from the village, which he sees as a miscarriage of justice.

Tensions are further heightened by the presence of Ephiny. Her storyline mainly takes place in *Xena: Warrior Princess*, but for now it is enough to note that she is mother to Xenan, a centaur son.[36] Ephiny and Xenan had briefly crossed over to *Hercules* in 'Prodigal Sister' (4.7), and Hercules had guest-starred in *Xena*, so there is enough overlap to make her acquaintance with Hercules plausible. In 'Sky High', Xenan is out with his cousins on a ritual hunt. While he never appears on screen, Ephiny knows he is in an area of the forest which will be covered by lava, so joins the party transporting the crystals to protect him. However, the group dynamic is just as explosive as the volcano, due to long-standing enmity between the Amazons and the Centaurs.

The episode explores the stereotypes of centaur behaviour that Nagus' son got caught up in, and that the village gang assume Nagus will follow; it also allows Nagus to demonstrate his own bravery and stoicism when he volunteers to carry explosive crystals up the mountain in a harness. Nagus is given the opportunity for some healing, since he and Ephiny are able to talk about the grief of losing someone you love when he realises her mate was a now-deceased centaur. The conversation closes with Ephiny observing, 'remember what I said before – people aren't always what they appear to be'. Although Nagus and Kurth never fully reconcile, Kurth atones for his crime by jumping into the volcano to trigger the explosion, saving the village and the local inhabitants. The reintroduction of a centaur into the series picks up on pre-established analogies drawn between centaurs and the African American community. The solution offered is rather uncomfortable – Nagus' justifiable anger that Kurth is given a stay of execution, interfering with official legal processes, is dismissed by Kurth's ultimate self-sacrifice, implying that judicial delay will ultimately be satisfactorily resolved. This optimistic message is far from the lived experience of African Americans encountering the American legal system, where institutional racism has created an overrepresentation of African Americans in prison populations. African Americans are seven times more likely to be incarcerated than whites.[37] In reiterating the theme that appearances do not signify monsters, so key to the earlier anti-racist episodes of *Hercules*' first phase, 'Sky High' inadvertently approves the mechanisms which underlie serial and oppressive miscarriages of justice.

After the return of Iolaus to the living at the end of 'Revelations' (5.22), monsters begin to creep back into dialogue associated with Hercules' identity, even if monsters to fight remain thin on the ground. It is as if Hercules needs Iolaus alive in order to be his full monster-fighting self. This resurgence paralleled Sorbo's slowly recovering health, which was allowing him to work some eight-hour days by the spring of 1999.[38] Yet, even though we see signs of a return to monstrous form in 'Darkness Visible' (6.4), as Hercules and Iolaus are summoned by their old battle companion Prince Vlad of Dacia to defeat vampiric *strigoi*, factors beyond the show's control took over. Sorbo had committed to star in the new show *Andromeda*, and was not interested in signing up for a further three seasons of *Hercules*. Although he offered to complete all twenty-two episodes of season six, the executive producer decided to finish after only eight episodes.[39]

This sudden end means the series has to conclude as best it can rather than with a climatic plot arc, but the final episode pays monstrous homage to what, in some ways, was the heart of the series. 'Full Circle' (6.8) revolves around a young boy called Evander, the son of Ares and Nemesis (who used to be goddess of divine retribution until she defied Hera and was made human). Evander has psychic powers which make what he wants happen. Zeus uses him to rescue Hera from the pit of Tartarus, where she was trapped at the end of season four, and the episode traces the unfolding consequences.

In their search for the missing child at the start of the episode, Hercules and Iolaus come to a village in flames. The culprit? A giant purple dinosaur with pink polka dots which farts fire, incinerating whatever happens to be behind it. As Hercules wonders, 'do you ever get the feeling the gods are running out of ideas?', we see a small child going 'Raaaargh! Raaaagh!' It is Evander, who has imagined this creation into being; rather than breathing fire at him, it blows bubbles. When he tells it to go away, it says bye in tones frankly reminiscent of the purple and green dinosaur Barney, popular on children's television in the nineties, before disappearing in a cloud of bubbles.

While Hercules is given 'proper' adversaries later in the episode, in the shape of three titans who are attempting to topple Olympus, I think the spotted dragon is an appropriate place for *Hercules* to finish its encounter with monsters. As an adversary, it is irreverent and playful; it fits perfectly into the series' constructed world, following the well-established fact that Evander can make things happen at will; it creates havoc which can be righted by the intervention of Hercules' strong yet peaceful masculinity; and it serves as a fitting end point for the journey monsters have taken over the course of the series. From the sincere but flexible engagement with Greek myth that characterised the first phase of the series to monstrosity embedded in the world of the characters but not necessarily visible on screen in the third phase, *Hercules* made classical monsters a staple of its version of antiquity. So great was their symbolic importance for how the series defined itself that even Kevin Sorbo's medical crisis could not displace them.

Tripping the Telefantastic in *Xena: Warrior Princess* and *Doctor Who*

After examining the world of *Hercules*, this chapter turns to two other examples of telefantasy, *Hercules'* companion series *Xena: Warrior Princess* and *Doctor Who*. Both take a very different approach to classical monsters, using them within a more traditionally episodic context. These case studies bring out diverse strategies for handling classical monsters, and for making them part of what appeals to each series' unique target audience. This chapter maps the ways in which monsters emerge on television outside the particular boundaries of *Hercules*, and charts some of the techniques used on a smaller scale to make space for monsters.

Xena: Warrior Princess

Xena: Warrior Princess was spun off from *Hercules* and debuted in September 1995. It continued to run for six seasons, building a wide fan-base and becoming a phenomenon in its own right. It aimed to combine the strength of the ancient world setting with a martial arts battle aesthetic, distinguishing itself from *Hercules* but allowing it to explore and further develop the same universe (Fig. 6.1).[1] Indeed, the greater success of *Xena* has led to the joint world being referred to as the Xenaverse, despite *Hercules'* chronological precedence.

Syndicated US television in the 1990s consciously applied the strategy of product differentiation, giving each individual series its own aesthetic and marketing it towards a targeted niche audience, and this manifested particularly clearly in telefantasy programmes.[2] Given the importance that *Hercules* placed on its titular hero's battles with monsters and gods, it made sense for the producers to find a different 'unique selling point' for *Xena* despite the two series' shared fictional world. The title sequence is again key to understanding how the series positions itself, at least initially. Visually, the introductory clip sequence

Fig. 6.1 Lucy Lawless as Xena.

includes no monsters, apart from one brief shot of a cyclops lifting a cage off Gabrielle, Xena's companion. Instead, the voiceover and accompanying images position Xena in a more explicitly political world than Hercules occupies:

> In a time of ancient gods, warlords and kings, a land in turmoil cried out for a hero. She was Xena, a mighty princess forged in the heat of battle. The power! The passion! The danger! Her courage will change the world.

Although it may seem a little grandiose, the immediate comparison that comes to mind is that between the *Iliad* and the *Odyssey*. *Hercules* takes on the magical and fantastic elements of Odysseus' adventures, while *Xena* draws on the world of the battlefield and political conflict that sits at the heart of the *Iliad*. The series are both equally invested in using classical myth to shape their own storytelling practices.[3] This observation is based on the initial position of both series, since we have already seen the monstrous take a back seat in *Hercules*, and the six seasons of *Xena* cover a great deal of ground in their turn. The fundamental distinction makes sense to a studio wanting to appeal to as many different audience demographics and tastes as possible. Such initial choices retain considerable power over the future direction of each series. It is, I think, no accident that Julius Caesar plays a critical (if deeply anachronistic) role in *Xena* whilst being limited to a single guest appearance in *Hercules* – political skulduggery and imperial expansion are much more in line with the interests of the former than the latter.

Another significant point of differentiation is the gender of the protagonists. The commercial motivation behind having a male and female series lead is fairly obvious, but there are a number of consequences that arise from the subsequent implicit gendering of the actions they perform. *Hercules* first appeared as a television series in January 1995, and *Xena* debuted in September. The same conflicting cultural trends of feminist advances and regressive backlash, driven primarily by concerns over women's reproductive and economic freedoms, shape them both.[4] However, Xena forms the vanguard of a new group of women warriors on 1990s television who mastered violence, did not rely on men for protection, and were fully in control of their sexuality.[5] Xena has warlords to overturn as symbols of the oppressive patriarchy rather than the monsters over whom Hercules demonstrates his masculinity. One could read her own rejection of the warlord role as the sign of a raised feminist consciousness. Conversely, Xena is positioned as the defender of the weak against the strong, drawing on underlying archetypes of maternal protectiveness which in turn defuse the threat of the aggressive and hostile woman taking on the establishment.

Xena also has great potential for queer readings and identifications, which catapulted it to cult status. The majority of scholarship on *Xena* focuses on the fan community which grew up around the show and its exploitation of the internet's capacity for community-building in the 1990s. The relationship between Xena and her sidekick Gabrielle was initially queer in subtext alone, much like the partnership of Hercules and Iolaus in *Hercules*, where innuendo-rich dialogue provided space for interpreting their relationship romantically from the first episode. Unlike *Hercules*, which often used the heterosexual relationships of its leading couple as a significant plot element, *Xena* responded to fan interpretations of Xena and Gabrielle as a lesbian couple by accepting them, even if the series never offered an explicit statement of canonicity.[6] From the historical perspective of homosexuality on screen, where queer identity has been synonymous with the monster, a popular television series with an established lesbian relationship at its heart was a major departure from the othering tradition. It offered a chance for queer viewers to identify with their heroines at a time when lesbian representation on American television was scarce.[7] *Xena* thus embraces the queer rather than punishing or repressing it, meaning the queer monsters of Hollywood do not belong in the Xenaverse.[8]

All this means that *Xena* has a much weaker investment in the monstrous, at least as manifested by non-humans, than *Hercules*. It is worth dwelling on an inadvertently revealing comment made in Sorbo's autobiography. In explaining his motivations for moving on to other projects, he notes his increasing frustration that *Xena* seemed to be prioritised by Rob Tapert, the executive producer and fiancé of Lucy Lawless, the actress who played Xena.[9] One example Sorbo gives of the favouritism he felt was shown explicitly mentions monster-related disparity:

> Rob also used *Hercules* as a testing ground. For instance, they built a new creature for my show, and four weeks later the spin-off got ten of them, resulting in that show having greater production value than *Hercules*.[10]

Sorbo's complaint emphasises the centrality of monsters to *Hercules*, but a close analysis of *Xena* reveals a much greater focus on warlords and other hostile individuals, including the gods. A close analysis of the first season neatly illustrates my point. In these initial twenty-four episodes, only six feature monster content, with monsters mentioned in dialogue in a further two. Contrast this with fourteen out of twenty-four episodes having explicit monster content in the second season of *Hercules*. While there are hardly any rent-a-monsters, the ground rules *Hercules* established for the shared universe still hold to some extent for the monsters which do appear. However, the monsters of *Xena*'s first season are organised around different nodes than those which appear in the first phase of *Hercules*.

The first episode makes it clear that viewers will not get the sort of monster-battling that they might have expected from *Hercules* ('Sins of the Past', 1.1). Xena passes through Potidaea, a small village being threatened by Draco, a warlord who happens to be an old flame. After rescuing some captive young women, including Gabrielle, and asking Draco to spare the village, she continues her journey back to her home town of Amphipolis. As she rides over a bridge, she is threatened by a blind cyclops. Rather than fight him, she uses her chakram (a circular metal throwing-weapon of Indian origin) to cut his belt, making his trousers fall down, and reducing him to a whimpering heap. In their ensuing conversation, Xena reveals that she originally blinded him, but their encounter involves no heroic combat. After advising the cyclops to take up another line of work, Xena rides on. When the cyclops captures Gabrielle in a cage as she follows Xena's trail, she adopts a new verbal strategy to get out of trouble: Gabrielle pretends that she is following Xena to kill her, and promises to bring back a tasty body part afterwards. The cyclops lifts the cage to let her out, and Gabrielle hurries on her way, muttering, 'Thank goodness for dumb cyclopses' (*sic*).

This first episode, following on from Xena's original appearance in the first season of *Hercules*, presents the warrior princess as a reformed character, even briefly attempting to give up her weapons until she realises she can use them for good. When she meets the cyclops, her decision to offer career advice rather than repeat the physical violence she inflicted when they last met signals she really has begun a new chapter in her life. The viewer would have found it rather peculiar if Gabrielle, an inexperienced village girl meeting her first monster, had beaten the cyclops in combat. Instead, the script uses the opportunity to establish her as a skilled teller of tales, since her escape relies on verbal rather than physical acrobatics. The programmatic first episode of *Xena* deliberately marginalises monsters, focusing instead on how Xena responds when her hometown and family come under threat.

While 'The Titans' (1.7) initially looks as if it will follow the *Hercules* model of writing a substantial plot around the monster of the week, it actually moves potential monsters into *Xena*'s preferred political mode. Gabrielle releases three Titans by reading a magical scroll using the correct metrical emphasis. When the Titan Hyperion realises she is not a goddess, he threatens the local village, and kills his companion and love-rival Crius for opposing him. In the end, the Titan Theia betrays Hyperion and prevents him from waking hundreds more Titans by helping find the scroll containing the chant for returning the Titans to stone, which Gabrielle duly recites. In the strictest sense, Titans are classical monsters, but this episode instead concentrates on their traditional enmity with the gods and their fatal love triangle. Their monstrous characteristics, unnatural size and strength are countered by their articulate speech and their costumes, which match stereotypical assumptions of clothing in the ancient world – Theia wears a flowing blue dress with pleats, while Hyperion and Crius have belted thigh-length tunics. Given the deliberate decision not to provide most of the cast of *Hercules* and *Xena* with 'authentically ancient' clothing, these costumes position the Titans as occupying the classical tradition, but lessen their monstrosity. Hyperion's megalomaniac desire to free more Titans and overthrow the gods is told as a cosmic version of the battles between warlords with which Xena is usually concerned, reshaping a monster tale into the preferred narrative mode for this series.

Two episodes follow the *Hercules* 'central monster' model – 'Prometheus' (1.8) and 'Mortal Beloved' (1.16). Following on from the hostile titans of the previous episode, in 'Prometheus' Hera binds the eponymous Titan to a rock, meaning that all of his gifts, including healing and light, slowly start to fade away from the world. Xena and Hercules team up to release him, with the added complication that they see this as a suicide mission – in order to break the chains forged by Hephaestus that are binding Prometheus, they will need to use a sword also made by Hephaestus. The resulting lightening blast will travel up the handle of the sword and incinerate whoever wields it, so Xena and Hercules spend a lot of time (and barely repressed erotic tension) vying to perform this self-sacrificial act. Xena gets to the mountain top where Prometheus is trapped first, but to reach him she has to weave her way through a field of unhatched eggs that are slightly taller than her. As she passes through, the eggs begin to crack and baby dragons burst out – or at least, people painted green and wearing green costumes, which are meant to make them look like baby dragons, conveniently armed at the point of hatching (Fig. 6.2).

These hatchlings have been foreshadowed in an earlier scene where Prometheus asked Hera why she was holding him captive. In response, she told him to observe other creatures which were more worthy of respect than mankind. In the conventional telling of the Prometheus tale, the Titan is sentenced to having his liver ripped out by an eagle for giving fire to humans. A viewer familiar with the story would now expect to see an eagle. Instead, we see something more akin to a dragon flying in the sky, although at a distance. Another earlier incident also draws on this narrative redirection. In order to discover how to release Prometheus, Xena must undergo a test of how much she is willing to sacrifice in

Fig. 6.2 Xena fights the dragon hatchlings.

order to gain knowledge. This involves pulling a tablet down the spine of a dragon skeleton through its mouth, which is held open by a rope being burned by a candle. The tablet is shattered to smithereens and turns out not to have had the answers written on it anyway; however, the presence of a dragon skeleton that must be overcome through skill rather than combat provides a neat mirror of the monster in the episode's ultimate confrontation.

As Xena and Hercules battle with the dragon hatchlings, the mother dragon appears, snatching Xena up in her claws – the brief shots permit a confusion between lizard and eagle until we are finally given a full-body shot of the beast in flight which reveals it is unmistakably reptilian. An exciting aerial sequence follows until Xena stabs the dragon in the neck with Hephaestus' sword. She throws it to Hercules, who deflects it with a giant rock towards one of Prometheus' chains. The chain shears in two, nobody is immolated, and Prometheus can free himself from the remaining shackles. The dragon serves as an unexpected monster-of-the-week, in which the use of the Prometheus story as a narrative base has deliberately confused viewer expectations. The dragon and its chicks come into play purely because of Hera, again following the *Hercules* trend that monsters are instrumentalised into evil by divine intervention rather than being inherently evil themselves.

Conquering monsters and thwarting Hera is much more in Hercules' line, so the plot of 'Prometheus' draws on the usual antagonists and underlying themes of a *Hercules* episode. Hercules' guest appearance explains why this is a monster-based episode rather than a warlord-based one, but the question still remains why the dragon is given the starring monster role. There is the possibility that the production team felt a giant eagle and its eggs would get too close to the giant two-headed roc and its chicks which featured in Harryhausen's *The 7th Voyage of Sinbad*. Alternatively, a giant eagle may not have seemed sufficiently monstrous, although the dragon performs no action that an eagle could not. We might also again be seeing the influence of Joseph Campbell's claim that the monster the hero must overcome should always be a dragon.[11] Whatever the cause, Hercules' presence signals that this episode follows the monster-of-the-week conventions established in the partner series.

While Hercules does not appear in 'Mortal Beloved' (1.16), it also fits the monster-of-the-week mould. Xena travels to the underworld, where the serial killer Atyminius has stolen Hades' golden helmet, trapped the good in Tartarus and is letting the wicked have the run of the Elysian fields. After meeting Atyminius, Xena and her dead ex-lover Marcus approach the tower where Hades is being held. In order to pass through the tower doors, they must first run the gauntlet of two adult harpies, who show us what the babies in *Hercules*' 'Beanstalks and Bad Eggs' (4.1) will become. Perhaps easiest to envisage as flying scaly gargoyles, the harpies harass Xena and Marcus from the air. Xena manages to destroy one, while the other grabs Marcus' waistcoat. She pulls him out of it, leaving the harpy distracted long enough for them to get inside the tower. Hades shows them a shortcut to the upper world, but after they have reclaimed the helmet they return to the tower. The surviving harpy attacks them and nearly throws Marcus off a cliff edge into a fiery chasm, but Xena manages to destroy it and just saves Marcus from dropping into the lava.

The harpies' function is to provide an impediment with suitably Greek overtones. They are located not in the realm of the living, where Xena usually operates, but in the realm of the dead and the supernatural. The monster at work in the realm of the living is in fact Atyminius. With Hades' helmet, he returns to the upper world and attempts to resume his criminal career as a serial killer with a penchant for brides on the night before their weddings. The serial killer has become one of the modern manifestations of monstrosity in popular culture, alongside the terrorist, precisely because we can no longer categorically recognise a monster when we see one.[12] While Atyminius exhibits certain physical characteristics of a stereotypical psychopath, including a fixed rictus grin while handling sharp objects, he becomes invisible when he dons Hades' helmet. The conventions of telefantasy demand an identifiable villain, but the helmet's powers of invisibility communicate the fear of the murderer who is impossible to pick out from a crowd.

I dwell on the serial killer because despite the appearance of harpies as monster-of-the-week, I would argue that the episode locates true monstrosity in Atyminius. The harpies offer an impersonal obstacle, with the added fantastical element appropriate for the underworld, but Atyminius' monstrosity is grounded and performed in the real world. The shift between realms generates the scope for introducing the harpies, but the episode focuses on a more modern manifestation of the monster.

Monsters appear in the dialogue of the show, as they do in *Hercules*, but more infrequently and with less investment in the monster as the arbitrator of character. As Gabrielle is pondering trying out for a place at the Athens City Academy of Performing Bards, Xena races in with the news that a cyclops is eating cattle in Keramis, and if they head off now they will be there the next day ('The Athens City Academy of Performing Bards', 1.13). This provides the excuse for Gabrielle and Xena to part ways, and for Gabrielle's storytelling expertise to be further established, but the cyclops and its not particularly monstrous hunger is never mentioned again, even when Xena and Gabrielle meet up again at the end of the episode. That a cyclops provides the narrative pretext for this episode makes sense following the framing of the cyclops as a comic rather than frightening figure in 'Sins of the Past' (1.1).[13]

More interesting is the dialogue from 'Warrior … Princess' (1.15), which sums up both expectations about monsters and how *Xena* deliberately ignores them. The premise of the episode sees Lucy Lawless playing both Xena and Princess Diana. Diana's father, King Lias, has asked Xena for her help in protecting Diana from assassins as she prepares to marry Mineus of Liberium. Xena swaps clothes with Diana and takes her place in the castle, sending the princess off to find Gabrielle and stay safe in the forest. Diana's eyes are opened to the suffering of her people when Gabrielle shares their already scanty meal with a hungry family. The daughter of the family asks 'Xena' to talk about her adventures, and Diana gamely improvises:

> Well! Like the time when I had to kill a lot of centaurs … not centaurs, ah, I mean cyclops! Hundreds of them! I took care of them all with my trusty round thing.

Some helpful assumptions emerge from Diana's sheltered impression of what heroes like Xena do. She assumes that Xena's bread and butter is battling monsters, confusing her with her opposite number Hercules. The first monster she hits upon are the centaurs, but Gabrielle nixes this idea with a shake of her head – centaurs are not appropriate objects of unmotivated violence. The move to the cyclops (*sic*) is not much better, but an eloquent shoulder shrug indicates that Xena might conceivably fight them. Diana's brief character sketch reveals both a belief that being a hero must primarily involve vanquishing monsters, and a clear sense of which monsters need vanquishing.

The fact that Gabrielle reacts so negatively to Diana's suggestion that centaurs are monsters brings up the last contact point between *Xena* and *Hercules*, namely the portrayal of the centaur race. Like *Hercules*, centaurs appear in the first season of *Xena*, but in a much more specific context – rather than explore the tensions between centaurs and humans in general, *Xena* emphasises the tensions between centaurs and Amazons. In some ways, this draws on established mythological links between the two groups, such as the friezes on the outside of the Parthenon in Athens. The battle between the centaurs and the Lapiths is featured on the south side, while the friezes on the west are usually read as a battle between men and Amazons. The conflict is established in the pivotal episode 'Hooves and Harlots' (1.10). After Gabrielle protects Terreis, an Amazon princess mortally wounded by a mysterious arrow, Terreis gifts her with her right of caste, or status within Amazon society, as she dies. This means that Gabrielle becomes Amazon royalty, and for the rest of the series will periodically be called back to the tribe at critical moments. At this stage, the narrative tension comes from the assumption that Terreis has been killed by a centaur's arrow. When the centaur Phantes is captured and his arrow seems to match that which killed Terreis, Xena must hunt out the true culprit – a warlord, Krykus, who wants to use the historical enmity between the Amazons and centaurs to capture more territory in the aftermath of the carnage.

'Hooves and Harlots' puts a lot of work into establishing the distrust between the two races. When Xena realises that the death is being blamed on centaurs, she asks the Amazon queen for some background:

> **Xena**   What problems do you have with centaurs?
>
> **Queen Melosa**   Disgusting animals. You know how they are. Near the river there's a village of centaurs and men. They want our hunting areas. And now they've gone too far. You should go.

The Amazons see centaurs as subhuman but also as a threat to their ancestral lands. Men and centaurs are conflated as equal dangers to the Amazon nation, significantly drawing on the idea that 'men are animals', which goes back to Circe turning Odysseus' sailors into pigs in the *Odyssey*. However, suggestions that the Amazon nation is under threat from external forces which seek to displace them are based on problematic visual and cultural parallels drawn between the Amazons and Native American tribes (Fig. 6.3). The use of the cultural traditions from a historically oppressed group, such as ritual dance and costume, by the dominant group (here production company Renaissance Pictures) perpetuates that oppression, particularly since members of the oppressed group are forced to take on the dominant group's customs (such as the use of English) in order to survive. That said, *Xena* is aware of these issues to some extent; the kinds of worries about centaurs *Hercules* explored around miscegenation are supplanted by a broader struggle the Amazons and Centaur both face for continued survival at the margins of human society.

'Hooves and Harlots' follows some distinctive patterns established by *Hercules* without going as far as to equate centaurs with African Americans. While the Amazons see both centaurs and men as other, the added bestiality of centaurs becomes a further point of hostility.[14] Yet *Hercules'* reiterated message about looking beyond appearances lies at the centre of this episode. When the Amazon

Fig. 6.3 Xena, Gabrielle and the Amazons in *Xena: Warrior Princess.*

Ephiny, a close friend of Terreis, comes to interrogate the captured Phantes, he attacks her for her prejudices:

Phantes   What would you know about centaurs? You despise us, you spit on us.

Ephiny   I had a friend who admired the centaurs. She didn't see you for the beasts you really are. She felt that one day we would work together. She thought you were brave and noble people.

Phantes   Well, if your friend liked centaurs so much, where is she now?

Ephiny   You killed her.

Phantes   I didn't.

Ephiny   She also told me that centaurs have a high sense of honour. Is that true? Could you swear on your father's name?

Phantes   I swear on the name of Tildus the Great, I didn't kill your friend. Not that the oath of a centaur means anything.

This exchange conveys Terreis' progressive views as well as the unfair prejudice that centaurs suffer. Phantes' oath goads Ephiny into joining forces with Xena to reveal Krykus' involvement in Terreis' death, forcing her to face up to her own bias. Similarly, when Phantes is freed, he tells his father Tildus, leader of the centaurs, that, 'I've also realised something about these Amazons. They aren't our enemies.' Xena also has the opportunity to prove herself a reformed character to Tildus, who she once fought with her army. The final message of the episode is that redemption is always possible, however hard the work might be.

Ephiny's change of heart has far-reaching consequences, as Xena and Gabrielle discover in the season finale, 'Is there a Doctor in the House?' (1.24). On their way to Athens, trying to skirt the war between the Mitoans and the Thessalians, they find Ephiny heavily pregnant, hidden under a pile of leaves. She and Phantes were travelling to Athens because he wanted their baby to be born there, but he was killed by a Mitoan war party. The trio, along with the wounded Mitoan general *incognito*, make their way to a Thessalian healing temple where Xena scandalises Galen, head priest of Asclepius, by actually doing some surgery rather than praying optimistically. Naturally, Ephiny gives birth, and the question raised by 'Outcast' (*Hercules* 2.5) of how precisely those hooves are handled is answered – Xena performs a Caesarean to bring a newborn centaur into the world just as the Mitoans are about to capture the temple.

Ephiny gets all the stereotypical 'going into labour in difficult circumstances' dialogue one would expect (including the obligatory 'the baby – I think it's coming!'). However, her pregnancy and the revelation that the baby's father was a centaur are critical to the plot. Because Ephiny is human, there is no sign that the baby will be a centaur, and she does not voluntarily divulge this information. When Marmax, the Mitoan general, asks why she and her husband wanted the baby born in Athens, she says that the Athenians are more tolerant, but declines to elaborate. When Marmax is encouraging her to push during her labour, he reveals an unexpectedly perceptive side:

> That was a strong kick. It's going to be one healthy little centaur. Yes, I've known since you said you wanted the baby to be born in Athens, because they're more tolerant – Phantes was a centaur.

The bloodthirsty general proves an able assistant during the caesarean section (as Gabrielle is at the time unconscious). He even holds the newborn baby centaur close to Ephiny as Xena sews up the incision. When the Mitoans rush into the temple, ready for carnage, he stops them and tells them he is ready to negotiate for peace. During their initial conversation, Ephiny explained her past with Phantes:

> **Marmax**   You don't know what tyrants these Thessalians are, they must be destroyed. My family was thrown to a pack of starving wolves for not bowing to their gods.

Ephiny   My husband was ripped apart by Mitoan hunting dogs while your men watched and laughed.

Marmax   This can't be.

Ephiny   Phantes was once my sworn enemy. Then I learned forgiveness, and from that I learned love. I just hope my child grows up to live in a world free from your blind hatred.

While at this point Marmax does not know Phantes was a centaur, the audience understands that his death by dogs is even more cruel in the context of hunting animals for sport and the overall dehumanisation of centaurs. However, Ephiny's comment about learning to love her enemy reveals a shift in her understanding of what makes a monster, and being able to see beyond her preconceptions. The newborn baby, shown precariously teetering on its hooves at the end of the episode, symbolises that move from hate to love; Marmax too is able to put down his anger after attending the literal birth of a new hope.

The monstrosity of centaurs becomes negated. Just as in *Hercules*, they are a people with their own culture who have become monstered by the attitudes others hold. In *Xena*, they are more frequently encountered through the perceptual lens of the Amazons rather than an independent culture as in *Hercules*. Interestingly, centaurs become a place to explore maternity, which becomes an important theme in later seasons. Xena left a baby with a centaur named Kaleipus, and her reunion with that child serves as an important pivot point in season three which has long-lasting implications for the series. After this event, centaurs fade out of *Xena*. Instead, subsequent seasons travel through a wide range of world cultures, including nods to China and India, and explore human cultural difference and similarity.[15]

With a sense of narrative completeness, *Xena* returns to Ephiny's son, Xenan, in one of its final episodes ('Last of the Centaurs', 6.17). A lengthy period of suspended animation at the end of season five put Xena and Gabrielle out of action for twenty-five years. As such, much of season six revolves around them finding out what has happened to old friends in the intervening quarter century. They find Xenan when Ephiny's spirit appears to Gabrielle and asks her to protect her son from the persecution of the local lord, Belach, who has placed a bounty on his head. After meeting Belach (who turns out to be the son of one of Xena's former warlord lovers), Gabrielle and Xena track down Xenan and Belach's missing daughter Nika – who is heavily pregnant. In the meantime, Belach has ordered the slaughter of Xenan's fellow centaurs in an attempt to track Xenan down.

When Xena, furious at the unnecessary carnage, confronts him before kidnapping him and taking him to view the mass grave, Belach exposes his main objection to Nika and Xenan's relationship:

> All this I have built, that is my achievement. But it means nothing without my daughter to give me an heir. I want a grandson to be loved and cherished, not some bastard offspring of a centaur.

'Last of the Centaurs' comes back to the problem that *Hercules* posed – the fear of miscegenation articulated through the conceit of interspecies relationships – as well as retelling Ephiny's storyline through her son. Xena even performs a second caesarean to bring the new baby into the world, although in a procedure without complications. Belach is eventually reconciled to his daughter's choices, after a dramatic standoff where Nika physically interposes herself and her newborn son between her father and husband, in a scene reminiscent of the intervention of the Sabine Women. Instead of leaving to start a new life, Nika and Xenan stay and settle on land which belonged to Nika's mother. Belach's sense of the centaur as monstrous, predicated on the belief that his daughter had been 'stolen' and that his legacy had been thwarted, is replaced by a model of integration of the 'monster' into the family. New birth once more signals hope, and, in turn, questions the parameters for defining the monster: where Xenan met Belach's fixed criteria, his infant centaur grandson destabilises them.

Xena initially positions itself as more concerned with the affairs of men than the wrongdoings of monsters. Over the course of its six seasons, *Xena* shifts its attention to supernatural and divine malfeasance, but monsters are never as conceptually central as they are in *Hercules*. The monsters who appear in *Xena's* first season have many similarities with the 'boss monsters' of the companion show, but this series sees them as interesting narrative fodder for individual episodes rather than as a central unifying theme.

Doctor Who

My final case study also comes from telefantasy, but moves beyond the world of *Hercules* and *Xena* to explore what happens to classical monsters outside an ancient televisual setting. Their appearances, as I noted earlier, are often brief, usually as a cameo or perhaps a central character in an individual episode. These cases are not made lesser by their appearance in popular culture, despite their frequent dismissal by academics as superficial or lazy. As Willis has argued, while it may be harder to interpret what is going on with these references, they are still part of a broader continued use of classical myth in popular culture.[16] The plasticity of myth allows popular culture to use it as an inspiration for revised and altered storytelling.

With that in mind, it is worth noting that most of the television series where classical monsters appear fall in line with Johnson's telefantastic criteria.[17] This rule of thumb applies even to examples ostensibly set in the real world. For instance, *Dexter* is a series about a loveable serial killer who hunts down murderers who escape justice. It uses the genre of the fantastic to ask viewers to suspend their disbelief and enjoy scrupulous vigilantism, pushing the boundaries of horror into the police procedural mode popularised by shows like *CSI*. The deliberate confusion of truth and fiction allows classical monsters to find a place even in a supposedly highly scientific and technical context. In *Dexter*'s case, one of the villains whom Dexter targets dresses in a Minotaur-esque helmet to hunt down the female victims he traps in a purpose-built maze. Telefantasy performs a balancing act between 'authentic' realism (so we can believe what is in front of us) and constructing impossible fiction (so that we can't believe our eyes). Such opportunities simply are not present in, say, *Coronation Street*, *Emmerdale* or even *Friends*, where social realism drives the narrative towards soap opera and away from the boundaries that frame reality. Since telefantasy deliberately plays with the borders between the real and unreal, monsters can slither in and become part of the show.

Telefantasy's other central characteristic is its deliberate reliance on and subversion of genre; that is, telefantasy uses generic verisimilitude to reinforce a sense of the familiar whilst at the same time undermining it. Thus, we see *Star Trek* episodes based around Westerns, *Hercules* episodes reimagining classic films like *Some Like It Hot*, and *Buffy the Vampire Slayer* branching into musical theatre. The fact that a viewing audience knows how a particular genre is 'supposed to go' means that by mostly conforming to those norms, telefantasy can shift expectations to provide plausible variety and entertaining viewing. For a format which sees jumping from one genre to another as an integral way of providing a range of plot settings, especially when the general direction of the series is vague and open-ended ('to boldly go where no man has gone before' means there's always somewhere else to go), classical myth provides a helpful source of familiar stories for series writers to tap. The flexibility of myth and its stock of ready-formed stories opens the path for classical monsters to work their way into telefantastic productions.

The specific case study I want to focus on pushes the limits of both time and space, and is known for monsters of all kinds. *Doctor Who* is a long-running and much beloved British science fiction series which first aired in 1963. Until the end of 1989, the programme ran using a 'serial' format, typically four to six short episodes bundled together into a single story. After a hiatus (and a not particularly successful film), it relaunched in 2005, following the twelve- or thirteen-episode season arc which had become dominant in the intervening fifteen years or so. The series focuses on the adventures of the Doctor, a regenerating Time Lord who travels across the universe in his/her time-travelling TARDIS with an array of human, alien and robotic companions.[18] On his/her travels, the Doctor encounters various new and exciting alien races, some of which display monstrous characteristics, and some beings which are purely and simply monstrous.

It's worth asking why *Doctor Who* bothers with classical monsters. As even a cursory viewing of the series makes clear, the writers conjure up plenty of alien races, humanoid and otherwise, to act as the catalyst for exploring what it is to be human. The non-humanoid aliens are not always monsters, but there is no shortage of villains. A particular favourite of mine are the Adipose ('Partners in Crime', 4.1), small white round cuddly aliens which are created from human body fat, neatly reflecting contemporary British society's panic over the supposed obesity epidemic. Given that the show has the ability to create monsters tailored to the anxieties of the audience watching at that precise moment, the choice to draw on classical monsters points to some different expectations about the function they are meant to play.

Part of the aim behind every encounter with the other in *Doctor Who*, monstrous or not, is to draw parallels, explicit and implicit, with humanity. From a classical reception point of view, this happens both through encounters with classical monsters, and in so-called 'historicals', when the Doctor and his companions go back through time to the classical period. These 'historicals' quickly encountered a setback – namely, you can't change the source material. *The Myth Makers* (1965), set in the final stages of the Trojan War, encountered a similar issue; the Trojans were presented as far nicer than the Greeks they were fighting, but had to be on the losing side.[19] Not all myths pose this problem, but it does lead to another temptation. As we shall see, *Doctor Who* has at times given into the seductive lure of a ready-made plot: the televisual format can rely on myth to provide a pre-packaged structure rather than taking the opportunity to seriously engage with the monster itself.

The first 'Classic Who' to incorporate classical monsters, in a manner which explicitly drew on the fictional nature of these stories, was *The Mind Robber*

(1968). The Doctor and his companions, Jamie and Zoe, are pulled into a strange void, populated by fictional beings, such as Gulliver, Rapunzel and a unicorn. The place is run by a Master Brain, which has as its puppet the Master of the Land of Fiction (not to be confused with the Doctor's arch-nemesis, the Master); they try and trap the Doctor into writing himself into a storyline so he can replace the Master. As part of this plan, the Master sends the Doctor into two scenarios involving classical monsters, the Minotaur and Medusa, to make him align himself with the pre-existing narrative and so come under the Master Brain's control. The extant narrative threads of the myths become precisely the danger that the Doctor has to avoid.

The first inkling we get of this is when the Doctor must remind Zoe and Jamie that a unicorn running towards them does not really exist, getting them to shout, 'It's not real!'; he notes that it existed because they believed in it, and that their belief was starting to affect him. When they find themselves in a labyrinth, the Doctor picks up a tempting ball of twine and comments that 'it's the classical way of getting through a maze'. Hence, it comes as no surprise that when Zoe and the Doctor reach the centre, they find human bones and hear roaring. Zoe tentatively recollects the story of the Minotaur, and we then see shadows of a horned bull upon the wall. Although we get a few brief shots of the Minotaur's head, the Doctor gets Zoe out of danger relatively quickly (episode three):

Zoe	Doctor, it's moving! It's coming closer! It's going to attack!
Doctor	Zoe, it's a legend! Another mythical beast like the unicorn!
Zoe	But it's there!
Doctor	No! The Minotaur is a mythical beast! Say it!
Zoe	The Minotaur is a mythical beast, it doesn't exist! It's gone!
Doctor	Yes. Yes, I fear we made it too, too difficult for it to stay.

Medusa poses more of a challenge. When the Doctor and Zoe return to the cave, looking for Jamie, they discover a statue which begins to come to life. Whether Zoe will give in to the temptation of looking at Medusa supplies the cliff-hanger between episodes three and four of the serial. Perhaps, oddly, not being able to see her makes it more difficult for Zoe to commit to her unreality (episode four):

Doctor	Don't look in her eyes! Don't look! The Medusa does not exist, you must believe that!
Zoe	I can see her fingertips [like ice?].

> **Doctor**   No, that, that's marble. Think of her as a marble statue of a
> legend!
>
> **Zoe**   But she's real! I've got to look at her, I've got to!

A sword materialises at the Doctor's feet, tempting him to slay Medusa; instead, he lets Zoe look at Medusa in a pocket mirror, and the statue becomes motionless again. This act reveals that the Doctor has a better understanding of Greek myth than the Master does. By taking a non-violent approach which fits with the pre-existing tale, he avoids the deception of the proffered narrative. The nature of the classical monsters as stories, told in parallel with the unicorn (the only other creature told to disappear through rationality), is what makes them dangerous in the world where the Doctor encounters them. *The Mind Robber* sees the risks of closed narrative pathways associated with myths, particularly those which privilege the hero's conquest, and understands the trap that these old familiar stories can construct.

Following *The Mind Robber*, 'Classic Who' primarily concerns itself with the Minotaur, giving the creature three further incarnations, all of which tell different stories about its origins and demise (although perhaps the issue of continuity was less of a concern in an age where internet streaming and DVD home viewing were more fantastical than anything the script writers could come up with). The first serial to give the Minotaur a serious conceptual role was *The Time Monster* (1972). The serial was influenced by the popular theory that Atlantis had existed, but was destroyed by a volcanic eruption at Thera.[20] Although the palace at Knossos had become strongly associated with the Theseus myth, the shared Minoan link allowed the scriptwriters to locate the labyrinth and its monster on Atlantis instead.

The plot revolves around the attempts of the Master to control Kronos, a Chronovore from outside time trapped within a crystal and worshipped by the Atlanteans until they realised how dangerous he was. After the Master fails to unleash Kronos through experiments in 1970s Cambridge, he summons the high priest of Atlantis and travels back in time to retrieve Kronos' crystal prison. The Doctor and his companion Jo Grant pursue him, and discover his plans to collude with Queen Galleia to stage a palace revolt and overthrow King Dalios. The plotters send Hippias, a member of the royal council, into a labyrinth beneath the palace where the Guardian protects the crystal. Jo (in splendid High Minoan dress) and the Doctor follow him, but are unable to prevent the Master from getting his hands on the crystal, summoning Kronos, and utterly destroying the city.

The Guardian is, of course, the Minotaur, although the Atlanteans do not call him that. King Dalios explains to the Doctor how the beast was created, and the name just slips out (episode five):

Doctor   But who is the Guardian?

Dalios   A beast. A man. You can take your choice. Once he was my friend, a firm counsellor, a great athlete. And just as I longed for the wisdom the years along could bring, so he craved great strength. The strength of the bull. And a long life in which to use it.

Doctor   Well, that's a harmless enough ambition, I should have thought.

Dalios   So too did I. But Kronos in his blind sport gave him his desire – not only the strength but the head of the bull. And so he has remained for the past five hundred years or more.

Doctor   The Minotaur!

Dalios   Please?

Doctor   No, it doesn't matter, please go on.

This origin story neatly avoids any possible suggestion of bestiality (always a difficult issue where the Minotaur is concerned), and instead lays the responsibility for the confusion of human and beast with Kronos. The creation of the Minotaur arises from human ambition combined with Kronos' inhuman sense of humour, reiterating the old adage 'be careful what you wish for.' King Dalios elsewhere mentions his own abnormally long life span, and the viewer can intuit that his desires have also been unnaturally fulfilled. Dalios speaks of the Guardian with real sorrow, and the characterisation of him as a man who was unlucky enough to get in the way of a capricious alien intelligence makes his monstrosity pathetic rather than fearsome.

The initial introduction of the Guardian is also compassionate. When the high priest mysteriously disappears, transported to 1970s Cambridge, King Dalios takes Hippias down under the palace to show him the secret location of the maze. When he opens the door, there is a great bellow; Dalios reassures Hippias that it is only the Guardian, and shouts, 'Return to your rest – it is I, Dalios!', before closing the maze once more. Hippias is understandably perplexed (episode three):

Hippias   What? Who was it? You said no other person shares the great mystery.

Dalios   The Guardian is a person no longer – a thing, a creature too horrible to imagine. Half-man, half-beast. Come.

The Guardian is given all the standard characteristics of monstrosity, suggesting a monster which pushes beyond the boundaries of the possible, increased by the fact the audience hears rather than sees him. Yet, when the Guardian does appear on screen, threatening Jo after she has been trapped inside the maze (episode six), generic expectations kick in – the Minotaur looks exactly like we 'think' he should, with a bull's head ending at the neck, a bare chest, and a loincloth from waist to mid-thigh. Although there is the possibility of creating an innovative Minotaur, the grounding of the serial's visual style in a hyperreal Minoan setting means that there is little scope for deviating from what viewers expect to see.

The final encounter with the Guardian is short and rather anticlimactic (although this is perhaps the least of *The Time Monster*'s problems). Jo runs around inside the mirrored maze, trying to avoid the beast, while the Doctor overpowers the guards outside to enter and rescue her. As Jo is cornered, Hippias unexpectedly comes to the rescue and wrestles the Guardian until it throws him through one of the mirrored walls, killing him. This gives the Doctor enough time to arrive and remove his cape before evoking another set of generic expectations, this time of the bull fight; the Minotaur, clearly having spent time in Spain on a new-fangled package holiday, obliges by charging the cape, whereupon the Doctor tricks it into running through another mirrored wall. It lies on its face, either insensible or dead, as the Doctor and Jo walk through the resulting hole and discover the crystal.

The Minotaur cannot be separated from its maze. Once the crystal has been discovered, both have served their purpose. Although the myth has been changed to meet the serial's aetiological requirements, fidelity to the mythic footprint continues to influence how far those changes go. The resurgence of the fixed narrative is perhaps better understood from the perspective of generic verisimilitude. *The Time Monster* primarily challenges our sense of normality with the idea of time travel and the revelation that Kronos is really a malevolent alien. As such, it does not have the scope to be more adventurous with the Minotaur.

The serial *The Horns of Nimon* (1979–80) offers Classic Who's third take on the Minotaur, again following the trend of making it an alien and in this way avoiding having to talk about bestiality.[21] The serial offers a more or less faithful rendition of the Theseus myth rather than using it as a 'stepping-off point' for an original narrative.[22] While *Horns* makes references which require a full knowledge of the myth to appreciate, such as the pseudo-anagram naming conventions (Skonnos for Knossos and Aneth for Athens, for example), most viewers will pick up on the sacrifices being taken to a beast with a gigantic bull's head which lives in a maze-like complex from which nobody ever returns. The deep penetration of the bones of the Minotaur myth into popular culture means that this sort of retelling becomes accessible precisely because the central monster is immediately recognisable. Unlike *The Time Monster*, which defers the appearance of the non-verbal Guardian, the Nimon (pronounced nye-mon rather than nih-mon) is introduced to us at the end of the serial's first episode and plays an important role in the plot.

The Doctor and his companion Romana encounter a Skonnan ship taking the last group of sacrifices to the Nimon. When their contract is fulfilled, the Nimon will supposedly give them advanced technology to replace their failing fleet and establish a second Skonnan Empire. The tributes from Aneth describe the Nimon as 'the great god of Skonnos! They say he's a terrible creature with great awesome powers,' although Romana thinks this sounds more like an insecure personality complex (episode two). It is also terribly convenient that the Nimon first appeared after a great civil war on Skonnos wiped out everybody but the army and Soldeed, the scientist and engineer who built the complex the Nimon inhabits. When Romana and the tributes enter the complex, they discover the Nimon's larder, consisting of the previous tributes in suspended animation, and the withered husk of a tribute whose life force has been devoured.

The Nimon obviously turns out not to be a philanthropic celestial traveller, but the vanguard of an invading force. After convincing its victim planet to build it a base and bring it tribute, it builds a giant positronic circuit that allows a capsule to be transported between points A and B almost immediately. The Nimon in Skonnos has just reached this point, and summons two more Nimons to help him prepare for transport. The monstrous masquerades under the banal. Soldeed was delighted to help the Nimon because he thought he was getting the better part of the deal (episode three):

> You get what you want by giving people what they want. If there happens to be a little imbalance, make sure it's in your favour. The Nimon is simple. Powerful, brutal, yes; scientifically advanced, yes; but simple in his desires. I fawn to him, a little; that satisfies his bestial ego and he gives us what I ask. I play the Nimon on a long string.

Soldeed is, naturally, horrified to discover the Nimon is not, as he was led to believe, the last survivor of his race. His collapse into maddened disbelief in part fuels his final decision to jam the Nimon's nuclear oven and make the complex explode. The Nimon can exploit Soldeed's own arrogance and greed because of his own smugness about outwitting it – once more the monster reveals our true selves.

The obviously recognisable monster takes on primary responsibility for signalling which myth we are occupying, although there are other small nods to specific details, such as Soldeed's long string. While the serial is fairly consistent with its retelling of the myth, from the point of view of the classical monster, it becomes the embodiment of monstrous reproduction. Skonnos is not the first planet that the Nimons have conquered using this stratagem. Romana is accidentally transported over to their current planet, Crinnoth, which has been all but sucked dry. The monster always manages to find a new place to go and a new way to get there – and even to get their own labyrinth rebuilt. It is precisely human weakness and vanity which creates the door through which the Nimon can enter.

The serial *Underworld* (1978), which moves away from the Minotaur myth, gives a final example of the power of mythic expectations in 'Classic Who'. The episode is a thinly veiled retelling of the Jason and the Argonauts myth. A crew headed by Jackson have been on a quest for a hundred thousand years for the race banks being carried by a rogue ship, the P7E (pronounced almost like 'Persephone'). As the Doctor arrives, the crew finally track the ship down at the core of a newly forming planet. They break the surface and descend to a system of caverns, at the heart of which lies the P7E and the control room where the race banks are stored. Over time, the computer has lost touch with reality and now sees itself as the Oracle, served by a seer class which have mutated into golden machines, while the guards and slave trogs are the humanoid descendants of the P7E's original crew.

The Doctor and his companion Leela encounter Idas, a trog whose father has been taken to be sacrificed to the Oracle. When the Doctor shows him a map of the tunnel system, the dialogue offers the first overt gesture towards the mythic model (episode three):

Doctor	Do you recognise that?
Idas	A tree, we call it a tree.
Doctor	A tree at the end of the world. Where are we?
Idas	Here.
Doctor	Where's your father? I see. Can we get from there to there quickly?
Idas	No.
Doctor	Why not?

Idas   It's forbidden.

Doctor   Why?

Idas   It's guarded by invisible dragons. Not even the guards can use it, only seers. They have special powers.

Doctor   So do I, Idas, so do I! The tree at the end of the world's always guarded by dragons. They're fire dragons, aren't they, with tongues of flame.

If this wasn't enough, at the end of the serial, the Doctor muses about another Jason who was on a long quest, looking for a golden fleece, and wonders whether myths might be prophecies of the future rather than stories of the past (episode six). While K-9 issues a resounding 'negative' to this proposal, the scriptwriters make no bones about the template that *Underworld* is built on. The idea that classical myth can somehow offer a universal truth owes much to Joseph Campbell's idea of the monomyth, an underlying mythic pattern to which all myths ultimately conform. While Campbell's theory has been compellingly critiqued for its erasure of any element of myth which did not fit his template, its popularity in the 1960s and 1970s may hold some responsibility for the cycle suggested as this episode ends.[23]

As part of *Underworld*'s adaptation of the Jason narrative, it duplicates the traditional dragon guardian of the golden fleece. First, we encounter the 'invisible dragons' mentioned by Idas in the exchange above. They turn out to be lasers guarding a gravity well, which Leela easily puts out of action with a blaster after identifying their locations by throwing an apple through the gateway. The second is the Oracle itself, which tries to trick the crew with a pair of fission bombs in place of the race banks. The Doctor locates the real race banks and sends the decoy banks back to the Oracle where they eventually blow up the planet. The fiery breath of the dragon is transformed into a devastating explosion, and the Doctor takes on the role of Medea in outwitting the monstrous guardian.

While the actions of the monsters don't deviate from the mythic script, the way the monstrous dragon of the Jason myth takes bifold form relies heavily on technology. Unlike the equipment of the Doctor and Jackson's crew, which might be mysterious to the serial's viewers but is under control, the dragon-lasers and the Oracle become monstrous because they are not understood as technological tools. Idas' fear of the dragon-lasers contrasts with the Doctor's blasé problem-solving. Autonomous technology with ideas of its own becomes terrifying; the Oracle computer in particular orders its subordinates around rather than being subject to human authority, like the well-behaved K-9.

With the reboot of 2005 and the beginning of so-called 'New Who', the series established a different relationship with 'historicals' and mythic motifs. The format of a series of episodes within an arc allowed the Doctor to hop back and forth in time, landing only for a brief moment in any given setting. That said, the ancient world remains rather off limits, although the writers do show a predilection for associating the classical with eternity. At one stage, an Auton version of Rory Williams, one of the Doctor's companions, waits for nearly two thousand years for a mysterious box called the Pandorica to open and free Amy Pond, his wife. The Auton took the form of a Roman centurion, standing at his post. Similarly, when the Doctor made a brief visit to Pompeii ('The Fires of Pompeii', 4.2), viewers who had slogged through the Cambridge Latin Course took considerable glee in spotting Caecilius, the *paterfamilias* of the family that introduces learners to Latin verbs and nouns, in the flesh. While the monsters which turn out to be behind the Pompeian explosion are not in any sense classical, the past still has a way of returning. When the Doctor later regenerates to take on the form of Caecilius, that too suggests the ancient world still lives.

Two episodes of 'New Who' engage with classical monsters, and both occur in season six. The overall arc begins and ends with the death of the Doctor at Lake Silencio in the Utah desert, engineered by a mysterious species called the Silence, who humans forget when they are out of sight. Questions of identity and self-identification are placed at the centre of the season's plot concerns. The familiarity of the monsters may be intended to offset the Silence; the show's producer, Steven Moffat, wanted to make them scarier than previous major adversaries.[24] The two episodes featuring classical monsters come in episodes three and eleven in a thirteen-episode series – that is, they occupy parallel structural positions in the season, two episodes after it begins and two before it ends. The familiarity of the classical monster and their narrative parameters perhaps make them 'safer' places for the season to go after beginning and ending with what the production team viewed as innovative, intensified terror.

'The Curse of the Black Spot' (6.3) takes place on a becalmed seventeenth-century pirate ship. Whenever a member of the crew cuts themselves, a mysterious siren begins to sing before appearing and seeming to zap the person into oblivion. Any injured person is marked by the appearance of a black spot on their palm. Those who are marked also become susceptible to the siren's song – as Captain Avery puts it, 'The music turns them into fools.' Slowly, more and more of the crew are apparently vaporised. After the siren takes the captain's son Toby, the Doctor decides to let her head for Rory, who has been washed over the side and is drowning. When the Doctor, Amy and the captain deliberately prick their fingers to be taken too, they wake up in a space ship trapped in a temporal rift in the same place as the pirate ship. Its alien crew died after succumbing to a human virus. The Siren turns out to be the virtual interface of the ship's sick bay, the black spots were skin samples, and the crew are held in suspended animation while the Siren keeps them alive.[25]

'The Curse' follows the formula of looking behind the scenes at a monster and revealing its true nature; the Doctor dismisses mumbles that the pirates are 'cursed' as an inappropriate human reaction to the scenario, and continually tries to puzzle out what makes the Siren tick. The episode interweaves maritime folktale with ancient myth (although Homer's sirens sit in a meadow next to the shore rather than being sea creatures themselves). The dialogue also conflates sirens and mermaids – the Doctor observes that, 'there are worse ways [to go] than having your face snogged off by a dodgy mermaid', before heading off to the TARDIS, and later reassures the captain that things can't get much worse since 'there's a stroppy homicidal mermaid trying to kill all'. The early hypotheses that the Doctor comes up with to explain the siren's behaviour draw on preconceptions about what a siren is, for instance that she can use water like a portal to materialise through. It later transpires that she actually manifests through reflections, but the assumption that something labelled a siren will behave in certain ways guides the Doctor's initial thinking.

Until the Doctor is forced to touch the siren himself, the idea that she must be deadly remains in play. As he prepares to go to the TARDIS, he moodily observes, 'she's out there now, licking her lips, boiling a saucepan, grating cheese'. That the siren turns flaming red and can throw fireballs does not help, although the Doctor eventually realises this is the programme's response to people who try to interfere with the people under its care and to the threat of infection. Her beautiful human form is explained by 'protean circuitry' that lets her 'become a human doctor for humans'. The strange reaction to her song arises as 'she anaesthetises people and then puts their body in stasis' in the alien ship's medical bay. Rather than being consumed, the crew's bodies are restored by their encounter with the siren (although given that simple cuts and grazes often trigger their transportation, this is perhaps not too much of a surprise).

The Doctor concludes that the ship must go back into space because despite being an essentially benign medical entity, the siren is still dangerous: 'I mean, imagine if the siren got ashore, eh? She would have to process every injured human.' Captain Avery decides to stay aboard for the sake of his son Toby, who has typhoid fever. While the siren can keep him alive, she cannot cure him, and a return to earth will mean his inevitable death. The episode ends with Captain

Avery piloting the alien craft into the wilds of space (since apparently one ship is much like another). Even though the nature of the siren's monstrosity has changed, out-of-control technology remains the underlying danger; however, properly interpreting and understanding her actions allows the episode to reach a generally positive outcome.

'The God Complex' (6.11) takes a similar approach to handling a classical monster, but the emotional tone differs. On this occasion, the Doctor, Rory and Amy are transported into a simulacrum of a seedy English hotel with no exit, along with other frightened people (including an alien) whom a mysterious beast is picking off one by one. Each of the captive 'guests' has 'their room', a bedroom inhabited by a particular horror so personal to the individual that it could not have been anything else. Once the room is discovered, a mysterious fervour overtakes the guest as they begin to repeat the phrase 'praise him', eventually seeking out the monster to be killed by it. Although the Doctor initially hypothesises that the monster feeds on fear, it turns out that it actually feeds on faith, which each person falls back on when encountering their most primal dread. The Doctor defeats the beast when Amy finds her room, where a tiny Amelia Pond is frightened that the Doctor will never return for her. By sacrificing her faith in him, he is able to give the beast the opportunity to die.

The reveal of the monster is suspended, but the episode gives some strong hints. The fear-infested rattrap hotel takes the place of the maze. We see brief shots of the monster's eye, its horns scraping the ceiling, its shadow, before the Doctor traps it in the hotel's hairdressing salon to work out what it is. We hear only half the conversation, as the Doctor thinks aloud in a way characteristic of the Eleventh Doctor while he also simultaneously translates the monster's bellows:

> You take people's most primal fears and pop it in a room. Tailor-made hell just for them. Why? Did you say they take? Aaah, what is that word? The guard? No, the – the warden. This is a prison.
>
> So what are we? Cellmates? Lunch? We are not ripe. This is what Joe said, that we weren't ready. So what? What, you make us ready? You, what? Replace? Replace what? Fear? You have lived so long, even your name is lost. You want this to stop. Because you are just instinct. Then tell me, tell me how to fight you.

The Doctor's reversal of the faith scenario shuts down a hitherto invisible programme that has been holding the simulacrum together. It transpires that the monster is both an alien and a Minotaur, and has been as much a captive as its victims. The collapse of the artificial environment reveals that they are in fact held on a prison space ship. The Doctor discovers that its central programming has developed glitches, getting stuck on a single setting and implicitly going rogue. The underlying maze and monster of the Minotaur myth are reimagined as an out of control disciplinary system, in line with Foucault's idea of the panopticon, where the prisoner is controlled precisely by always being seen. This wayward prison draws on contemporary social fears of unaccountable systems of justice which claim to be transparent whilst being the exact opposite. In a neat twist of *The Horns of Nimon*, the predator itself becomes the prey, trapped for the benefit of its host population:

Amy   What is it? A minotaur or an alien? Or an alien minotaur? That's not a question I thought I'd be asking this morning.

Doctor   I mean, it's both, actually. Yeah. Here we go. A distant cousin of the Nimon. They descend on planets and set themselves up as gods to be worshipped, which is fine until the inhabitants get all secular and advanced enough to build bunkers, prisons.

Unlike the Nimon, this monster has a message for the Doctor, which it gives to him as he translates its dying observations:

Amy   What's it saying?

Doctor   An ancient creature drenched in the blood of the innocent. Drifting in space through an endless shifting maze. For such a creature, death would be a gift. Then accept it. And sleep well. [The Minotaur growls.] I wasn't talking about myself.

It does not take a genius to work out that the Minotaur was talking about the Doctor. Whether this prod to his conscience is what prompts him to drop Amy and Rory off at a rather nice terraced house with an upmarket sports car outside at the episode's conclusion is not made clear; however, when he parts with Amy, he explains that he is doing so while she is still breathing. 'The God Complex' refashions the Minotaur myth for the purposes of the episode and the series arc. The Minotaur becomes linked to our deepest personal fears, even if only because they evoke our most deeply held faiths, and a counterpart to the Doctor himself.

'New Who' has been consistently fascinated with the Doctor's own ethical position within its constructed universe. The most significant development on this front has been the introduction of the War Doctor, a figure who stands outside the normal numerical naming conventions for the Doctor's regenerations, and disowned the identity of Doctor to fight in the Time War. The Minotaur speaks to that darker corner of the Doctor's character, pushing that boundary between monstrous appearance and monstrous being.[26] As well as sacrificing Amy's trust in the Doctor, the Minotaur invites the audience to question their faith in him, too.

Changing the channel

Where does looking at classical monsters in *Hercules*, *Xena* and *Doctor Who* leave us? First, they show us that telefantasy set in the ancient world soon runs into problems with classical monsters. The narratives are limited, they can only be reset with difficulty, and once a particular story has been told, returning to it can be challenging. While *Hercules* sets out its stall as primarily concerned with monsters and their conquest, it was beginning to move towards a less monster-heavy episode structure even before its star's health issues imposed changes. Despite sharing the same telefantastic universe, *Xena* does not claim to engage with classical monsters, using them to provide occasional episode fodder rather than as a central thematic idea.

Second, *Doctor Who* helps clarify the other possibilities available to the telefantastic genre when engaging with classical monsters. Since the series is not set in the ancient world, it is under no obligation to focus specifically on classical monsters. The science fiction setting offers a range of aliens (which may or may not be monstrous) to act as antagonist to the Doctor and his companions. While this potential range may initially make the classical monster seem redundant, the nature of telefantasy works in its favour. The need for generic familiarity to balance out unbelievable content, the constant striving for sufficient verisimilitude to carry off the fantastic, makes the pathways of classical myth as appealing as the conventions of crime whodunnits or the spy thriller as a recognisable framework to carry off unbelievable aliens or time travel. The decision to make that generic shift, to use that preformed mythic narrative, not only opens the door to the classical hero, but to the classical monster too.

The already flexible boundaries of telefantasy allow the classical monster to slip in, particularly since it is a convention of this kind of programme that any available material can be reshaped to further the interests of the series and its contemporary audience. Perhaps this explains why classical monsters do not tend to appear in television which is not somehow telefantastic, and why strict remakes of myths are far less common than they seem to be in cinema. The drive for authenticity which caused such problems on the silver screen seems either to scare television producers off altogether, or leads them to expand the supple borders of telefantasy to imaginatively accommodate monstrosity. The classical monster can thus find a space which is not restricted by its prior incarnations or some earnest sense of the authentic. The need of telefantasy to have something familiar for audiences to grasp does not cancel out its own propensity for the incredible.

The final two chapters of this book will explore this suppleness, the ability to fit into alternative narratives and to take shape in particular ways. Two iconic classical monsters, Medusa and the Minotaur – the two with which *Doctor Who* first grappled – will be our guides to the terrain on which they are making new homes.

Thoroughly Modern Medusa

It is said that the ruler of the sea violated her in the temple of Minerva: the daughter of Jove turned away and covered her chaste face with the aegis, and so that this should not have happened without punishment, changes the hair of the Gorgon into snakes.

Ovid, *Metamorphoses* 4.798–801

Medusa, so they say, was a priestess in the temple of Athena, until she caught the attention of the god Poseidon. The god, mindful only of his own pleasures, raped her and amused himself. This would have been outrage enough, except that he did so in Athena's own temple, dishonouring the space that should be holy to the virgin goddess as well as the woman who served her. (Poseidon and Athena had never got on, not since the business at Athens when the city made her its patron for her gift of the olive tree and disdained his gift of a saltwater spring.) But rather than take her revenge on the god who showed her such disrespect, Athena turned on her faithful priestess, and transformed her into a monster. Her hair swam into snakes, her eyes blazed, and anyone who caught her gaze turned to stone. She lived with her two sisters, the Gorgons Stheno and Euryale, until Perseus came, seeking her head on the order of king Polydectes, a quest designed to kill. Perseus beheaded her, and from her blood sprang the winged horse Pegasus and the giant Chryasor. As Perseus flew his prize home, drops of gore fell onto the Sahara, and bred poisonous snakes. Once Perseus was done with his grisly trophy, his mother protected and her suitor turned to stone, Athena took the head and bears it still on her shield, a terror to all who behold the goddess.

These are the more or less familiar bones of Medusa's story that we can excavate from the ancient sources.[1] There are problems with this myth, as with them all, caused by the number of versions in circulation. Apollodorus, compiling a handbook of myths in the first or second century AD, gives us three Gorgons, with serpents for hair, tusks, bronze arms, gold wings and the power of turning people to stone with their gaze. For reasons unexplained, Medusa alone is mortal and so the only one whom Perseus can slaughter.[2] Hesiod, writing a poem about the origins of the gods much earlier in the eighth or seventh century BC, also reports two ageless sisters and one mortal one.[3] Ovid appears to have first introduced Medusa as a human rather than a mortal monster in his *Metamorphoses*, published around AD 8. He is unconcerned about how this might affect her relationship with the other two Gorgons, and writes them out of his version.[4] Ovid's innovation has become the classic story, his weaponised rape victim replicated in the myth collections which in turn feed the imaginations of those creating popular culture today.

Since classical antiquity, Medusa has (as we would expect) fascinated and repelled in equal measure. She has been reimagined as an adversary and an ally, depending on your point of view. Freud took her up as a symbol of psychosexual formation, arguing in his short essay 'Medusa's Head' (published posthumously in 1922) that Medusa was created by a small boy seeing his mother nude and realising the actual possibility of castration. The snakes forming Medusa's hair should be understood to represent female pubic hair. Erich Neumann, a psychologist influenced by Jung, argued in *The Origins and History of Consciousness* (1949) that Medusa's tusked mouth represented the devouring womb of the great mother whom the hero must slaughter, and that the snakes were aggressive phallic symbols. By contrast, the French theorist Hélène Cixous turned these misogynistic interpretations upside down in 'The Laugh of the Medusa' (1975), reading Medusa as the disruptor of male systems of meaning, creating subversive havoc with her delight.

These theoretical preoccupations lead to interpretations which are obsessed with the moment of Medusa's beheading and the nature of her gaze: what does the notion of being looked at by a calcifying figure mean? What about when she looks at herself? The disembodying of Medusa and the elevation of her look (compared to the relative powerlessness of most female gazes) lead to considerations of identity and the nature of petrification within this sort of world. Equally, her disempowered body asks questions about voyeurism and who gains pleasure from watching, since her corpse becomes fetishised precisely at the moment of her death; is she reduced to the powerless object of the male gaze? I mention these rather intellectual debates as they neatly illustrate the dance which takes place around Medusa – around her sexuality, her power, her agency, her appearance. Popular culture shifts and alters what side of Medusa it puts forward with as much variety as is found in psychoanalysis and critical theory.

The image of Medusa retains considerable power within the current political sphere. The famous images of decapitated Medusas created by Cellini and Caravaggio have provided ample opportunity for enterprising users of Photoshop to impose the faces of female politicians on Medusa's own features. Theresa May, Angela Merkel and, in particular, Hillary Clinton have been subjected to this treatment, which places them in the position of the conquered monster.[5] Medusa thus becomes a symbol of female power stepping outside its bounds, yet brought to heel – exterminated by the righteous male order, cut down with the power of a narrative told again, and again, and again. The sight of the fallen body becomes a sight of pleasure for those who wish to see the defiant female defeated.

As I have said, and shall continue to say, there is no value in treating the various iterations of Medusa, or any other monster, as flowers to press in an album, or butterflies to dose with formaldehyde. I want to map out some of the shapes that these different versions take as they manifest in popular culture. The space available to them might allow no more than the misogynistic stereotype – the devouring mother, the emasculating viewer, the uppity female who needs to be punished – or it might allow an inversion of that stereotype, the liberating, powerful figure who destroys the patriarchy with a glance. It might allow other readings, drawing on that queer indefinability of the monster or Medusa's own powerful gaze, approaches fashioned by possibilities rather than preconceptions of how the story 'should go'. Here is the value in exploring the movements of popular culture, although (as we saw with the lure of the preset narrative in telefantasy) the temptation to slip into something culturally comfortable lies in wait.

Equally, not all planned receptions are successful. I was particularly excited in 2014 when Sony Pictures Animation announced they had acquired an animated comedy titled *Medusa*, to be directed by Lauren Faust, the creative director and executive producer behind the highly successful *My Little Pony: Friendship is Magic*. Faust announced in November 2015 she was no longer attached to the project, citing 'creative differences', and its status on IMDB is currently 'unknown'. The desire to take a story in a particular direction may end a tale and its retelling before it has begun.

With that in mind, let us begin a brief and incomplete charting of some recent sightings to populate Medusa's atlas and join some dots. Naturally, this account does not pretend to achieve completeness, but these case studies help foreground important nodes in her story where retellings gather and new tendrils become possible.

Medusa on film

Perhaps the best place to begin considering the different ways Medusa manifests is through a comparison of how she is handled in three recent films – the original *Clash of the Titans* (1981), the 2010 remake of *Clash* and *Percy Jackson & the Olympians: The Lightning Thief* (2010). Each film takes a distinct approach to her story. Considering the versions offered in similar narratives helps us get to grips with what can be at stake in her various incarnations.

The Medusa created by Ray Harryhausen for the original *Clash of the Titans* has become iconic, with her snake tail now taken more or less for granted when considering what a Medusa should look like.[6] The echoes of his vision reach out into many other media; for instance, the influential video games *Age of Mythology* (2000) and *Zeus: Master of Olympus* (2000) both featured Harryhausen-esque Medusae, and have shaped people's engagement with the myth as much as the original film did. Harryhausen's Medusa is deliberately ugly; her fully scaled skin marks her as fully monstrous. She is first introduced to the plot when Perseus asks the Stygian witches how to defeat the Kraken, and they tell him to get hold of Medusa's head – 'a titan against a titan!' as one witch gleefully cackles. She lives under a traditional Greek temple, filmed on location at ruins on Paestum, and her lair is shadowy, lit by flickering braziers and with the drip of rainwater in the background. The island she inhabits is located on the edge of the underworld; although Perseus travels there in a ferry piloted by a skeletal ferryman, he treads the line between the two worlds rather than crossing it, meeting Medusa on the border upon which she dwells. As well as her fearsome gaze, she is armed with a bow and arrows, which let her goad her prey out of hiding and into her line of sight.

The encounter is incredibly tense and drawn out; there is a great deal of cat-and-mouse as Perseus lures Medusa into position and steels himself for the decisive blow. Even the acquisition of the head itself poses problems, since its poisonous blood is strong enough to corrode the temple flagstones and the snakes continue to writhe. Medusa presents a significant challenge and, as the voiceover makes clear when Perseus brandishes the head outside the temple, is a central part of the hero finding and fulfilling his destiny. In this retelling, Medusa is firmly incorporated into the film's world. She is given a specific place, and an implicit role in the monstrous cosmology which makes the Kraken a titan (even if nobody in the film ever explicitly explains how that system works). She also retains her own distinguishing characteristic, that deadly gaze, which makes her a desirable and a dangerous foe.

Yet, while we see where she lives, there is no indication of where she has come from. The film makes no attempt to offer an origin story, which is in keeping with its broader attitude to the supernatural in the film's world – the only monster thus explained is Kalibos, whose transformation as punishment from Zeus is a key plot point. Otherwise, monstrous features of the landscape are as normal and unquestioned as the fact that the gods have temples and sometimes choose to manifest in them. Medusa's rape by Poseidon, presented as the faithful consort of Perseus' antagonist the goddess Thetis, is utterly elided from the script. This is particularly odd in a film which is happy to address the sexual aggression of the gods and Zeus in particular. Thetis recounts, to general laughter, the time Zeus turned into a cuttlefish to try and seduce her, and she turned into a shark in response. But this Medusa, the film implies by its silence, has always been monstrous, and so Poseidon is allowed to remain an untarnished factotum of the Kraken.

The 2010 *Clash of the Titans* references many touchstones of the 1981 Medusa, although inevitably with a twist that either exaggerates or outdoes them (as the 2010 *Clash* can't bear to be inferior to its predecessor). Her dwelling is shifted over the Styx into the underworld proper, and has become a prison rather than a home (much like the Minotaur's labyrinth). She behaves as if she is playing a game with the humans entering her lair rather than as a huntress stalking her prey, although she is also armed with a bow and arrows. The biggest visual shift, though, is in her physical representation. Although her body is still fully serpentine and her lashing tail has become longer, she has a highly stylised feminine face and her décolletage has been enhanced.[7] She has become more recognisably female – or, perhaps more accurately, her representation is more in line with a sexualised feminine stereotype despite the fact she has a tail.

The suspense which accompanied the 1981 Medusa more or less disappears in the 2010 sequence, which creates a dynamic action scene where Perseus, his companions and Medusa hunt each other through temple ruins set above a chasm filled with flaming magma. The resulting sequence looks designed to translate almost seamlessly to a companion video game, but also changes the balance of power in the interaction – rather than Medusa dominating her space while Perseus needs to negotiate it, both Medusa and Perseus' team face a hostile environment full of sudden drops, falling rocks and unsteady surfaces.[8] The space itself becomes an antagonist, which means that Medusa has to be conquered as a group effort rather than a solo feat as in the 1981 *Clash*. In the process, a number of the crew die, sometimes quite dramatically, so Perseus can achieve his goal.

A shift in attitudes towards women over the three decades between the two *Clash* films results in a Medusa who offers a great physical challenge but also appears more sexualised. The combination of Medusa's heightened strength and her hyper-idealised femininity mean that she must be monstrous, being both too female and not female enough. Her destruction is justified by the salvation of the self-sacrificing Andromeda. (That Andromeda will turn out to be a reasonably competent general in the sequel, *Wrath of the Titans*, is neither here nor there.) The ultra-attractive woman is presented as monstrous, at least in part because of her separation from the upper world and the rest of humanity, but also because of her origin story. For the 2010 *Clash* makes the surprising choice to offer a full narration of Medusa's rape by Poseidon and her subsequent punishment by a pitiless Athena, offered by Io, Perseus' guide and later love interest. Yet any suggestion that this might lead to a more sympathetic approach to acquiring her head are firmly dashed when Perseus turns to his team as they enter her lair and instructs them to not 'look the bitch in the eyes'. This implicit victim-blaming is to some extent necessitated by the plot requirement that Medusa be a properly conquered antagonist, but there is a strange disjunct between mythological precision on the one hand and what might be the expected emotional response from the characters on the other.

Finally, the Medusa of *Percy Jackson* occupies entirely new ground.[9] Like the source novel, the film is set in the modern era, and operates under the conceit that the gods and monsters of the classical world live in parallel to the human world, with humans blissfully unaware of their existence and the havoc it occasionally causes. Medusa needs a form which can pass in this scenario, and comes up with a pleasingly fitting dwelling – an abandoned garden centre which Percy and his companions stop at early in their road trip to Hades to rescue Percy's mother. As they explore, they are separated. Annabeth, daughter of Athena, comes face to face with Medusa, who initially appears as an elegant woman in a leather trenchcoat with a turban and wrap-around sunglasses. She soon announces her relationship with Annabeth's mother:

Medusa　You have such beautiful hair. I once had hair like that. I was courted. Desired by many suitors. But that all changed because of your mother, the woman who cursed me. Who turned me . . .

Annabeth　Don't look!

Medusa　. . . into this. They say the eyes are the window to the soul. I hope you find my eyes – attractive.

She removes her turban, then her glasses; the camera focuses in on her snake-encircled visage, giving the viewer the sight that Annabeth cannot and must not have. Later, when Medusa's snakes tell her that there is another demigod in the garden centre, she ruminatively says, 'Son of Poseidon. I used to date your daddy,' before pushing a line of statues down domino-style to where Percy is hiding. Although Percy is caught, Annabeth drives a truck into the garden centre and sends statuary flying, giving him a chance to escape. As Medusa picks up his discarded iPhone, she sees him coming up behind her in the reflection before he decapitates her – an advertorial twist on the usual shiny shield.

This Medusa differs from the two *Clash* Medusas in several significant ways. The full snake tail pushes the film's conventions of just-normal-enough too far, and is instead replaced by a fluid body-covering coat and a set of camera angles that never show Medusa's feet. Sinuous physical acting on the part of Uma Thurman strongly suggests slithering without needing further visual cues.[10] Medusa is not overtly sexualised, an understandable choice in a movie which wants a PG rating. This is the only Medusa of the three who speaks, and thus the only Medusa who is in command of communicating her own story. Her speech also becomes hypnotic as she tries to convince the teens to look at her. The power dynamic is further complicated by the fact that she is positioned as an adult, giving her the authority of a grown-up despite her clear goal to harm Percy and his friends.

Her words gesture towards a historical hinterland that Percy and Annabeth don't know anything about, a world of adult sexual agency already rendered inexplicable by Percy's mother's choice to remain with his horrible stepfather (it later transpires his body odour has disguised Percy from monsters). The film implies that Medusa's accusations mean nothing to Percy. While Annabeth fills in some backstory (like the fact that Medusa's eyes will still work post-decapitation), the film itself doesn't close the story gap. The link between dating Percy's daddy and being cursed by Annabeth's mother is left entirely unspoken, so it is only through pre-existing knowledge or further research that the connection comes to light – otherwise this exchange of dialogue is just another confusing remark in a world that Percy already finds utterly alien. That said, the words Medusa speaks draw on her own embitterment, and the possibility of revenge on the children of the individuals who caused her suffering is clearly attractive. This is also the only example where Medusa talks to another female. That the exchange focuses on intergenerational female conflict places the emphasis of the underlying story on the wrong done by Athena in the original narrative, as does the more neutral language of dating used to describe Medusa's relationship with Poseidon.

What does placing these three cinematic portraits of Medusa next to each other achieve? First of all, it clearly illustrates (as if there were any doubt at this stage) that contemporary manifestations of Medusa are far from cohesive, although they may share some points of contact. Even something as simple as appearance does not provide consistency – while the snake-hair and the dangerous eyes are consistent, each portrait takes a different approach to the bottom half, and to the subsequent issues of movement raised by that choice. Two Medusae do not have speech, or rather are not given the opportunity to speak in coherent sentences; the third not only has complete grasp of her voice box, but speaks at length and with authority. The visual line between human and snake, and indeed beauty and monstrosity, is movable, and affects how each manifestation of the monster functions within its setting.

Second, this comparison helps map out the points of the Medusa story which generate fascination, and which areas cause narrative disruptions. The battle between monster and hero is repeatedly circumnavigated – perhaps this is not surprising, given these three examples are all in one way or another retellings of myths, but I want to single out that locus of conflict as key, not least because it inevitably pits male and female against each other. Medusa's origin story proves particularly challenging – one version erases it, one version simultaneously acknowledges and diminishes it, and one version alludes to it knowingly. The villain of the piece can be Athena or it can be Poseidon. The sexual element can be coerced or consensual. None of these decisions about the origin story are neutral.

Third, and not unrelatedly, the comparison brings out the significance of gender to retellings of the Medusa story and to monstrosity more generally. For the 1981 *Clash*, gender is subordinate to monstrosity. Harryhausen's creation emphasises the monstrous physical qualities of Medusa's body over the sexual ones, which in combination with the lack of origin story effectively desexualises Medusa, diminishing gender as a vector of tension between her and Perseus. The 2010 *Clash*, by contrast, takes advantage of the shift in standards of how women's bodies can be depicted on screen to give Medusa a body as sexualised and feminine as CGI will permit, and allow her an erotic identity (however compromised) through telling her origin story. The effect is to make her a sexual monster, hyper feminine and hyper-threatening at the same time, in contrast to the human masculinity of Perseus himself. The Medusa of *Percy Jackson* embodies a more restrained sexuality (understandable given the target audience), but projects a threatening agency which taps into adult relationships that are totally foreign to the film's protagonists. That she is framed almost as Percy's father's ex activates all of the stereotypes about rejected older women and patterns of revenge which have become staples of twentieth and twenty-first-century soap operas and thrillers. The fact that Medusa can be used to embody two conflicting negative female stereotypes, sometimes even at the same time, points to her as a place for monstrous femininity.

Medusa's head: Decapitation, representation and viewing

I turn to how Medusa has been handled in recent popular literature, although her story appears to have been relatively overlooked as a source of mythical inspiration. I should note that I am not including what might be called 'faithful retellings', or stories which explicitly market themselves as a version of the Medusa myth for children – what happens in these adapted 'entry-level' texts would need a discussion of their own.[11] What I am interested in is the sort of text in which Medusa has found space to dwell beyond the predictable borders of the enclosure provided by ancient myth. Peculiarly, or perhaps not, these appear to be less abundant than one might anticipate.

The fertile slopes of Young Adult (YA) literature and the light comedic novel move away from Medusa as a significant character, choosing to focus more generally on the lives and loves of deities and demigods as opposed to specific mythic episodes. Even though the protagonist of the *Percy Jackson* series is named after Perseus, the series encompasses the full range of classical myth and its inhabitants rather than being limited to one particular story. Alternatively, YA fiction seems drawn almost magnetically to the myth of Hades and Persephone, a ready-made story of love against the odds, provided you're willing to ignore the fact that that the heroine is abducted against her will by her uncle. Either way, Medusa seems to be of little interest to these genres. Honourable mention should be given to *Dusssie* by Nancy Springer (2007), which features a teenage girl whose entrance to puberty is marked by her hair turning into snakes, just like her mother and her aunt Medusa. The link made between burgeoning female sexuality and the monstrous is pretty clear, as is the sometimes terrifying arrival of one's first menstrual period and the discovery that one's hitherto acquiescent body has a firm mind of its own.

I noted that perhaps Medusa's failure to find life in the written word should not come as a surprise. Medusa is a monster of sight and of vision; she not only needs to see and be seen, but she represents that which cannot be seen without paying a fatal penalty. Maybe it is inevitable that she finds life in the places where she can be seen, an almost ironic multiplication of the unseeable in our age of digital reproduction. That one of her most abundant, and domesticated, presences is as the logo for the fashion house Versace marks a fitting link between her need to be seen and yet unseen, a signifier that everybody understands but nobody looks at for its own sake, lost as a status symbol, yet powerful through the assimilation to the brand (Fig. 7.1). Fashion's monstering of its models, with aggressive and chronic thinness *de rigueur*, freezing extravagant looks through the eye of the camera, makes a haute couture house an even more attractive place for Medusa to dwell.

That is not to suggest that Medusa's reception is alive only in her image. The importance of her vision and the sight of her can become a helpful point of orientation for written as well as visual representations, as it does in Tim Powers' *Medusa's Web* (2015). When Scott and Madeline Madden return to the decaying Hollywood mansion where they grew up after the suicide of their aunt, along with their cousins Claimayne and Ariel they are caught up in a supernatural mystery which revolves around the existence of so-called 'spiders'. These are eight-limbed symbols which transport the viewer backwards or forwards in time, either into their own or somebody else's body. The exchange is completed when somebody else looks at the 'spider', cementing the switch. The same spiders can be used multiple times, making them 'dirty', although 'clean' ones can be

Fig. 7.1 The Versace logo.

created by photographing them and printing them out. The experience of looking at a spider involves an initial timeless phase, a feeling of falling through massive incomprehensible shapes, and then an encounter with the other time.

While this paranormal phenomenon draws heavily on arachnid imagery, the connections to Medusa are developed throughout the book. She is embedded in the landscape of the novel through a Medusa mosaic wall in the mansion gardens:

> The face was no more than six inches across and made of only twelve flat stones, black and white – two black rectangles for the eyes, a smaller one for the mouth, white triangles for the cheeks and a fan of them for the forehead – but the tendrils of the snaky hair spiralled out in all directions across the rest of the wall, in a variety of shades of purple against a gold background. Madeline remembered how they seemed to glow, even to pulse, in the coppery light of late October afternoons.[12]

The Medusa wall becomes a landmark where the characters encounter each other, but also points to the important relationship between Medusa and the mysterious existence of the spiders. It emerges that all of the spiders descend from one original, known as the Medusa, located near Taranto. At one stage in a spider vision, Rudolph Valentino describes his experience of seeing it as a child to Scott:

> 'My friends and I went into the caves, and in one I saw the very old fresco, in the deep tunnels.' He smiled and raised the film can. 'It was this one, the mother of them all, the Medusa. The government dynamited that tunnel, later. People said the Vatican ordered it.'[13]

During a subsequent visit, Scott learns that the spiders are 'apparently two-dimensional creatures who have no conception of time or spatial volume', and that their relationship to the 'big spider', the Medusa, means they are all linked together.[14] The monstrosity of breaking down our linear experience of time becomes linked to a monster who has herself transcended time.

Medusa's Web focuses on the issue of looking or not looking at Medusa in her various spidery incarnations. At the start of the novel, Ariel uses a spider for the first time in four years, and much of the language around spider consumption echoes that around substance addiction, including the term 'spiderbit' for those who have used spiders but are trying to give them up. This enterprise is more difficult than it sounds – spiders appear in cracked plates and glass without warning, and the protagonists often find themselves faced with a rogue spider which needs dispatching. For instance, Scott becomes suspicious when Claimayne is cross that Ariel won't fetch him a coke from the kitchen, and discovers a spider in a cracked kitchen window which he breaks properly;[15] when he returns to the house on another occasion, he discovers Ariel and Madeline pinned in the kitchen by a broken plate of cookies which Ariel is attempting to get rid of.[16] These unexpected spiders have to be looked at covertly, with peripheral vision, or through glasses with distorted lenses sold by spiderbit shops. Characters even face being forced into viewing spiders against their will by wheelbugs, people who try to exploit spider users. This imagery gives Medusa even more heads, making it increasingly difficult not to look at her.

The plot hinges on the existence of a so-called exorcism film, once in the possession of Rudolph Valentino but missing in the present day. Shots of the original Medusa were set to black frames spinning at the correct rate to make it stop. Watching it should freeze it, thus disconnecting the spider dimension from ours and deactivating the spiders here. The only downside is that whoever watches the film is likely to die – staring at Medusa remains fatal. Scott nobly volunteers to watch, hoping to save his sister from a similar fate. While he survives, the film reel combusts in the unoiled projector he has used to show it, destroying the final traces of the original Medusa. This is not quite the equivalent of decapitation; Scott describes the Medusa as falling out of our reality, but that is not the same as leaving all realities.[17] The role of Medusa in *Medusa's Web* moves away from explicitly engaging with her mythic context, but focuses on the key characteristics of seeing and non-seeing as gateways to monstrous experiences. Sight and agency are to some extent defused as methods of interacting with the lesser spiders, but the final visual encounter with the Medusa herself remains both sought after and avoided, desirable and dangerous.

A similar emphasis on the significance of vision for Medusa, albeit more grounded in her own mythological tradition, drives *The Medusa Amulet* by Robert Masello (2011). The novel takes the famous statue of Medusa by Benvenuto Cellini and the account in the artist's autobiography of conjuring spirits in the Colosseum to build an adventure mystery premised upon the idea that Cellini encountered and beheaded Medusa in a mystical marsh (Fig. 7.2). He brought rushes and lake water back to our world along with the decapitated head. The rushes were encased in silver to create a wreath which turned the wearer invisible. He cast a small silver amulet with Medusa's head on the outside, and a mirror on the inside, under which he placed the lake water. If someone looks at the mirror in the moonlight, they are transformed not into stone, but into immortal beings. Cellini himself undergoes this process, as does his muse,

Fig. 7.2 Cellini's 'Perseus with the Head of Medusa', Florence.

model and lover Caterina, and his assistant Ascanio. The couple are separated when Cellini is kidnapped, and both assume the other is dead.

Although this 'origin story' is told in flashback through the novel, the bulk of the plot follows the attempts of an art historian, David Franco, to track down the Medusa for a mysterious woman who is willing to acquire it at any cost. (The woman is, naturally, Caterina, hoping for her own death if she can destroy the amulet.) While Medusa herself only appears at the start and the end of the novel – as a hissing monster to be decapitated, and then as a disembodied head kept in the vault of a Parisian townhouse – her artistic representation lies at the heart of the plot. David follows leads in papers provided by Caterina which show evidence of Cellini making the Medusa mirror, but has to battle past the received wisdom that the Medusa of the Perseus bronze is the only one which he ever sculpted. That bronze, too, becomes critical for the plot, as it is where David meets Olivia, a tour guide with an incidental side interest in Nazi conspiracy theories, with whom he becomes romantically entangled.

Nazis play more than a passing role in the plot. While Medusa appears primarily as an artefact, her monstrosity is displaced onto others. The amulet was stolen from Cellini during the Second World War by none other than Hitler himself, who has also taken over the mansion in France, the Chateau Perdu, where Cellini reinvented himself as the Marquis di Sant'Angelo after staging his own death. When Sant'Angelo first encounters Hitler, he 'felt the imminence of something powerful … and evil'.[18] As his underlings attempt to explain the significance of the amulet, Sant'Angelo uses his magical powers to bore into Hitler's mind, only to discover that 'the Führer's power was greater than anything he had ever encountered, as if he were channelling the devil himself'.[19] In the end, Sant'Angelo jumps out of a castle turret to escape, leaving the amulet behind. The monstrosity of Medusa becomes embodied in one of the greatest monsters of the twentieth century – and his death, too, echoes that of Medusa. David and Ascanio infiltrate the Chateau, taking Hitler by surprise. Armed with Cellini's own *harpe*, the Greek-style sword used to decapitate Medusa, David hews off Hitler's head. As he does so, 'it felt as if the blade was acting on its own, hungry to complete some ancient labour'.[20] The curse of immortality means that just before Ascanio and David set off a gas explosion to destroy the Chateau and its inhabitants, David has the unnerving experience of seeing the decapitated head, alive, under the arm of a trusted henchman.[21]

The reader knows this is not David's imagination from an earlier flashback, where Medusa's death was again re-enacted by Marie Antoinette, whose court Cellini frequented in the guise of the first Marquis di Sant'Angelo. The French queen was accidentally exposed to the amulet after it was sent to her as a gift by the Vatican, which had originally confiscated it from Cellini. Although the Revolution occurs too soon after the exposure for him to be sure that she has become immortal, he follows her to the guillotine, first by impersonating a priest and then by donning the bulrush wreath to become invisible. Cellini believes he is mistaken, until Mademoiselle Tussaud comes to take the death mask of the executed queen:

> Taking up her hairbrush, Tussaud pulled the bristles roughly through the tangled mat of hair, once, twice, but on the third stroke – just as Sant'Angelo felt sure that his worst fears had not been realized – the eyes of the queen flew open, in an expression of utter bewilderment and horror.[22]

The marquis quickly dumps the head into a nearby barrel of quicklime, ensuring a swift demise, and substitutes a replacement head while Tussaud recovers from a faint. Sant'Angelo takes swift and brutal revenge on those responsible for the queen's execution and humiliation, marking out this particular reiteration of Medusa's beheading as monstrous for its innocent victim rather than the wickedness of its target.

Both *The Medusa Amulet* and *Medusa's Web* exhibit a fascination with Medusa's head and the power it conveys even when separated from her monstrous body. In a peculiar way, the head itself becomes an independent entity, a daughter plant to the maternal monster, yet remains fully empowered with the authority, danger and fear of Medusa whole. Rather than the moment of decapitation, where the Perseus story revolves and spins, these examples find a place for a modern aegis, summoning danger rather than warding it off, a warning of a monster dismembered but not defused.

Reclaiming the narrative

The previous tendril of receptions takes Medusa's objectification to its natural conclusion and obsesses over her decapitated head. Another tendril rejects this kind of narrative, which operates by focusing on Medusa's victimhood, and instead seeks to reclaim the story and empower Medusa. Many examples occur in Young Adult fiction which looks to the classical world for inspiration. YA literature has proved to be an incredibly imaginative and resourceful emerging category of writing, primarily characterised by its targeting of a 'young adult' audience. Precisely how this should be defined is the subject of considerable debate among writers, publishers, libraries and academics, but most agree that the 'target audience' of YA is in their mid- to late teens, and that the actual readership of YA extends beyond this demographic in both directions.[23] The popular perception of YA is that it mainly contains paranormal romance and sparkly vampires, as characterised by the *Twilight* saga by Stephanie Meyer (2005–8). However, YA reaches far beyond these scenarios, and can handle complex emotional situations with more honesty and daring than much so-called 'adult' fiction. Oddly enough, YA shares with telefantasy the characteristic of being a generic magpie – while individual novels settle into (for instance) a historical period piece, contemporary soap opera or apocalyptic drama, the genre as a whole is free to travel between forms, depending on how the author perceives the needs of the plot (and, in all honesty, what has recently sold well to the target demographic).

Given this generic flexibility, it was inevitable that YA would settle on classical mythology. Well-known examples include the popular *Percy Jackson* series, which hovers on the boundary of children's literature and YA, and the *Hunger Games* trilogy, which claims strong influence from the myth of Theseus and the labyrinth.[24] I want to look at Kelly Keaton's *Gods & Monsters* quartet and its heroine Ari Selkirk, whose strange regenerating silver hair has always marked her out as different. Ari was given up for adoption at the age of four, spent some traumatic years in state care, and finally ended up in a supportive foster home with a pair of bail bondsmen. The first novel in the series, *Darkness Becomes Her*, opens as Ari learns her mother committed suicide six months after admitting herself to an insane asylum.[25] The novel is set in a parallel universe where not one but two Katrina-style hurricanes have hit Louisiana, and made the city of New Orleans unrecoverable. The state sold it off to the Novem, nine influential families, who now run it as an independent country. Ari's mother at first appears to have been one of those suffering from post-traumatic stress disorder (PTSD) after the hurricanes, believing that snakes were trying to grow out of her head – something that sounds more than plausible to the doctors who knew how snakes had been pushed in-land with the flood waters.[26]

As soon becomes clear, Ari's mother was not imagining things. Ari's grandmother also died at the age of twenty-one, and her mother before her. The whole family labours under the original curse laid on Medusa, who gave birth to a baby girl before Perseus beheaded her. Athena has hounded the female line descended from that baby ever since. Each woman has to face the growth of the gorgon inside her as she reaches maturity. As is typical of YA, *Darkness Becomes Her* revolves around the question of Ari's identity, culminating in the revelation of her Medusan ancestry, and the second book, *A Beautiful Evil* (2012), continues the theme as Ari comes to terms with her inner gorgon and the petrifying power she can access through it. All this takes place in New Orleans, now a private fiefdom surviving mainly through tourism to its carefully preserved French Quarter, but also a haven for demigods, shapeshifters, witches, warlocks, vampires and other supernatural humans. Many of the defining tropes of YA literature, particularly in paranormal romance, are on show here, but the reimagining of Medusa through her descendant offers the scope for a particularly pointed conflict.[27]

The node of the Medusa myth from which *Gods & Monsters* grows is the transformation of Medusa by Athena, retold when Ari undergoes a magical flashback.[28] The moment of rape by Poseidon and then betrayal by Athena is sharp and confusing – 'first raped and now blamed', says the narrative, explicitly bringing in contemporary ideas of victim-blaming which are common in feminist discourse around how rape is treated in the media.[29] Ari is driven by anger at the injustice Medusa suffered, explicitly wanting to take revenge on Athena for all the suffering and pain caused down the generations since the original curse. In turn, the presentation of Athena in the novels turns away from the benign goddess looking out for humankind, and instead gives us a psychopath who killed her own father and many other divine relatives. She first appears wearing a moving body suit made from the skin of the Titan Typhon, establishing her villainous credentials beyond doubt.[30] Her cruelty (both of the casual and calculated varieties) towards Ari and her friends is based on her belief that, as ultimately her creation, Ari is hers to own and command. Rather than confronting an overbearing high school principal, as might occur in other YA, Ari must face down a disciplinary system, an abusive pseudo-family, created and articulated by the goddess of war herself.

Ari's growing confidence with tapping into her inner gorgon naturally addresses the YA theme of coming to terms with our personal demons. There is also the literal demon which must be controlled, and this aspect speaks to a darker part of adolescent identity shift, the move into sexual maturity, into independence, and indeed into being *female* in a patriarchal and misogynist society. We meet Ari at seventeen, after the moment of menarche, and the books track her transition out of secondary education and into the adult world. Her autonomy and sexual agency mark her out as socially other – perhaps not so much in the uprooted and unnatural world of New Orleans, but certainly to the world undisrupted by the hurricanes. Ari's femininity, in all its forms, is monstered explicitly by her ancestry and implicitly by her rejection of stereotypical gender expectations.

Yet Ari's monstrosity, initially frightening and alienating, becomes empowering as she comes to terms with her own body and abilities. Positioning a Medusa stand-in as the heroine of the quartet reclaims the monstrous, especially in terms of the misogynistic tradition which swirls around contemporary Medusas. Ari's identity as the God Killer becomes a positive attribute, her sexual freedom a token of her commitment to her adopted community and humanity (however unusual), and despite Athena's attempts to make her see herself as ugly, those around her think she is beautiful. Reclaiming the monster in this instance does not mean weakening the monster; the entirety of Ari's narrative focuses on taking control of that power and developing it to its fullest potential. The monster needs to be released rather than contained in order to overturn Athena's repressive and abusive regime.

An alternative narrative of reclamation drives *The Deep End of the Sea* by Heather Lyons (2014). Lyons has written within the Young Adult and New Adult genres, but identifies *Deep End* as an 'Adult Mythological Romance' on the FAQs section of her website.[31] Like *Gods & Monsters, Deep End* is written in the first person, putting the reader literally inside Medusa's skin. The novel is set in the contemporary world, as Hermes finally convinces Medusa to let him take her case to the Assembly of the Greek gods, to force Athena to reverse her curse. The Assembly finds in Medusa's favour, compelling Athena to change her back. Medusa ends up staying at the home of Persephone and Hades on Olympus as she recuperates and learns to use legs again. She also gradually realises that Hermes has been quietly falling in love with her for the last two millennia, allowing them to finally consummate their relationship.

Despite the other gods' attempts to keep it from her, Medusa discovers that Poseidon has been stalking her, convinced that she is 'his' because of the original rape (not helped by a quirk which means once a god has fallen in love, it's forever). After an attempted abduction and Poseidon taking his case against Hermes to the Assembly, Medusa is sent into hiding in Jackson, Wyoming. She has to deal with the possibility that she will never see Hermes again, and face the inevitable grief of losing a romantic relationship after believing for so long that her monstrosity made such a thing impossible; she also finally has the space and opportunity to reflect on her experience being raped and reclaim that part of her life. Along with taking self-defence lessons, she eventually plucks up the courage to attend a support group for survivors of rape and sexual assault, and comes to terms with not only the experience (which still gives her flashbacks) but also her feelings about herself, Poseidon and, indeed, Athena.

Lyons focuses on the emotional impact of being an unacknowledged victim over such a long period of time. Medusa has internalised a lot of hatred while in isolation on an island in the middle of the sea, contrary to rumours of her demise at the hands of Perseus. The sheer physicality of the emotions she experiences comes through in a particularly dramatic scene as Athena is made to reverse her curse before the Assembly:[32]

> Athena lurches to her feet. 'She desecrated the sanctity of my temple with her overzealous, whorish libido!'
>
> An imaginary fist punches my stomach. Before I break the rules and start shrieking, Hermes also stands up, visibly shaking. 'You think she *chose* that? She was *raped*, you idiot!'
>
> His words echo across the room. I cannot bring myself to look at Poseidon, but I know, just know, he is still staring at me.
>
> His hands, on me. Blood, on the floor.

The central issues of victim-blaming, of responsibility and of divine immunity come together in this key judgement scene, where Medusa is not only unable to speak but forbidden to. She must rely on Hermes to speak for her as she seeks justice. Her agency develops over the novel, until she floors Poseidon with a deeply satisfying roundhouse kick as he fails to comprehend that she has chosen Hermes over him.[33]

The lifting of the curse is only the first of many steps in Medusa's recovery, although it has the immediate effect of removing her snake tail and 'the Girls', as she refers to the snakes on her head. The restoration of her normal hair and legs marks the removal of visible monstrosity and the danger Medusa has posed to anyone who catches her eye. It also removes physical obstructions to intimacy – while no mention is made of the biology involved in the return of her legs, it is significant that her initial sexual encounter with Hermes is framed as her first since Poseidon raped her, implying that Athena's curse removed her genitalia and with them her physical capacity for sexual pleasure. The ability to finally look Hermes in the eyes without the fear of turning him to stone removes another barrier to intimacy – as made clear in the opening scenes, Medusa always dons mirrored wrap-around shades when he visits, protecting both him from petrification and her from the guilt of harming him, but also creating an effective obstacle between them.

The removal of what Medusa has perceived as her monstrosity, both in terms of her form and her deadly power, might have been assumed to be the end of the recovery story, but what *Deep End* makes clear is that the damage done goes more than skin deep. Medusa must rebuild her confidence, take control of her own sexuality, come to terms with her past trauma, and confront her assailant before moving on with her life. Medusa's physical monstrosity becomes a metaphor for the physical violence of rape and the harm that does to a body, while the emotional journey then goes on reflects the kinds of psychological damage which survivors of rape and sexual abuse must confront. The use of an actual support group located in modern day America, where Medusa draws strength from other women processing similar experiences, explicitly both frames Medusa's experience as rape (as it is unquestionably positioned throughout the novel) and makes her emotional journey reflect those of modern women. The novel becomes, if not therapeutic, then certainly inspirational, a tale (as the blurb on the dust jacket puts it) 'of reclaiming a life after tragedy'.

Deep End gives Medusa back her agency without glossing over the injustice she suffered or the impact it has on her life. It situates monstrosity not in Medusa's appearance, but in the harm done to her. By the end of the novel, not only has

Medusa regained her human appearance and her sense of identity, she has also discovered that she is really a god, transcending the problem that mortality posed for her relationship with Hermes. She has been transformed by the experience, and given the key to her true divine identity which otherwise might have remained hidden. Medusa herself is freed of monstrosity, humanised and actualised, while the horror of the monster is instead layered on to Poseidon, the abuser and stalker. The shift to empower Medusa does not diffuse her inherent monstrosity; rather, it reveals where the true monster resides, in the predatory, entitled and manipulative male.

Medusa in space

While my case studies so far have made Medusa easy to see and be seen, she also finds more allusive ways to manifest. One example of this oblique reception comes from *The Medusa Chronicles* by Stephen Baxter and Alastair Reynolds (2016). The novel is an extended homage to Arthur C. Clarke's novella, *A Meeting with Medusa* (1971).[34] The story's hero, Howard Falcon, suffers a catastrophic dirigible crash and is brought back to life with pioneering surgery which permits him encounter intelligent alien life forms during the first manned mission to Jupiter. The novella ends as Falcon wheels off to a press conference with an ominous observation that he will be needed as an intercessor between machines and men in the future – and it is this future that Baxter and Reynolds explore.

The Medusa Chronicles are ostensibly named after the alien intelligences Falcon encounters, who occupy one of the outermost layers of Jupiter. They are jellyfish-like creatures of massive size which float through water vapour:[35]

> The *Ra* was a tremendous craft, its envelope of fusion-heated hydrogen more than eight hundred metres long. But the medusa was more than three times that length, an oval-shaped continent of creamy flesh from which that inverted forest of tentacles dangled, some as thick as oak trunks, Falcon knew, and some so fine they ended in tendrils narrower and more flexible than human fingers.[36]

As Falcon has learned through long and patient observation, the Jovian medusae have a complicated culture of their own, using songs to share memories of individuals and events.[37] The medusae become emblematic of Falcon's wider fascination with Jupiter, and the mysterious nature of its inner core. His love for them as a species is used as a lever to force him to act as a supposed peace ambassador to the machines in the novel's final phase, set in AD 2850. These peaceful creatures do not seem to interlock with their classical predecessor.

However, Medusa has undergone a radical reshaping. I would argue that we should read Falcon himself as a Medusa figure, drawing on monstrous allusion and hybridity. As Clarke's original novella established, only experimental cyborg surgery in the 2080s saved Falcon's life. *Chronicles* makes it clear that he subsequently occupies a unique position, since the technology used to keep him alive does not become humanity's preferred route to extending life. In part, this is the result of the evolution of intelligent machines, who disappear at the end of twenty-second century and reappear as a sovereign race rather than a servile one. Falcon, his few remaining biological parts trapped within a mechanical chassis, comes to stand for an uneasy alliance between human and machine at precisely the same time as the respective nations are sizing each other up before engaging in increasingly destructive warfare. The decisions made by Falcon's surgeons in the 2080s turn out to have far-reaching consequences, as his cyborg form leads him to become both useful as an appropriate ambassador to the machines, and suspect for being too much like them to trust.

Falcon's mechanisation means a constant stream of upgrades, tunings, overhauls and similar technological interventions are required to keep him operational. They constantly change his shape and his appearance, although his face remains the same – as described at the opening of the novel by a captain of the navy, 'the face your mother gave you, even if it's become a somewhat immobile, leathery mask'.[38] Increasing human competence in electronic engineering makes his physical form more sensitive and mobile, but he ultimately remains a machine with an undercarriage, never becoming fully anthropomorphic. The reactions of some of his fellow audience members when he attends the first performance of a Neutrino Symphony in Antarctica, around 2108, are typical:

> He heard few direct insults that night, but he could fill in the blanks: that he was neither human nor machine, but an unnatural mixture. His very movements were strange, even insectile, as if, in his metal shell, he wasn't a man but a giant upright cockroach. That he was, in short, an obscenity.[39]

What makes Falcon a Medusa is his hybridity – halfway between human and machine, neither one nor the other, crossing the boundary between the like-us and not-us in a genre which is concerned about the influence of technology, the place of the human in the grand world of progress. His face becomes that which is frozen rather than that which freezes. The attempts to save his life have made him monstrous. That Falcon is male is an artefact of the original Clarke story which inspired the novel, but equally the gender shift serves to reemphasise both the tendency of sci-fi to prioritise the male and the versatility of the classical monster to take whatever form necessary for its new environment.[40]

At the end of the novel, Falcon and his robot counterpart Adam are both, in effect, sacrificed by their respective communities. They meet in the outer layers of Jupiter ostensibly to negotiate peace; when Falcon shakes Adam's robotic hand, he also transfers a logic virus through technology the humans stole from the machines. The only possible way to save the machines from contamination is for them both to drop into the heart of Jupiter – a noble self-sacrifice for the sake, hopefully, of peace. In the process of falling, Falcon and Adam encounter increasingly severe pressures. Adam is able to morph his mechanical body to survive, but Falcon's antiquated mechanical systems and biological components don't stand a chance. Adam offers him the chance first to be contained within Adam's own mechanisms, and then, slowly but surely, to be assimilated into the machine in order to survive and continue the journey to the heart of the planet. Finally, Adam jettisons what is left of Falcon's neurons, and replicates his neural wiring within a structure which can survive the intense pressures of their environment:

> So Howard Falcon completed the long journey that began with the crash of the *Queen Elizabeth*. He had stood between two worlds for long enough, between human and Machine – useful to both, trusted by neither.
> Equally feared.
> Now he was one with the Machines.[41]

With the final expulsion of all biological matter, Falcon's incorporation into the machine becomes complete – and Adam becomes the engine of replicating humanity, combining them into the entity the novel then refers to as Falcon/Adam, containing two distinct consciousnesses in one physical being. The conversion process is enacted upon Falcon by Adam, but ultimately transforms both.

While Medusa appears in *Chronicles* more indirectly than she does in my other case studies, she allows an exploration of mechanical monstrosity, or rather its potential for fear. Falcon's unique circumstances position him as the ideal interrogator of the dread of the machine, while his ultimate assimilation foreshadows the destruction of the human/machine binary. Medusa's presence under the narrative's surface emerges at these moments of technological critique and hybridity, revealing that *Chronicles* situates monstrosity much more on earth than on Jupiter.

Reclaiming Rihanna

My final Medusa is, on the surface, both profoundly uninteresting and wearily predictable in its misogyny. The December 2013 edition of the men's magazine *British GQ* celebrated its twenty-fifth anniversary with a photoshoot directed and conceived by Damian Hirst featuring the singer Rihanna. In that shoot, Rihanna took on the persona of Medusa. The final photos showed her sporting a CGI-added shock of snakes, a (coincidentally?) seashell shaped silver thong, cosmetic contact lenses to give her reptilian eyes, and not a great deal else beyond an occasional helpful python. This, it seems, is a development of the Beautiful Medusa theme and the associated ideas of the monstrous feminine, the woman who must be conquered because of the danger she poses, which in turn is linked to her implicit sexual power. For Medusa to be snake-haired and just-about-naked takes the implicit sexual threat she poses to Perseus and his pursuit of heteronormative bliss with Andromeda and reifies it. A key selling point of *GQ* and similar men's magazines has been the salacious pictures of celebrities they publish, excused, superficially, by the high art combination of a classical theme and a prominent Young British Artist.[42]

The photos also draw on the tradition of seeing the racialised other as a symbol of the exotic. This colonial habit goes back as far as the public exhibition of Saartjie Baartman as the 'Hottentot Venus' in various European capitals during the early 1800s, where the viewers' primary interest was the size of Baartman's buttocks.[43] The display of black bodies for the visual pleasure of white viewers, often using the excuse of scientific observation to justify sexual abuse, constructed inhabitants of colonised countries as aberrations from the norm and thus acceptable objects for objectification. While Rihanna's appearance on the front of *GQ* presents her as beautiful in a way that was barred to Baartman, the increased presence of racialised bodies presented positively in popular culture does not remove historic racist assumptions about those bodies and their behaviour.[44] For Rihanna to appear as an actual monster adds a layer of historically informed racism to the sexism already on display.

Yet there is more at work in this choice of image than first meets the eye. First of all, the Rihanna/Hirst Medusa has been *constructed*, of necessity – one of the photos from the shoot recorded Hirst arranging a snake on top of a plaster head sporting a mesh hairnet, presumably for digital addition to the original photo of Rihanna. Consequently, the image is understood both as real and non-real, crossing the boundary of order and control; the magazine's front cover features Medusa-Rihanna as a way-marker for readers opening up the *GQ* universe, celebrating the fiction of the 'GQ life' that the magazine had sold for quarter of a century. The daring of putting Medusa on the cover, too, generates that frisson of danger, albeit repurposed in a culture where semi-nude photography of women's bodies is not as acceptable as it once was – will Medusa turn you to stone for catching her undressed? Medusa threatens both the reader and the magazine itself with destruction.

The choice of Medusa as an avatar for Rihanna also deserves more unpicking. At the time of the shoot, Hirst was working on his Venice exhibition, *Treasures from the Wreck of the Unbelievable*. The conceit of the exhibition is that the displays were rescued from a shipwreck off the coast of East Africa, a not implausible fiction, given the number of Greek and Roman bronzes that have similar provenances. The tradition that Medusa herself came from Libya or somewhere else in North Africa could also be projected onto the shipwreck's location.[45] Hirst's creation was storytelling in the broadest sense, as much about building the historical and museological world which surrounded his art as the statues themselves. The show as a whole displayed the strong influence of Ray Harryhausen. A pair of sculptures of Kali fighting a hydra (one encrusted with coral, the other not) borrowed heavily from Harryhausen's visual art in *Jason and the Argonauts* (1963) and *The Golden Voyage of Sinbad* (1973). It is not surprising that the severed head of Medusa appeared in the exhibition, although one might not have expected the same head to appear three times, in crystal glass, malachite and gold, the facial expression fixed slightly differently in each case. Having made Rihanna into a live Medusa, Hirst is happy to kill off his creation, bringing the myth to its natural end, albeit transforming the head into stone rather than the viewer.

In an interview for *GQ* about the cover shoot, Hirst offers enthusiastic but vague reasons for working with Rihanna.[46] The work on *Treasures* was underway, and Rihanna appears to have been as keen as Hirst on the *GQ* opportunity. What about Medusa, in particular, spoke to Rihanna? It is not the only time she has drawn on the classical world to shape her self-presentation. She has consistently used Egyptian mythology as a reference point for her persona, including a tattoo of the goddess Isis kneeling with outspread wings across her breastbone. In November 2017, she featured on the cover of *Vogue Arabia* as Queen Nefertiti, generating both enthusiasm and complaints about a black woman from Barbados representing the queen rather than an Arabian or black African woman. Rihanna's long-standing connection with Egyptian mythology creates an easy way for an audience familiar with her star image to 'read' and understand her as Medusa.[47]

In her deliberate engagement with history she travels the same path as Beyoncé, whose own photographs offer a masterclass in reclaiming the established iconography of Western art and combining it with African visual traditions to mould her public image. The photograph accompanying Beyoncé's 2017 pregnancy announcement strongly evoked the visual tradition associated with the Virgin Mary, in particular the Virgin of Guadalupe's mandorla of flowers and blue robe.[48] More recently, the video for 'APESHIT' by The Carters (the duo of Beyoncé and her husband Jay-Z) was filmed in the Louvre Museum. It featured hip-hop dance moves and scenes of Black American life, intercut with iconic works of the European artistic tradition – including Géricault's *The Raft of the Medusa* (1818–19). For Rihanna to deliberately align herself with antiquity as a way of controlling her own image would be a way of tapping into a discourse of authority from which people of colour have historically been deliberately excluded.

From this perspective, the choice of Medusa and her serpentine locks takes on extra significance. Medusa's hypothesised African origins have led to her being interpreted as a black woman with dreadlocks who was monstered by Europeans. This reading was, for instance, central to the London-based Barbadian poet Dorothea Smartt in constructing her one-woman performance piece *Medusa* in 1993:[49]

> I thought to myself: Medusa was probably some black woman with nappy hair, and some white man saw her and cried: a monster!, and feared her, and so told stories about her dangerous potential. To see her more clearly, I studied anthropology and thought about the first encounters of white men in Africa, and how they might have viewed and feared these strange and fantastic creatures: black women. What did early explorers see or think they saw? That's what I ask, in a sense, in performance.

Smartt's interpretation draws on a history of African hair which saw the enslaved Black population of the USA have their hair shaved as one of many ways to separate them from their home cultures, and then forced to improvise ways of caring for hair which significantly differed in texture to that of their White enslavers.[50] Differences in hair and skin also contributed to a hierarchy of the enslaved, where those with lighter skin and straighter hair were given easier domestic duties, and those with darker skin and more kinky, curly hair were assigned to field work. This colourism continued after emancipation, as wider society was more accepting of those Blacks with lighter skins and straighter hair, hence the promulgation of skin-whitening products and hair treatments which promised to smooth the way to jobs, marriages and social integration. The painful history behind Black hair means that it is still categorised as 'good' or 'bad', depending on how kinky or frizzy it is, and that 'nappy' hair can be used as an insult.

There were kick-backs against the imposition of this White beauty standard on Black bodies, not least since multiple hair cultures exist among the African American community. In the interwar period, the women of the Church of God in Christ, a Pentecostal denomination, showed their commitment to the Holy Spirit and living a Sanctified life through their external appearance, meaning their plain clothes and unprocessed hair set them apart from other Black women in urban areas.[51] For a brief period in the 1960s, the rise of the Black Power movement made wearing natural hair and Afros an explicitly political sign of racial pride, particularly on college campuses. Even though the gradual acceptance of more natural styles by mainstream White culture opened up styling options, Black women still experience the regular microaggression of people touching their hair without permission – this kind of unwanted encounter is so common that one artist even made a video game to highlight its ubiquity.[52]

In this context, possessing serpents as hair changes the rules of the game. By choosing to become Medusa, Rihanna inverts the standard associations of 'good' hair with straightness and pliability, embracing the inherent unruliness of snakes. They have the autonomy to resist any form of control which might be imposed on them, departing from hierarchies of hair texture in the most extreme of ways. Yet, should these exotic locks be treated as public property, to be approached without permission, to be touched without warning, then they will not passively stand for it. They will bite back. They embody the threat and disorder that Whiteness sees in Black women's hair and, in turn, offer protection from the institutionalised systems of violence which have historically devalued and damaged wearers of such hair.

Finally, the Medusa myth had particular weight for Rihanna personally in 2013. In March 2009, following the wide circulation of photographs showing Rihanna's badly bruised face, her partner, the singer Chris Brown, was charged with assault and making criminal threats. Brown pleaded guilty to felony assault in June. Rihanna cultivated a public persona which acknowledged her past abuse whilst linking it to erotic violence as a sexual preference, in particular in her albums *Rated R* (2009) and *Loud* (2010), the latter of which began with a song titled 'S&M'.[53] The couple seemed to be reconsidering their relationship throughout 2012, with Rihanna confirming to *Rolling Stone* in January 2013 that they had started dating again. Brown stated that the relationship had ended in

May. The Medusa shoot took place in September, after first being mooted two months earlier.

Rihanna had spent the four years before the shoot at the centre of a highly visible discussion about domestic violence, fuelled by the celebrity gossip industry and the increasing prominence of social media. Her identity as a victim/survivor/enabler had been debated and dissected in hundreds of forums, with varying degrees of sympathy. Many felt that she had been too lenient to Brown in light of his behaviour towards her, actively rejecting approved social patterns for handling perpetrators.[54] To take on the identity of one of the most famous victims of sexual violence in the ancient world, to bring her back to life, and to unapologetically stand in the public eye, daring the public to look back, becomes a further statement in the dialogue between Rihanna and her public, another element in her star image. By taking on the power of the monster, in an explicitly fantastic way, she augments the fantasies of female violence and revenge against abusive men which had featured in her post-Brown albums – only, this time, her gaze extends her revenge to everyone who seeks to dehumanise her, not just her perpetrator.

***

Tracing tendrils of the Medusa story helps us see points of particular power within the narrative, where the monster can most easily burst out and reimagine herself. Certainly, the underlying myth has a general structure, with a fixed grammar and sequence of events. However, just as ancient writers in antiquity were quite comfortable with exploring mythic variants, so modern receptions develop from different nodes in the narrative pathway, helping the monster to modify whichever aspect of its monstrosity is most adaptable. The moment of Medusa's beheading and death belongs to Perseus, and as such places Medusa as the antagonist who must be defeated, regardless of where and when that tale is told. Yet, the danger of her gaze, the horror of her rape and her inherent duality between human and non-human all offer powerful and fertile spaces from which new incarnations can spring.

Lost in the Minotaur's Maze

*The scandal of the family grew, and the abominable adultery of the mother lay
exposed by the strangeness of a monster with double form; Minos resolved to
remove the shame from his marriage, and to imprison it within a home with
many winding places and lightless dwellings.*

Ovid, *Metamorphoses* 8.155–8

The Minotaur, so we are told, was born of a bestial union between human and
animal, and from man's greed. To gain the throne of Crete, Minos sacrificed to
Poseidon, asking for a sign that the gods wished him to become king. Poseidon
sent a magnificent bull from the sea, but instead of sacrificing it as he had
promised, Minos kept it for himself and substituted another animal. The gods do
not look kindly on those who disregard their vows, and Poseidon was no
exception. In revenge, he made Minos' wife Pasiphae burn with desire for the
bull. To sate her longing, unnatural both in object and cause, she enlisted the
master craftsman Daedalus, who created for her a hollow wooden cow, covered
with cowhide. As she sat in it, the bull came and mated with her as if with a real
cow. Of this cross-species union, the Minotaur was born, half-man and half-bull,
a sign of Minos' disgrace. Minos had recourse to Daedalus once again, who built
a winding labyrinth in which the king shut the monster, away from the eyes of
all, but not forgotten – an Athenian tribute of young men and women was
brought every year and fed to the beast, until Theseus, newly acknowledged
prince of Athens, came as tribute and left as conqueror, taking the Minotaur's
half-sister Ariadne with him.

The myth of the Minotaur, compared to that of Medusa, is comparatively
stable in our ancient sources.[1] Sometimes he is named Asterios, other times
simply called the Minotaur. Hyginus tells us Pasiphae's passion came as
punishment from Venus, to whom she had not sacrificed for many years.[2]
Bestiality remains the penalty for dishonouring the gods. The tales which spiral
off the Minotaur – Theseus's journey home in his ill-starred, ill-sailed ship,

Ariadne's abandonment, Daedalus' imprisonment and Icarus' disastrous flight – all spring from the core narrative in which the Minotaur is created by human folly, contained by parental shame and fed on human flesh.

Ovid refers to the Minotaur as a 'half-bull man and a half-man bull' (*Ars Amatoria* 2.24); visual representations in children's books capture the variety made possible by this description. Some give the Minotaur a perfectly human body and a bull's head, while others have him transforming at the waist.[3] While some modern representations keep him a ravening monster whose defeat by Theseus marks a just end to a reign of terror, others explore the experience of being trapped inside a prison through no fault of your own. Reading the Minotaur sympathetically leads to explorations of what life would be like for the monster outside the labyrinth – although often the two are inextricably linked.

Psychoanalytical readings of the Minotaur myth have been as prominent as those of Medusa. A Freudian interpretation of the myth sees the labyrinth as the human psyche, the place for shutting away the bestial within ourselves; retracing Theseus' steps, we defeat the Minotaur as an act of repression – yet one which does not defeat the true monster, that which is us, since we have projected it onto the beast we have killed.[4] There's a symbolic appeal to seeing the human mind as a labyrinth with a monster at its heart to be unravelled, particularly as an allegory for the psyche seeking to come to grips with the brutish repressed but always fearing its return. Jung saw the Minotaur as one of the embodiments of the fearful Great Mother, which the hero must defeat on his journey to an independent self, with entry to the labyrinth as a symbolic return to the womb. The power of this image for understanding our battles with our inner monsters has been particularly appealing in the post-psychoanalytic era. Picasso's work, for instance, shows us a Minotaur who loves, drinks, sleeps and rapes, using the monster as an allegorical way to articulate the painter's feelings about masculinity and power (Fig. 8.1).

Arthur Evans' excavations at Knossos in Crete in the early 1900s offered a further imaginative route into the legend. The Minotaur's mythological link to Crete meant that the compelling archaeological finds from the dig – including wall paintings of bull leapers and the richly decorated bull's head rhyton (libation vessel) made from serpentinite – created fertile ground for aetiological reimaginings of the myth. To put it another way, the evocative finds allowed authors to ask what the *real* story behind the Minotaur was. One deeply influential example (certainly as far as I am concerned) was Mary Renault's *The King Must Die* (1958), told in the first person from Theseus' perspective, where 'Minotaur' becomes the honorific title used for the king's heir, and the fearsome half-bull half-man is created by a ceremonial mask, made of gold with glistening

Fig. 8.1 The 'Minotauro bebiendo con una muchacha' (Minotaur drinking with a girl) by Pablo Picasso.

crystal eyes. The possibility of recapturing the 'true' story of the monster, not a particularly prominent feature in responses to Medusa, presents a different avenue for popular culture to explore what the beast inside the human might look like.

As with Medusa, I am not attempting to create a comprehensive chart of monster sightings, to catalogue and classify within precise limits (only to become obsolete as soon as the manuscript reaches my publisher). Rather, I want to outline the landscape, the plains and the ridges, which characterise the terrain that the Minotaur travels over. In what follows, I will not go back over ground covered in the discussions of the cinematic Minotaur in Chapters 3 and 4; instead, I move into new territory.

Minotaurs in London

What do place and space have to say to the Minotaur, whose is as closely tied to his labyrinth as Dick Whittington is to London? The Minotaur finds himself relocated to London with a perhaps surprising frequency. The meeting between monster and city seems at first sight a little anomalous, but comparing three examples of different Minotaurs (and different Londons) brings to the surface some central issues at stake in the decisions that popular culture makes about representing the creature.

The first example occurs in Neil Gaiman's *Neverwhere* (1996), in which Richard Mayhew is pulled down from the capital into the parallel city of London Below; he must fight through many trials in order to save his companion, the Lady Door, and, in the process, he begins to belong more to the lower city than the upper. One significant point in this journey occurs when he and his companions must pass through a labyrinth inhabited by the Beast of London. This episode owes much to the Minotaur myth, not least because the word 'labyrinth' is used to describe the Beast's dwelling place. When Richard and his companions first see the beast, the description is deliberately and vastly bestial – Richard thinks, 'It was the size of an ox, of a bull elephant, of a lifetime.'[5] The Beast expands to contain all possible beasts, goring one of Richard's companions, and when Richard kills it, his overwhelming sensory experience is of 'the shit-and-blood animal stench of it'.[6] Richard anoints his eyes and tongue with the blood of the dead animal, which allows him to navigate the labyrinth with ease. At a stretch, one might see this as a distant echo of the rituals held in the Mithraeum discovered under London's streets in honour of the god Mithras, an idea gathered from a shared consciousness of the city's history.

The Minotaur myth underpins the connection between location and monster that *Neverwhere* builds in this episode. The good old-fashioned blood magic Richard performs to take the blood of the conquered and acquire its powers for himself means that previously uninterpretable space becomes simple and familiar. The act of tasting the Beast's blood, too, is represented as totally natural. Richard has had a repeated dream of killing the Beast, and when the dream is realised, in a sense Richard comes home – the experience is not alien but instead embedded within his identity. This pivotal moment grounds him in London Below, a space against which he has struggled since he entered it, and where, ultimately, he will be more at home than in London Above. The Beast shares the Minotaur's deep associations with the labyrinth as well as its horrendous bestiality.

A Freudian reading, too, aligns the Beast of London with the Minotaur. The Beast is trapped deep below the city – buried, as it were, beneath. The battle with the Beast can be read as a battle with the repressed, with Richard rising glorious as a newly incarnated saviour;[7] his victory means Richard sheds the last vestiges of supposed civilisation and instead is freed to participate in the more 'genuine', and certainly more sincere, society of London Below. *Neverwhere*'s encounter with the Minotaur story is less about the Minotaur itself and more about the psychological shorthand it provides as part of a hero's journey. In order for the monster to do the work of the repressed, it materialises as utterly bestial, the complete antithesis of Richard's sanitised and smugly sophisticated life in London Above.

Sara Douglass takes a completely different direction in *Hades' Daughter* (2002), the first in the Troy Game quartet. The central conceit is that the golden period of the ancient world existed because cities had mystical labyrinths built into their foundations; Ariadne destroyed them in revenge after Theseus abandoned her on Naxos. A new labyrinth was almost built under what is currently St. Paul's, but Asterion, the Minotaur, had conserved enough strength to prevent its completion. The quartet traces characters through a series of reincarnations as they fight either to complete the Troy Game or to destroy the Labyrinth entirely. Over the centuries, the positions of the characters change. The flash-forwards in *Hades' Daughter* to the Blitz, when the fourth book is set, do not reflect the gradual transformation of Asterion and his position as an ally rather than an antagonist as the characters seek to defeat the Troy Game itself, which has grown self-willed and powerful beyond all measure. However, Asterion's introduction in the first volume sits at the other end of the spectrum to *Neverwhere*'s Beast.

Asterion is positioned as the antagonist from the outset of the quartet. Ariadne made a pact with him that he would teach her the magic of darkcraft she needed to destroy Theseus if she would destroy the Game and accept his rule over her. She betrays him when her descendants begin to build a new labyrinth in which to trap him. His quest for revenge and then for control of the Game drives the first phase of the quartet's plot. The first time we encounter him is when Ariadne summons him after his death, and realises the damage that Theseus did to him:

> Theseus' sword had cut into Asterion's body in eight or nine places: across his thickly muscled black throat, his shoulder, his chest, both his flanks, laying open his belly. The wounds were now bloodless lips of flesh, opening and closing as Asterion's chest rose and fell in breath (*and why did he need to breathe at all, now that he is dead?*), revealing a rope of bowel here, a lung there, a yellowed cord of tendon elsewhere.
>
> Ariadne swallowed, then very slowly lifted up her eyes back to Asterion's magnificent head.
>
> It was undamaged, and for that she was profoundly grateful. The beautiful, liquid black eyes still regarded her clearly and steadily from the bold countenance of the bull, and his graceful horns still curved unbroken about his broad brow.[8]

Reading about a monster is a different experience to seeing it on screen; our first encounter with Asterion is framed with an uncanny vivacity, exploiting the taboo Ariadne breaks by summoning him back from the dead. Given that the reader cannot look at him, the description needs to help generate a mental vision of the character, and is thus marked by his physicality. The transition between bull and human is seamless – Ariadne marks no break in physical continuity, the breaks instead appearing in Asterion's skin. The emphasis on the physical will prove to be thematically significant. Asterion goes on to inflict plenty of damage on other people's bodies in subsequent books, but he also takes on the *form* of other bodies, almost possessing them, an ability all the central characters in *Hades' Daughter* possess. The boundary between flesh and identity becomes porous, although the person remains the same.

Ariadne's description of Asterion's appearance is both hideous and yet a surprisingly loving way to look at a corpse. The horror comes from his butchered torso rather than his hybridity, and the beauty of his physique counterbalances the carnage with desire; his bloodless wounds are themselves sites of hideous appeal. Asterion's bull shape is secondary in making him monstrous. Rather, his monstrosity is expressed through his moral character. His possession of speech, despite his bull head, lets him plot and scheme. Throughout *Hades' Daughter*, he is characterised as articulate and intelligent, goading his opponents to nudge them into an error. One such occasion happens in a flashforward to the Blitz, when Asterion appears in his true form, 'his naked, muscular man's body topped with the blue-black head of the bull'.[9] He is heard before he is seen, moving out of the shadows when challenged before vanishing into London fog. When he holds his interlocutor by the chin, the physical contact is a gesture of power and control. The bull's head becomes almost kingly.

While the main locus of Asterion's monstrosity is his desire for power, the labyrinth exerts its pull on all the characters, drawing them back to St. Paul's and the city of London. The repetitive curves of a labyrinth are mimicked both in the repeating arcs of the narrative and the steps of the characters rewalking the plot – Asterion's monstrosity becomes manifest in his desire to control these moves in the Game, making him bestial in his violence but frighteningly human in his ability to scheme, manipulate and abuse. Given that fundamentally he is positioned as deviously and hideously human, with his bull's head incidental to his terror, the passage of the centuries allows Asterion the space to transfer his affections to his daughter – and, in the process, the quartet reveals that the true monster is not the Minotaur, but the Troy Game itself.

The third example I want to use to triangulate our initial mapping comes from Charlie Fletcher's *Stoneheart* (2006), again the first of a trilogy. *Stoneheart* is a Young Adult novel, and operates on the central conceit that the statues in London come to life and feud between themselves. The statue 'gangs' are divided into humans, known as spits, and non-humans, known as taints. The trilogy's protagonist is a teenager called George, who discovers he has inherited the power to be a Maker from his recently deceased sculptor father. *Stoneheart* tracks how he adapts to this new reality, alongside his new friends Edie, a glint or person with the ability to plunge back into the past, and the Gunner, one of the statues from the Royal Artillery Monument at Hyde Park Corner. He is also pursued by the London Stone, rather brilliantly cast as the book's villain with the help of its henchman the Elizabethan alchemist John Dee, now known as the Walker. The pair send a number of taints after George, culminating with Michael Ayrton's statue of the Minotaur located in the Barbican (Fig. 8.2).

Fig. 8.2 'Minotaur' by Michael Ayrton in the Barbican, London.

When the statue is first set on George's trail, the reader is given a lengthy description to help them visualise it:

> Above it crouched a powerful figure, black and shiny in the rain, the wetness coursing over its hunched and massive body, reflecting the surrounding streetlights. It was an unmistakably male figure; below the waist, a man with strong over-muscled legs bent to spring out of the rushes at any unwary passer-by. But his principal feature was in the predominance of muscle and bulk curving up from the waist; not the muscle of a man, but the raw brutal power and bulk of a full-grown bull. The shoulders hunched massively below a bull's head topped by aggressively pointing horns; and so well had the sculptor shaped it, that the sound of enraged snorting seemed to lurk about it, even though it never – to the normal eye – moved or breathed at all.[10]

The description of the sculpture as 'unmistakably male' is a child-friendly euphemism to describe the erect phallus on the actual statue, no doubt a surprise to parents taking their children on the walking tour suggested by the map in the book's frontispiece. Yet, *Stoneheart* shares the same fascination with the physicality of the Minotaur as my previous two examples, and finds other ways of articulating the underlying sexuality which the statue so visually embodies. The point of transition for this Minotaur between the creature and the man occurs not at the neck but at the waist – its heart and mind are all bull.

When this Minotaur snatches Edie as a way to entrap George, the interaction between its twin identities of man and beast becomes obvious. The statue cannot speak, emitting 'a bull-roar of pure fury and hunger and sound' as it grabs her, evoking her hard-wired fear and communicating the Minotaur's own 'keening pain'.[11] It does not have the grasp of language that Asterion does, relying on animalistic sounds and noises which explain why it is aligned with the taints rather than the spits. However, it later displays rational judgement through its behaviour as it appreciatively smells Edie, licks her to almost provide a taste test, and paws her flesh 'like a butcher testing his meat'.[12] The statue's human intelligence expresses itself through the unmistakable actions of a creature anticipating dinner. The human traits which facilitate the desire to consume, communicated by acts of smell, taste and touch, signal that the Minotaur's monstrosity goes beyond its physical appearance.

Another form of monstrosity is more subtly communicated, given the intended audience of the novel, but is equally as pressing. The language of leering and panting, of groping and heavy breathing, positions this Minotaur as both a hungry hunter and a sexual predator. Where Medusa's sexual threat sometimes came from her own sexual agency, the Minotaur's comes from actual sexual violence. The novel drops pointed hints about the Minotaur's inclinations: the Walker comments that children excite the Minotaur's appetites and threatens that he will let the bull do whatever it wants to 'the girl-child'. The Gunner offers a vague 'not as such' to George's question about whether the Minotaur will eat Edie, and asks whether George knows what the Minotaur does to little girls.[13] Edie is about twelve, so multiple layers of monstrosity are implied in the Minotaur's unspoken desire. That initial signifier of being 'unmistakably male' finds a way to express its toxic half-man half-bull masculinity through the traces of an inexpressible sexuality, drawn precisely from the point at which the transition from man to bull occurs.

What becomes clear through the novel is that division is an essential characteristic of the statue's monstrosity. As the Gunner explains the nature of their new enemy to George, 'man half of him hates the bull part, and the bull part thinks the man part's what makes it unhappy'.[14] Being pulled between two identities, the literal incarnation of Ovid's half-man half-bull, means the statue suffers eternal conflict. The second novel in the *Stoneheart* trilogy, *Ironhand* (2007), casts further light on this internal schism when Ayrton's statue of Icarus begins to hunt down George and Edie for killing the Minotaur. The Minotaur 'had the same mad split at its core' as the Icarus, while the Icarus cannot understand 'who or what it was – man, machine, animal or bird ... that's why it lived its life in a scream'.[15] While the Minotaur statue reached some kind of internal truce to follow the London Stone's bidding, the Icarus, trapped inside its wing mechanism, has been pushed into permanent mental incapacity by its inability to reconcile its warring parts. What this tells us about the Minotaur is that the split between man and beast is a fundamental psychological characteristic which tears its identity apart. The monstrosity that accompanies it exists as much inside its own head as in the world. The two statues also raise the question of the moral responsibility of their Maker, who created these creatures with this fundamentally unliveable discontinuity in their identities; the final volume of the trilogy, *Silvertongue* (2009), explores what precisely makes a statue a taint or a spit, further asking how permeable the boundaries between human and non-human become within the artistic practice of sculpture.

Reading these three manifestations of the Minotaur myth brings out the importance of place for the story. All three are set in London, which offers a particularly fertile place for reimagining the labyrinth. A simple comparison of the street maps of the City of London and, for instance, downtown Manhattan brings out the straight lines of the one and the twists and curves of the other, while the winding map and corridors of the Tube's underground world can be daunting to a novice user. The city offers a historical palimpsest, layers upon layers of past history down to the London Mithraeum and beyond. The current Crossrail construction project and expectations that building work excavations will take archaeology into account are making the richness of London's past even more visible, reminding us of the stories under our feet. London becomes pliant and flexible, and in turn tells us something about where contemporary culture feels monstrous fights for identity take place – in arguably *the* urban jungle of the Anglophone world. City environments surround us with threats to our sense of who we are, dislocate us from our communities and place us under pressure. The Minotaur dwells in London because that is where we fear demons are lurking, waiting to devour our young. The hero in these three narratives somehow comes to understand himself in a city which offers the same fundamental challenges as the ancient labyrinth in its modern architecture. Other spaces in which the Minotaur appears may make themselves equally revealing.

A second point of interaction is the question of how hybridity plays out in practical terms. What does it *mean* to be half-human, half-beast? Which part of you makes decisions? I come back again to Ovid's description of the half-man bull and the half-bull man, capturing both the dilemma and the fascination of this monster, the fundamental boundary crossing between human and not human, and where individual manifestations place the Minotaur on that possible spectrum. *Neverwhere* removes the human entirely, focusing on the beast in the maze to be conquered and so transcended. *Hades' Daughter* gives us a Minotaur who might as well be human, whose monstrous aspect becomes visible only rarely, although he is known by his deeds. *Stoneheart* treads the middle path, where the monster and the man are embodied in equal measure, fighting for control and never achieving it, instead coming to an uneasy truce. The ratio of beast to human becomes an important factor for the monster's actions, its decisions and the agency which it can display.

A parallel practical issue surrounds how to depict the Minotaur's body, and how to handle that issue of boundary crossing. What is to be done about the physical aspects of the beast, not least of all its genitalia? *Stoneheart*'s elegant ellipsis displaces the discovery from the text; *Hades' Daughter* fetishises Asterion's corpse before undermining issues of bodily integrity completely through the plot device of reincarnation. *Neverwhere* avoids the question by going all beast. Writers have a choice about what to show and how to show it, while film makers cannot evade the issue. Given the sensibilities of their target audiences, one can understand why those dealing with screens tend to send their Minotaur out in a loincloth.

A third general theme comes from the way in which the Minotaur is inevitably tied to questions about masculinity, whether through the need of a Theseus-figure to vanquish it and prove his authority, or through its own sexual appetites. In *Hades' Daughter*, Asterion's strong sexual drives eventually temper themselves as part of a move towards domesticity and a paternal protectiveness towards his daughter, the long cycle of the years engendering a transformation from beast to civilised being. Richard cannot reclaim his own masculinity without conquering the Beast of London. The traces of sexual violence in *Stoneheart* cast dark shadows in a YA novel, but once again come back to this feeling that the Minotaur is a monster inseparable from powerful and dangerous masculinity.

The three versions help us understand which points in the Minotaur story attract attention, and which deflect it. One almost deafening silence emerges over the question of the Minotaur's origins. *Stoneheart* gets around this by discussing the Minotaur-as-statue rather than the Minotaur-as-being, shifting questions of origin onto the Minotaur's Maker rather than requiring the target audience of children to engage with the tricky issue of bestiality. *Hades' Daughter* mentions that Asterion is Ariadne's half-brother, but that is as far as the discussion of his parentage goes, and there is no mention of what caused him to have a bull's head in the first place.[16] The narrative of rebirth into a fully human body elides the need to discuss his original shape. Given the amount of sexual violence that the novel otherwise is happy to narrate, often in graphic detail, the evasion of the taboo of interspecies sex is even more marked. Should the reader consult the glossary at the end of the book, the entry for Asterion reads 'the name of the Minotaur at the heart of the Cretan labyrinth, son of King Minos' wife and a white bull, and thus half-brother to ARIADNE, the MISTRESS OF THE LABYRINTH' – the dry recitation of basic mythological facts defuses the need to engage in imaginative reconstruction. *Neverwhere*, by allusively referring to the Minotaur through the Beast, is able to pass over the issue entirely.

Another key narrative moment is the Minotaur's conquest and defeat, which reflects almost a post-Freudian cultural consensus of seeing the Minotaur as representing deep and personal inner demons which we must overcome in order to become our true selves. This emphasis on what the myth 'means' inevitably lends itself to a particularly irredeemable monster, and a hero whose victory is presented as critical for the survival of the world. Richard's defeat of the Beast of London not only cements his developing identity as a hero-saviour, but is an essential step in thwarting the Angel Islington's quest for world domination. The Troy Game in *Hades' Daughter* seeks to trap not just the Minotaur but all the world's evil within the labyrinth, making Asterion the symbolic embodiment of perfect wickedness (although that quality will gradually transfer to the Troy Game itself). *Stoneheart* requires George to trust in his own power as Maker to form the bullet that saves him and Edie from certain death at the Minotaur's hands, facing up to the truth about his identity. The instrumental nature of the Minotaur as a figure of evil to be overcome invests the central moment of monster-hero conflict with wider psychological significance.

As a counterpoint to this fascination with the act of despatch, two of these retellings also gravitate to the question of what happens *after* the hero's moment of truth. Certainly, the *hero's* use for the beast is fulfilled at that point, but what happens to the beast itself? *Stoneheart* partially evades the issue of death by using the conceit of statues, allowing the Minotaur statue to both be and not be its mythical predecessor and giving the monster a life which has not been cut short by Theseus. *Hades' Daughter*, by contrast, not only frames the Minotaur's death at Theseus' hands as one of the central betrayals within the wider quartet, but revels in the question of what the Minotaur's afterlives look like as Asterion bounds from body to body, both himself and not himself as he wreaks havoc. The question of what the Minotaur does after Theseus perhaps arises from a natural comparison with his sister, Ariadne. We know what happened to her after Theseus, who took her half-way to Athens and abandoned her on the beach of Naxos, to the tender mercies of the wild god Dionysus. To wonder what happened to the Minotaur, what really happened in the maze between the hero and the monster, and whether the hero told the truth, becomes a possibility in a world where the indisputable authority of the patriarchal story has finally become questionable. Equally, the Freudian approach itself invites this opportunity – just as the monster always resurrects itself, the animal drives within the human psyche are never fully extinguished, merely suppressed. That the Minotaur will return, somehow, in some guise, is an inevitability if it has come to represent our deepest inner psychological conflicts.

A myth in the modern world

One quite extraordinary manifestation of the Minotaur, which both respects and rejects these nodes of connection, comes in Steven Sherrill's *The Minotaur Takes a Cigarette Break* (2003). The novel is set in contemporary North Carolina and charts the day-to-day life of the Minotaur, or M, as he gets by working as a line cook, living in a trailer park and mending cars for his landlord as part-contribution to the rent. *Cigarette Break* follows the Minotaur as he attempts to interact with humans, deal with misunderstandings, and find a space to live within an increasingly complicated world which has no room for him. Although initially it appears that nobody notices his bull's head, people then appear to notice but gloss over it, until he encounters children asking honest questions and testosterone-driven teenagers who mock his appearance without understanding the consequences. The mythological monster is embodied and active, yet also unreal, in that his powers have dimmed over the preceding centuries, and he is now too tired to create the sort of carnage he once could.

It is not just the Minotaur who lives like this. M watches a television advert for a telephone escort service run by Hermaphroditus, which creates a surge of recognition in him and is the reader's first sign that this might be a mythologically complex world.[17] Later, he meets a dryad working as a clerk in a petrol station with a name badge indicating she is called Laurel, who has all the physical signs of her mythical self but experiences no echo of recognition when she looks into the Minotaur's face.[18] She, it seems, has forgotten her past completely, while the Minotaur himself often notes the fuzziness which has intervened in his memories. While initially one is inclined to put this down to the mix of man and bull in his psychology, the meeting with Laurel indicates that this may be a result of the passing of time. As a more detailed understanding of this world emerges, it becomes clear that prejudice against 'freaks' of mythology is as rife as prejudice against other minority groups.

This interface between myth and reality reflects the ancient Greek under-standing of supernatural space, the possibility that at any moment you might round a corner and come face to face with a god or monster (just as a child runs around the corner of a drugstore aisle and barrels into the Minotaur's hip).[19] The challenge then becomes, given the erosion of the space between the ancient labyrinth and the modern city, how this mythical creature inhabits a non-mythical space. The novel's italicised prologue concerning 'bargains struck' closes with 'from the back the Minotaur skulks into a tepid eternity; high, the costs of living'.[20] Tepidity is precisely the word for the Minotaur's modern existence, grounded in simple rituals and habits, things which might have seemed or could have become extraordinary washing over him into the waves of undifferentiated time behind him.

The nature of the boundary between human and bull is outlined through the minutely detailed account of the Minotaur's grooming ritual, a celebration of meditative monotony.[21] He uses a currycomb to attend to his fur, followed by veterinary conditioning oil, with special balm at the place where his body transitions from one to the other, and grooms his horns with a knife, sandpaper and an emery cloth. The point of transition, the bodily sign of change, 'remains tender, painful at times'.[22] Earlier in the novel, it is described as 'scarlike' while the 'transitional skin' is 'gray and flaky', the line primarily visible under his pectorals with a contrasting change of skin colouration on his back.[23] His vestigial tail, the last detail of bodily otherness the reader learns about, is revealed only in a moment of deep personal vulnerability.[24] The preoccupation with the Minotaur's body is underscored by the way in which, for instance, his horns constantly get in his way in chairs, cars and narrow corridors, and by two serious physical accidents he suffers as part of his work as a line cook. The nature of embodiment, of being trapped in a body which behaves in different ways and follows different rules, becomes a central focus for the Minotaur's actions and motivations, mirroring to some extent his ponderous thought-processes as they try to bring together the simple desires of the bull with the complex drives of a human.

It will come as no surprise that one of these drives is sex, which pervades the novel – in a dream sequence, the Minotaur even dreams of Pasiphae in her 'moment of cramped ecstasy', coming as close to bestiality as any of the case studies in this chapter.[25] Yet the Minotaur does not become the marker for the exaggerated hypermasculinity we might expect. While he is comfortable with some of the sexualised banter among the kitchen staff, he is put off-balance by strongly performative jock masculinity and casual objectification of women when he spends a Monday afternoon with two of the waitstaff. Although his own sexual encounters have, in the past, been numerous and not always consensual, the novel makes it clear that although he may have urges, he is now more discerning. Those urges lead him to two intimate encounters with his colleagues (both waitstaff rather than kitchen workers), which both end in differently disastrous ways.

I pause to note the decoupling between M's sexuality and monstrosity, particularly as he is overtly interpreted as bisexual. Given the explicit link between queer identity and monstrosity that has been well established in American popular culture, as well as a general tendency to erase bisexual identities, the narrative's acceptance of M's choice of partners takes the reader on a queer journey which does not rely on the gender identities of those involved to generate catastrophe. The problems instead arise from M's own struggles with interpersonal relationships.

The first encounter, with David, an enthusiastic Civil War reenactor, is a disappointment more in terms of results than in consequences. After going over to David's flat late one evening, the Minotaur and David spend the night curled up together on David's Murphy bed. In the morning, the Minotaur leaves while

David feigns sleep.[26] Although they spend the night lying next to each other fully clothed, the experience has all the emotional intimacy of a one-night stand. When David and the Minotaur meet at work the following day, David has no intention of discussing what happened, and the Minotaur leaves the next steps in his hands.[27] David's emotional awkwardness, coupled with his perceived effeminacy, combine to make the encounter a failure in terms of sexual outcomes, but a success in that the relationship between the Minotaur and David is not damaged, and neither seems harmed by the encounter. The act of celibate intimacy, of allowing his partner to decide the way forward, marks the Minotaur's engagement with the sensual.

Indirectly, this encounter makes the second possible, since it leads to one of the waitstaff stripping off in the restaurant as the Minotaur is carving a side of beef, distracting him and making him cut deep into his thumb with the carving knife. His colleague Kelly offers to take him to an emergency clinic. She talks without really waiting for the Minotaur to say anything, fills in his paperwork and comes with him as the wound is stitched together. As she drives the Minotaur home, Kelly volunteers that her step-father is black, although he cannot work out why it seems so important to her to say this;[28] presumably is an awkward way to bridge the gap between them by signalling that she is comfortable with people who are somehow other, picking up on established racialised links between monsters and darker skin tones.[29] The Minotaur then plucks up the courage to tell her his day off is Monday, and they agree to meet.[30]

On their first date, for date it is, the Minotaur enters Kelly's apartment, and views her collection of fancy goldfish, although as the narrator observes, this is a deceptive term:

> But the word *goldfish* can be misleading, as can *beautiful*. Most of the fish have very little gold in their colouring. And the characteristics enhanced by breeding and eagerly sought by aquarists could just as easily fall on the other side of that tenuous aesthetic line and into the domain of the horrific.[31]

While the link between Kelly's passionate parenting of her fancy goldfish and her relationship with the Minotaur is never made explicit, her affection and devotion to her fish maps onto her sympathy and openness to the Minotaur's body. Their second encounter outside work comes when the Minotaur drops by her apartment to find her setting up a hospital tank for one of the fish suffering from dropsy, which subsequently dies; in a combination of *eros* and *thanatos*, the drives towards life and death that Freud argued powered all human behaviour, in her grief Kelly kisses the Minotaur, which opens up the way for a physical sexual encounter (all the while, the Minotaur watches the clock, worried about being late for work).

Again, it is Kelly rather than the Minotaur who initiates this development, and the first stages of the encounter go well.[32] She traces the Minotaur's scar of transition with her tongue, 'sweet rapture'.[33] Her reaction to the tail, of which he is embarrassed, and of which the reader has so far been unaware, is, 'this is amazing', honouring his body for its reality rather than what she thinks it should be (perhaps this is why David, in contrast, froze).[34] However, as he becomes caught up in the moment, M misses some important physical and verbal signs that Kelly is beginning to have a seizure. He watches, detached yet worried, as the seizure takes its course – and then, his brain operating more as bull than man, he checks she is breathing, gets dressed, and (in what seems to him an obvious move) takes her money so that he can use it to buy a corn dog trailer his landlord is selling in which they can travel around the country together, a new start for them both.

His failure to explain that this is what he is doing, to Kelly or anyone else, leads to the novel's climactic ending, when a group of angry co-workers and Kelly arrive at his trailer and he risks branding or worse; the mood is that of a lynch mob. However, when M's landlord emerges from his trailer, he reads the situation and understands M's intent without explanation. He defuses a hostile situation into one which is shamblingly embarrassed about itself and, as it dissipates, offers hope for the new business partnership. *Cigarette Break* takes us perilously close to the edge of violence, of breaking open the past and returning to the half-memories, except with the Minotaur in the position of victim rather than as perpetrator, led down the wrong road by the bull in him. It is human intervention, his landlord's perception and familiarity with the beast, which reframes him:

> But standing there in his torn pajamas, his dirty shirt, his heavy shoes, the Minotaur in all of his bullishness seems something other than evil now, seems vulnerable, seems pitifully human.[35]

Being bull and human, needing to find ways of living that negotiate the divide, to manage the confusions and the misunderstandings which nearly go so catastrophically wrong, are part of the Minotaur's life now. To continue being part of the modern world, he must find a way to be himself in a society which offers precious little sympathy.

It is not just people who pose this challenge, as his continual perturbation with automatic doors illustrates:

This might be taken as a portent for his perpetually diminishing ability to fit in, to function in a world rapidly growing dependent on technology. But he doesn't think that far ahead.[36]

As I read this passage, I found myself marvelling at a piece of classical reception that is wondering how much longer this sort of classical reception can go on – how can the Minotaur survive in a world where technology is taking over, where, *Cigarette Break* seems to suggest, space for him will soon disappear?[37] Yet, funnily enough, it is precisely in cyberspace that the Minotaur finds another space in which to manifest.

Technological minotaurs

Given the nature of cyberspace as fundamentally undefined and easy to get lost in, along with the sense that computers are themselves somehow complex and unknowable, the properties of modern technology are fertile soil for the Minotaur. The monster has been making space for itself in this realm since technology started to appear in popular culture.

For instance, Stephen Coonts' novel *The Minotaur* (1989) is a Cold War-era thriller which revolves around a secret design for a new Navy aeroplane, and a leak within the Pentagon, code-named the Minotaur, who is passing information on top-secret military projects to the Soviets. It is fair to say that the technology upon which the hacking depends has not aged well; the wonder of the hero, Jake Grafton, at the powers of a floppy disc and password now raise a smile rather than the astonishment which it presumably did at the time of publication. However, the maze-like web of technology which the supposed hacker must navigate within the Pentagon's security system remains labyrinthine, as does the building itself – when Jake arrives, he gets lost in its twisting passages at least once. The irony is that there was never actually a Minotaur at all: the mole was in fact the secretary of state, and the 'Minotaur' was a plot coordinated by the highest levels of government to smoke out Soviet sleeping agents. The Minotaur that Jake was tracking turns out to be mythical, but given the amount of carnage that the search for this non-existent figure has caused, the secretary of state certainly looks in line to inherit the monstrous mantle.

More conventionally, Alan Gibbon's novel *Shadow of the Minotaur* (2000) presents the Minotaur as both a real and cybernetic threat inside a virtual reality (VR) videogame designed by the protagonist's father. The game, a Greek myth vehicle called *The Legendeer,* turns out to be a dastardly plan to weaken the barrier between our world and that of the mysterious villain, the Gamesmaster, through the medium of video game narrative. Phoenix must embrace the peril of being sucked into the virtual world to rescue his abducted parent as well as his best friend, Laura. The final level the hero must navigate is a retelling of the story of Theseus and the Labyrinth, although the Gamesmaster and his minions do their best to change the familiar story and ensure Phoenix's doom. The Minotaur is situated as the ultimate villain, the final boss, whose defeat is critical to the player's victory.

However, the Minotaur has a looming presence right from the beginning of the book, when Phoenix accompanies his father inside the game as a beta tester. The monster becomes more and more terrifying each time Phoenix encounters it as the Gamesmaster manipulates the game-world to stack the odds against the hero, yet Phoenix always has the get-out code of 'game over!' until he enters into the game for real. The final encounter has thus been foreshadowed throughout the book. The Minotaur lurks not only in the labyrinth but also on the edges of Phoenix's mind, as he is always aware that the only way for the game to end is by facing the monster. Technology multiplies the Minotaur, allowing Phoenix to play out the battle again and again, just as a computer game can be played multiple times. The repetition of the monster is not a loop, since the Gamesmaster's constant interference ensures there is always a new twist to fighting it; for instance, the Minotaur suddenly appears with a club where he was programmed to rely only on brute force.[38] Virtual reality ensures that whenever Phoenix thinks he has figured out how the monster works, it always has another surprise for him.

Shadow would be categorised by its author as children's literature, but the line between what counts as writing for children and Young Adult fiction is generically blurry.[39] Phoenix is fourteen, so his teenage experience of gaining greater autonomy within the adult world maps onto the discovery of a new realm which operates according to unfamiliar rules and contains monsters to conquer. The Minotaur, in that sense, becomes a representation of the terror of adulthood, not least because the figures which line up against Phoenix are mainly adults, exploring the unequal power dynamic that exists in the lives of young people wobbling on the boundary of in/dependence. The Minotaur's manifestation in the realm of video games also serves as a way for the monster to access a new generation, as it comes to meet them on their ground rather than in the places their parents and grandparents frequented. This particular manifestation reinforces the way in which a monster adapts to the places and spaces which humans move to, finding ways to make itself fit into a new medium rather than being left behind.

A final technological Minotaur appears in *The Helmet of Horror*, Victor Pelevin's 2006 contribution to Canongate Books' series of short novels retelling classical myths. The novel is told entirely through the medium of an internet chat room message board, with speakers coming in and out, describing their shared experience of typing on keyboards fixed to desks, watching words appear letter by letter on screens set into the walls of the identical bedrooms they find themselves in. They eventually explore outside, each discovering their own peculiar labyrinth or landscape. The thread is initiated by a chatter called Ariadne, although all the other interlocuters are given 'internetty' names like Organizm(-: and Nutscracker. It is through Ariadne's descriptions of her dreams that the chatters begin to piece together what is going on and understand the frankly bizarre situation in which they find themselves.[40]

The Minotaur takes on a different guise for each interlocutor, changing to best suit each of them and the location in which they find themselves. He appears to Ariadne in a dream as a massive figure wearing a dark floor-length tattered robe and 'a bronze helmet, like a gladiator's mask' on his head; two horns emerge from the front of the helmet and run along the sides before merging into the back again.[41] She is also informed by one of the two dwarves that accompany him that his name is Asterisk, an obvious riff on Asterion. Romeo-y-Cohiba sees him as a tall person on roller skates wearing a sombrero, an ice hockey goalkeeper's mask, a full goalkeeper's uniform and holding a double-headed hockey stick, evocative of the double axe which decorates the bedrooms of the chatters.[42] IsoldA has a brief glimpse of a man, again extremely tall, 'dressed all in black and gold like an eighteenth-century gallant', with a mask in the shape of the sun on a stick in front of his face.[43] While each of these manifestations are peculiarly relevant to the viewer, the precise nature of that relevance is left opaque.

The only feature of the Minotaur which is consistent every time he is seen is his completely covered head. Ariadne, in a second dream, is treated to a lengthy lecture by one of the companion dwarves on the nature of this headpiece, properly called the Helmet of Horror. A complicated and (one suspects deliberately) obfuscatory discussion of the various components of the Helmet follows as the chatters try to understand how it works. Nutscracker's career background makes him think of virtual reality, and he begins a lengthy examination of the ways in which virtual reality helmets can affect perception and decision-making. He also introduces the idea of the Helmholtz, a person immersed in a VR environment, and subject to whatever the programmers decide to make them feel. The helmet, the Minotaur's key signifier, becomes about the nature of technology and our interaction with it. Just as the human–beast interface of the Minotaur originally raised questions about categorisation, the human–machine fusion takes us into the world of the cyborg and invites the reader to explore how free this supposedly liberating technology actually makes us.

The precise workings of the Helmet, and the relationship of the various chatters to its component parts, remains unclear. While some passages of *Helmet* offer precision and explanation, others serve only to confuse and baffle, so that readers following along the chat-log format are as perplexed as some of the participants themselves. The novel ends with a faux-resolution, as the chatters start to doubt the Minotaur's existence, summoning Theseus and bringing the 'traditional' myth to a close. They then recall they have a shared purpose, the goal of luring the Minotaur into the Helmet, so that everything can exist. Ideas of continuous repetition have been central to the paradoxical descriptions of how the Helmet works, again reflecting the way in which myth itself is recycled and renewed, but also highlighting the futility of that aim – whenever the chatters, in whatever incarnation, get close to bringing the Minotaur into the Helmet, he escapes. Yet, when the Minotaur has been seen, he has always been wearing the Helmet, despite one of its characteristics being that it is so stuffed full of parts that it has no room for anyone's head. Perhaps this is one way to come at the question of bestiality with which, as we have seen, fresh incarnations of the Minotaur find it so difficult to engage – instead of reflecting on the physical impossibility of conception between human and bovine, *Helmet* instead locates the unthinkable act of becoming in the interface between user and technology. If the reader cannot get their head around the relationship between the Minotaur, his helmet, the chatters and the world they occupy, then their confusion parallels the bemusement of working out the logistics of copulation, conception and birth of a beast–human hybrid child.

Technological minotaurs, then, demonstrate two conflicting qualities. From one perspective, the Minotaur finds spaces in the digital realm to make his own with ease, drawing on fresh veins of human terror in response to the threats of this unexplored territory. The appeal of the Minotaur as a vehicle for exploring this new world is perhaps best understood through comparison with the figure of the cyborg, which Donna Haraway has argued is generated where 'the boundary between human and animal is transgressed' as well as by the leaky barrier between human/animal and machine.[44] Its bridging between two domains of existence draws deeply on the sense of impossibility which the

Minotaur's parentage relies upon. Yet, at the same time, these Minotaurs seem either fixed in their tracks or evasive, discovering technology locks them into place or using its possibilities to avoid being seen. The problems encountered by CGI monsters on film, the false allure of the hyperreal, still face digital Minotaurs on the page, but written texts have built-in trapdoors which allow an escape into the digital.

Minotaurs and misunderstanding

The last place in which modern Minotaurs gather is created by the intersection of the Freudian approach to seeing the Minotaur as the monster within ourselves and the desire to aetiologise, to find the 'true story' behind the myth. In this realm of retellings, the Minotaur becomes a human with a developmental condition of some sort which makes them monstrous to those around them; monstrosity is moved from the condition that the character may have to the misunderstanding and hostility that they encounter as a result.

The Double Axe by Philip Womack (2016) is intriguingly literal and aetiological. The main plot revolves around a conspiracy to summon the shadow god to ancient Crete, and the mystical People of the Mountains manifest at significant times to ensure the downfall of this plan, but the Minotaur is a creation of fibs, gossip and half-heard rumour. The story is narrated in the first person by Deucalion Stephanos, second son and latterly heir to King Minos of Crete. He is thirteen when the book opens as he kills a white hind in a hunt, an act which brings down a curse upon the house of Minos. When he first mentions his younger brother, Asterius, he says that he will 'be in his room with his nurses', and that he wants to bring him some wooden toys he has whittled, giving the impression that Asterius is a toddler.[45] When we meet him in person, again Stephan describes him using language which might apply to a younger child:

> My little brother Aster was sitting by the side on a stool, clutching his nurse's hand. He moaned – even he could tell something bad was happening. I went over to him and stroked his head, and from my pouch gave him the little wooden toys I'd made. He rocked back and forth, and set them out on the ground.[46]

Stephan eventually mentions that Asterius is in fact ten, and he is described as ill or sick. A promise of healing convinces Minos and Pasiphae to hand him over to the high priestess Myrrah and agree to the sacrifice of the tributes from Athens. However, as Stephan discovers, the priestess intends to kill Asterius, and use his royal blood to summon the shadow god. The tributes are told that the Minotaur waits for them in the middle of a temple-maze (constructed by a coerced Daedalus). This is Asterius wearing a bull-mask, while the actual killings are carried out by Myrrah and her priests. Stephan and his sister Ariadne manage to get into the maze on the last night of the tribute killings to save Theseus and Daphne, the last female tribute, yet they cannot defeat the shadow god without Asterius joining them, to work as one and repel the darkness. While it is always clear that Asterius is vulnerable, both as a child and as someone with a developmental disability, he is not marginalised or instrumentalised; instead, he plays a critical role in saving the kingdom and is rewarded with a golden crown and the title of Shield-sword.

The story of the Minotaur grows out of gossip that Queen Pasiphae and the architect Daedalus had an affair, which then grows into the familiar mythic story that Daedalus made a mechanical cow for Pasiphae to allow her to sleep with a bull. Ariadne hears the rumours when she goes to the market in disguise, while Stephan hears servant girls making jokes about someone's horns emerging – rumours about Asterius that are cemented by his seclusion in the temple. Myrrah's decision to use that rumour to justify her slaughter of the Athenian tributes again creates the monster out of a child – yet, once it has been produced, it must be slaughtered as Asterius emerges from the labyrinth, *sans* horns. At the novel's end, Stephan overhears some courtiers talking about the collapse of the new temple, with one overexcited boy claiming that Theseus slew the Minotaur, and that he saw the shadow of its horns on the wall and its bones on the temple floor.[47] The monster grows up over the disabled child, constructed by the words of people who do not know him and never see him, built from shadows and whispers. After Asterius steps out of that shadow and is honoured for his actions, the monster keeps going, albeit in its own story – *Double Axe* does not keep Asterius trapped within the monster that others manufacture around him.

Ruth Rendell, writing under the pen name Barbara Vine, takes a different tack in *The Minotaur* (2005). This crime novel lingers on English eccentricity as seen through the eyes of Kerstin, a young Swedish woman who has come to be a live-in carer for John Cosway. John lives with his widowed mother and his four sisters in the rambling and ancient Lydstep Old Hall. While Kerstin is twenty-four at the time of the novel's main events, she narrates it some forty years later, allowing her to comment on her youthful self's actions with the wisdom of hindsight. This proves critical in how the reader is introduced to John and how Kerstin's own reactions to him are framed. She arrives thinking she will work as a carer for a schizophrenic, but instead finds herself expected to be an impassive companion for a man she herself describes as zombie-like.[48] She soon discovers that Mrs. Cosway is drugging her son with medication provided by the family doctor, who (it transpires) is her lover of many years' standing. Kerstin has some medical background, and so enquires about the necessity of the prescription of barbiturate and chlorpromazine. Dr. Lombard informs her it is necessary to prevent John's psychosis taking hold and stop him being violent.[49]

After Mrs. Cosway suffers a fall down the stairs and is hospitalised with an ankle fracture, John refuses to take his medication from Kerstin or his sister Ida. Kerstin starts to notice differences in his behaviour, such as an increased awareness of his surroundings and more verbal interaction with her.[50] She makes a trip to the nearest public library, where she looks up one of the drugs John has been taking and discovers it may be responsible for the tremors he suffers, which informs her decision not to force the issue.[51] As the stupefying effects of the drugs wear off, John begins to become more functional, if not necessarily engaged. Dr. Lombard's death means that Mrs. Cosway finds it impossible to get another doctor to prescribe the same high dosage without a proper examination of the patient. Consequently, more and more traits of what Kerstin retrospectively identifies as Asperger syndrome emerge.

The presentation of John's diagnosis is mediated through the older Kerstin's greater knowledge base – 'everyone knows about autism now' – but as events unfold, she does not directly challenge John's established diagnosis of violent schizophrenia. His formal re-diagnosis takes place outside the events that the novel recounts.[52] The use of the older Kerstin's voice means that while the reader can contextualise John's behaviour, and his family's reactions to it, the novel presents the younger Kerstin's experiences without retrospective or enlightened diagnosis. The fear and loathing generated by John's unmedicated behaviour is unaffected by the reader's understanding of his condition.

John's monstering becomes explicit through his association with the library at Lydstep Old Hall. When Kerstin first arrives, she has been told to expect a maze, but can't find one anywhere in the grounds. It turns out to be the library, which is always kept locked in order to keep John out of it. Kerstin eventually takes the opportunity to enter the library with Zorah, the youngest sister, and discovers a maze created by bookcases placed to create narrow passages, lined with leather-bound books, and eventually leading to a square space at the centre holding a bronze lectern in the shape of a young man with outstretched hands.[53] Zorah tells her that the next time she comes in, she must bring a ball of wool with her, as Theseus did into the lair of the Minotaur. Her older sister Ella also refers to the myth of 'what's-his-name in that place in Crete' when she brings Kerstin in for a second time.[54] As the effects of John's medication wear off, he spends more and more time in the library (the key having conveniently been 'lost'), sometimes falling asleep there. He occupies himself, among other things, with maths problems.

It is from the centre of the library labyrinth that John must be fetched on the day of the novel's inevitable murder, of which he is accused. Kerstin and Ella hear a terrible noise and come down to the drawing room, to find the oldest sister Ida and Mrs. Cosway with bloody hands, John curled up on the sofa keening, and the corpse of the second sister Winifred on the floor, her head and face crushed by a Roman glass vase that lies shattered on the floor. Mrs. Cosway and Ida both maintain John was responsible, and the police take him away, yet his hands are unbloodied and uncut. Kerstin also doubts the story because the Roman glass vase was the only thing to which John had an emotional connection. She attributes his wails to deep distress at its destruction. His retreat into the library, and to proving Pythagoras' theorem, take him back to comfortable, familiar things – which are all somehow linked to antiquity.

Mrs. Cosway, Ida, Winifred and Ella consistently fail to understand John's attachment to these objects. They represent the tradition of classical education that John's status as a wealthy young English man at this period should have entitled him to, but that his condition has prevented him fully accessing. In a way, his family emasculate him, since women were also historically denied access to classical learning. Their attempts to isolate him from what might be categorised as the elite male's inheritance go hand in hand with their unwillingness to engage with his actual condition. Mrs. Cosway's desire to keep him as sedated as possible is essentially a way of not having to deal with the reality of her son's personality which, while difficult, is not vicious. With the exception of Zorah, who is broadly sympathetic to John but more concerned with scoring points off the rest of the family, John's relatives try to cut him off from his true identity and bury his monstrosity. With the chemical suppressant removed, John becomes the Minotaur within his literary labyrinth once more. Yet, he is not violent – Mrs. Cosway attributes violence to him as a displacement of her anger and frustration at his condition. Instead, just as John's Minotaur-esque tendencies re-establish themselves, brutality bursts out in Winifred's death – and, eventually, in the destruction of Lydstep Old Hall and the labyrinth. Mrs. Cosway saw the monster, but misunderstood where danger actually lay.

And here, I think, is the shared point about these Minotaurs of the mind – they are always fundamentally misunderstood. Our modern knowledge of developmental conditions like autism and Asperger's means we are much more aware of the characteristics associated with them, so the sorts of othering which has targeted these unseen disabilities is changing the way in which it manifests. The kind of antagonism seen in *Minotaur* has replaced the supernatural monstering which edges around *The Double Axe*. In both cases, the hostility is misplaced. These Minotaurs participate in the trend of sympathetic readings of the beast, separating out otherness (and it is undeniably other to the neurotypical narrators) from malevolence.

***

As we follow behind the Minotaur on his way to find different labyrinths in which to dwell (or, perhaps, different routes through what is ultimately the same labyrinth), our steps take us through a variety of terroirs of terror, in which the constant focus is the thin dividing line between human and animal. The fascination with the nature of identity marks the Minotaur's manifestations, along with a strong sense of associated place which brings the labyrinth along for the ride. The underlying idea of a threatening not-quite-human occupying a threatening place creates the scope for the appearance of new monstrous tendrils as we generate new spaces to occupy and need fresh ways of articulating the threats which come with them. Yet, regardless of how human the Minotaur may seem, the beast will always return.

Epilogue

The Sirens Still Sing

In the autumn of 2016, the Naked Truth Project, a Christian charity, published a video to the hosting platform Vimeo, which promised to share some basic practical steps for people wanting to stop using pornography.[1] The video drew on the unlikely stories of Jason and Odysseus escaping from the sirens to communicate key tips to its male viewers – avoid what you can, ask others for help and pursue the better song (just as Jason asked Orpheus to sing louder than the sirens). The threat of the sirens, sexual and visual rather than (as in Homer) aural, becomes the threat of pornography, luring men onto the rocks of damaged relationships.

In the video, a desire to be 'authentic' battles with the need to present the heroes as, well, heroes. The producers of the video know that the sirens originally appeared as women with bird wings rather than fishtails, and present them in this more 'accurate' way.[2] This attention to the sources is, however, absent in the accounts of the myths themselves, in particular the story of Odysseus. The Homeric sirens are dangerous because of the sweetness of their song. They threaten Odysseus' safe homecoming by embodying the temptations of knowledge, not sexual allure. While the video voiceover notes that Odysseus asked his crew to block their own ears with beeswax and tie him to the mast, ignoring his pleas to be released, it erases the fact that the hero presented as a role model in fact wishes to have the dangerous pleasure of hearing the sirens' song himself, and coerces his crew into a dangerous situation in order to fulfil his own desires.

I opened this book by saying I was tired of heroes. I am still tired of heroes, particularly when they try to pull this kind of nonsense, brushing their own faults under the carpet and blaming the monsters for the mess. The video that the Naked Truth Project produced is yet another example of the challenge that classical monsters face in the modern world, and have faced, time and again, in my case studies – a cultural desire to be 'genuine', whatever that might mean, which results in slavish hero-worship, making the classical monster a cipher at best and sword fodder at worst. Yet, negotiating this tension, the embeddedness of the monster in the hero narrative and its independence from it, is at the heart of understanding how classical monsters work within popular culture, and why they behave differently to the other monsters who proliferate in mass media.

Although classical monsters might not inspire knee-trembling terror in us, they are still capable of asking us difficult questions about what our culture values and whether the boundaries we think we have established actually stand firm. Their fearsomeness comes from their unknowability – we cannot recover what they meant in antiquity, and we never know which form they will take when they emerge this time. They have resisted attempts to bring them under control, preserving their freedom to define themselves and take on new forms in order to keep interrogating us. Their power, their *impact*, comes from their amodern consistency, their insistence on being both ancient and contemporary and their refusal to compromise on their inherent ambiguity. Looking at classical monsters in the round, as opposed to obsessing about pinning down a single tendril, allows us to appreciate the ever-shifting shape that they take as they move among us.

This book has made the first gesture towards unpicking the complex function of classical monsters in their contemporary guises. I hope that anyone reading this book who might, in their day job, be in the position to nurture a fresh tendril of a classical monster into being will now think more carefully about those dominant narratives, their function in flattening out what classical monsters can do, and the possibilities created by giving the monsters room. Equally, for those readers who in their daily lives encounter rather than create classical monsters, I hope I have given some insight into why there is more to them than meets the eye, and that you understand the value of looking the monster in the face.

Above all, this book has wanted to show that there is another way of doing things. We *can* be tired of heroes. We *can* turn to the monsters. And, in doing so, we can learn about another significant way in which classical culture continues to interlace with the evolving forms and ideas of modern society.

Take me back to the monsters.

Notes

Introduction

1   Hardwick (2003) offers an excellent overview of how classical reception works and what's at stake in it. This book does not extend to the reception of ancient Egypt or the ancient Near East. I hope others will cover these areas in future.
2   Augoustakis and Raucci (eds) (2018) address this question.
3   Lowe and Shahabudin (eds) (2009) survey the debates around looking at this kind of cultural artefact.
4   Children's books with classical content are nothing new, see Maurice (ed.) (2015b).
5   Nisbet (2006), xiii.
6   Asma (2009), 1–15, summarises these key characteristics.
7   For those needing their centaur fix, I recommend Maurice (2015a).

Chapter 1

1   The advert is viewable at: https://www.youtube.com/watch?v=LTC7zlCR2w0 (accessed 2 April 2019); a 'behind-the-scenes' video is at: https://www.youtube.com/watch?v=GF-xUDcP7Ac (accessed 2 April 2019). In the inspiration board featured in the second video, the siren is labelled a 'mermaid'; I am allowing myself this definitional liberty, given the close relationship between the monsters. See Berman (1988) for more on the slippage between the two.
2   Cohen (1997).
3   See, e.g., Felton (2012) and Lowe (2015).
4   Marshall (2018) discusses classical reception in the *Dungeons & Dragons* franchise.
5   Hassig (1996) explores medieval bestiaries and their monsters. The essays in Tobin and Acereda (eds) (2004) consider the Pokémon phenomenon, including issues of cultural localisation faced in moving beyond Japan.
6   Buckingham and Sefton-Green (2004), 21–2.
7   Rose (2000) takes an encyclopaedic approach to monsters in general.
8   Nisbet (2011), discussing *P.Oxy*. XXII 2331.
9   Mayor (2000), 22–53 reaches this conclusion as part of a wider argument that the Greeks and Romans knew about and engaged with the fossils of large vertebrate species.

10 Cohen (1997).

11 Mittman (2012), 6.

12 Ibid., 8.

13 Köster (2014).

14 For instance, the essays in Levina and Bui (eds) (2013) claim to offer an overview of monster culture in the twenty-first century. There are multiple considerations of vampires, zombies and werewolves, but no classical monsters.

15 The hermaphrodite would now be located within the intersex community. Greek and Latin used the masculine-gendered nouns *androgynus* and *hermaphroditus* to identify intersexed bodies.

16 Sedgwick (1990), 160–6.

17 These films were strongly influenced by the Japanese *kaiju* tradition, exemplified by *Godzilla* (1954).

18 Weinstock (2012), 276.

19 This systemic injustice created the Black Lives Matter movement, which was established following the acquittal of a White man who murdered the Black teenager Trayvon Martin.

20 Haraway (1991) explores the significance of this particular breakdown of boundaries.

21 Weinstock (2012), 277.

22 Felton (2012), 127.

23 Barton (1993), 81.

24 Benshoff (1997) fully investigates the history of the homosexual monster in Hollywood cinema.

25 Click, Lee and Holladay (2013) analyse how Lady Gaga has built relationships with her fans, built on a message of self-acceptance.

26 Douglas is known to classicists because of the impact her work had on the study of ancient religion, not least the proposal that her analysis of the Lele tribe's relationship to the pangolin should inform our understanding of the Roman Vestal Virgins. See Beard (1980) and (1995).

27 Carroll (1990), 33–4 offers a helpful summary.

28 Prince (2004).

29 Ibid., 128.

30 References are to the Freud (1919 [2003]) Penguin translation.

31 Ibid. (1919, translation 2003), 157.

32 Ibid., 155.

33 Halberstam (1995), 116.

34 Ibid., 119.

35 Felton (2012), 103.

36 Foucault (2003), 43–8.

37 Ibid., 48.

38 Attebery (2014), 115.

39 Joseph Boyden's *Three Day Road* (2005), which features a member of the Cree tribe becoming a Windigo, illustrates the sensitivities in play. Boyden's claims to indigenous heritage have come under intense scrutiny, raising questions about whether he was entitled to use this cultural material as he has done.

40 Haraway (1992), 299.

41 Braidotti (2002), 22.

42 Ibid., 11–12.

43 Haraway (1992), 300.

Chapter 2

1 Asma (2009), 283.

2 Booker (2001), 140.

3 Carroll (1990), 34–5.

4 Simpson (2014), 45–9 and 99–105, considers these issues in relation to the Mohawk nation at Kahnawà:ke.

5 Carroll (1990), 99.

6 Strauss Clay (1993), 111.

7 Ibid., 113.

8 Pache (2011), 43–69.

9 Green (2007), 147–84, explores the significance of the *rex nemorensis*.

10 Ovid, *Metamorphoses* 3.138–252.

11 Ovid, *Metamorphoses* 8.260–444.

12 Von Stackelberg (2009) analyses the ways the Roman garden was experienced as liminal and interstitial.

13 Newby (2012) explores the use of violent mythological landscapes in Roman domestic design.

14 Felton (2012), 105.

15 Carroll (1990), 35.

16 Felton (2012), 105.

17 Cohen (1997), 4–6.

18 Wood (1984), 181.

19 Attebery (2014), 11–12.

20 Murnaghan and Roberts (2017) explore the tradition of children's books which retell myth.

21 Carroll (1990), 12.

22 Ibid., 16.

23 Ibid.

24 Cohen (1997), 20.

25 Marshall (2018) surveys seven D&D bestiaries from 1974 to 2014. At the lowest count, fifteen classical monsters are represented (1974), with the highest count at twenty-five (1995).

26 Marshall (2018).

27 Duffy (2018).

28 Adams (1986), 31.

29 Benjamin (2008), 22–4. Although a piece appeared under the same title in 1935, the second version (which Benjamin had wished to publish originally, and of which this is a translated edition) was not published until 1989.

30 Benjamin (2008), 26.

31 Ibid., 31.

32 Ibid., 35.

33 Haraway (1992), 300.

34 Ibid. (1988) explains why these claims to objectivity should be understood within their specific historical contexts.

35 Nisbet (2006), 24–30.

36 De Lauretis (1984), 139.

37 Haraway (1988), 581–2.

Chapter 3

1   Cohen (1997), 16.

2   Keen (2015). Dyer (1986) argues that the star image is carried between film productions, so a star is understood in terms of their previous as well as their current role. Carlson (2001), 52–95 explores the operation of this 'haunted body' on stage.

3   Michelakis and Wyke (eds) (2013) provide an invaluable introduction to classical themes in silent cinema.

4   Solomon (2001) surveys the first two phases. The essays in Pomeroy (ed.) (2017b) offer in-depth analysis of all three phases.

5   Solomon (2001), 131.

6   Ibid., 322.

7   Rushing (2016), 100–35, analyses skin and muscle in the peplum tradition, although omitting monster-fighting as physical spectacle.

8   Wyke (1997), 71.

9   Radford (2017) explores the influence of the House Un-American Activities Committee on *Ben-Hur* (1959) and *Spartacus* (1960).

10 Hughes (2011), 1–27, Rushing (2016), 12–18 and Pomeroy (2017a) discuss this in more detail.

11 Hughes (2011), 3, identifies the bison. Tony Keen believes it is a European bison (personal correspondence, July 2018).

12 Rushing (2016), 14.

13 *King Kong* foreshadows the framing of the monster as an object of sympathy as well as fear.

14 Harryhausen and Dalton (2009), 133.

15 Keen (2013).

16 Harryhausen and Dalton (2009), 49.

17 Ibid., 98.

18 Ibid., 131. Harryhausen had been anxious about costuming since *Earth vs. the Flying Saucers* (1956). Budgetary restraints meant he was 'reduced to designing a suit for actors', and he felt the aliens looked 'collapsed and phoney' (Harryhausen and Dalton, 2009: 81).

19 Keen (2013) explores the implications of the Greek elements in the *Sinbad* films.

20 Harryhausen and Dalton (2009), 113.

21 OKell (2013) considers the influence of Harryhausen's Cyclops on later representations of the monster.

22 Harryhausen and Dalton (2009), 106.

23 Apollodorus 1.9.16–28.

24 Harryhausen and Dalton (2009), 151.

25 Ibid., 165.

26 Ibid., 246.

27 Ibid., 246.

28 Ibid. (2011), 116.

29 Ibid. (2009), 265. Torjussen (2016) traces the Kraken from its Norse origins to *Clash* and beyond.

30 I explore the significance of landscape and monsters in the two *Clash of the Titans* films in Gloyn (2013).

31 Harryhausen and Dalton (2009), 272.

32 Ibid.

33 Ibid., 8.

34 Stoichita (2008) explores 'the Pygmalion effect' in cinema through the blurring of the lines between body and sculpture.

35 Solomon (2001), 83–90.

36 Pallant (2011) explores the film's place within the *peplum* genre.

37 Pallant (2011), 179.

38 This interpretation draws on the Christian tradition of seeing Hercules as an allegory for the moral life or Christ's own fight against evil; see Stafford (2012),

202–15. Rowland (2016), 71–101 explores how Christians in the Middle Ages responded to Hercules' relationship with his wife Deianira.

39 Blanshard and Shahabudin (2011) outline Scarfe's particular aesthetic contribution.

Chapter 4

1 *300* was preceded by *Sin City* (2005), based on a comic book set in the American west created by Miller. Rushing (2016), 54–7 analyses the formal aesthetic.

2 Diak (2018) argues for labelling these films and their fellow travellers on television as 'neo-pepla'.

3 Raucci (2015) explores how modern incarnations of the Greek hero have been marketed to audiences.

4 Solomon (2001), 21.

5 Courcoux (2009), 38.

6 This concept of the hyperreal was developed by Baudrillard (1994).

7 Hesiod, *Theogony* 319–324.

8 Ogden (2013), 98–104, surveys the evidence for the Chimera.

9 Apollodorus 2.3.1-2.3.2, Hyginus *Fabulae* 57.

10 The video is available at: https://www.youtube.com/watch?v=SiwS1HLwrS4 (accessed 21 February 2019).

11 The video is available at: https://www.youtube.com/watch?v=OhBqwCTGG5w (accessed 21 February 2019).

12 Lacey (2012).

13 LaSalle (2012).

14 Neumaier (2012).

15 Whitty (2011).

16 Chapter 2, p. 39, explains the heliotropic gaze.

17 The Labyrinth appears in the Percy Jackson books as a monstrous space in its own right, but the films have not got that far.

18 Riordan (2013), 51, 86.

19 Salzman-Mitchell and Alvares (2017), 322, argue that the garden centre's New Jersey location signifies 'a wasteland, a desolate and abandoned place'. Chapter 7, pp. 146–7 explores the ways this Medusa manifests monstrosity.

20 Given that this made-for-television movie's plot creates a new episode in Odysseus' journey, features Homer as a member of Odysseus' crew, gives Persephone world-conquering ambitions and concludes with the creation of vampires, this is probably for the best.

21 The line does not appear in Coen and Coen (2000), 60, which ends at 'see ya in the funny papers!'

22 Coen and Coen (2000), 51.

23 Davies, Shaw and Tierney (2014), 1–2.

24 Ibid.

25 Lindsay (2016), 183–4; Kermode and del Toro (2006).

26 Kermode and del Toro (2006).

Chapter 5

1 Harrisson (2017) analyses *I, Claudius* in detail.

2 Hobden (2017) explores how ancient world documentaries appeal to ideas of authority.

3 Johnson (2005).

4 James (2011), 137–49, offers an extended reading of this episode.

5 Willis (2017).

6 The shorter-lived *Hercules: The Animated Series* (1998–9) does some similar things, limited by its cartoon format and intended audience.

7 As Cyrino and Safran note in relation to myth on the cinema, 'in texts created for poplar audiences, whether the story feels true to the viewer's experiences and fantasies is more important than ensuring faithful replication of source material on screen' (2015a: 2). Lees (2016) outlines some conflicting ideas of authenticity in play with material on screen.

8 Johnson (2005), 4.

9 Hills (2002), 137.

10 My thanks to Nick Lowe for pointing this out to me.

11 Weisbrot (1998), 54.

12 Virgil's version is at *Aeneid* 2.203–227.

13 Campbell's *The Hero with a Thousand Faces* (1949) attempts to identify a monomyth to which all stories ultimately conform. This approach usually smooths out differences between narrative traditions and erases any features which don't fit his pre-designated pattern.

14 Apollodorus *Fabulae* 2.4.8.

15 Weisbrot (1998), 10.

16 Ibid., 8.

17 Chapter 1, p. 11 discusses Cohen's Monster Theses.

18 Weisbrot (1998), 192.

19 Ibid., 230.

20 DuBois (1982), 31–2.

21 See Chapter 2, pp. 27–8.

22 Felton (2012), 105–13.

23 Faludi (1993) offers a still relevant analysis of the backlash phenomenon.

24 Whelehan (2013), 88–90 outlines the continuing difficulties faced by older women in Hollywood.

25 Weisbrot (1998), 202.

26 Ogden (2013) provides an overview of the *drakōn* in antiquity.

27 The Hercules narrative, especially Sophocles' *Trachiniae*, reveals the hero as an abuser. Rowland (2016) explores how the play's reception history has highlighted this theme of domestic abuse.

28 This may be a deliberate pun on herpes.

29 Sorbo (2011), 34–6.

30 Ibid., 113, 161.

31 Ibid., 151, 164.

32 Ibid., 182.

33 Ryfle (1998), 117–18.

34 The original King Ghidorah has three, so this may be an attempt to circumvent copyright.

35 This again shows the influence of Joseph Campbell; see p. 88. I am reminded of two episodes in *Buffy the Vampire Slayer*, which conflate high school graduation and the defeat of a newly ascended demon ('Graduation Day' Parts One and Two, 3.21 and 3.22).

36 Ephiny's storyline is discussed in Chapter 6, pp. 120–4.

37 See Western and Pettit (2010).

38 Sorbo (2011), 219.

39 Ibid., 220–3.

Chapter 6

1 Weisbrot (1998), 5.

2 Johnson (2005), 90–1.

3 Willis (2017), 112.

4 See Chapter 5, p. 98.

5 Early and Kennedy (2003a), 5.

6 See Jones (2000), 14–15.

7 Viewers might have seen the first televised lesbian wedding in *Friends* as Ross's ex-wife married her lover (1996); Ellen, the main character in the series of the same name, coming out on television and in real life (1997); Willow discovering her lesbian identity before trying to destroy the universe in season four of *Buffy the Vampire Slayer* (1999–2001); and the Showtime premiere of *Queer as Folk* (2000).

8 The representation of the relationship is not overwhelmingly positive. Caudill (2003) explores how Xena's 'dark side' offers a specifically erotic thrill in the show's episodes and fan responses.

9 The couple married on 28 March 1998, while Xena's third season was airing.

10 Sorbo (2011), 222.

11 See Chapter 5, p. 88.

12 Weinstock (2012), 276.

13 Willis (2017) analyses this episode further.

14 Contemporary tropes about the threat of specifically black male sexuality are absent, in that centaurs never pose a distinctively sexual threat.

15 *Zena*'s move from West to East creates some serious problems with Orientalism; see Kennedy (2003).

16 Willis (2017).

17 Johnson (2005).

18 At the time of writing in May 2018, Jodie Whittaker had debuted as the Thirteenth Doctor in the 2017 Christmas Special, and season eleven of so-called 'New Who' was eagerly anticipated. By me, at any rate.

19 Keen (2010), 106. Homer's *Iliad* provides precedent for the sympathetic portrayal of the Trojans. Potter (2018), 169–72 explores the historical context in which *Doctor Who: The Myth Makers* (1965) was produced.

20 Keen (2010), 107 and Potter (2018), 174.

21 See Potter (2018), 177–8.

22 Keen (2010), 109.

23 See McMaster and Sundaram (2017), 42–3.

24 Sheldrick (2011).

25 Potter (2018), 181, reports audience responses to this reveal.

26 McMaster and Sundaram (2017) explore the role of classical material in constructing identity in *Doctor Who*.

Chapter 7

1 Ogden (2013), 92–8, summarises the ancient sources for Medusa. Topper (2007) argues for the development of the 'beautiful Medusa', with a focus on Classical red-figure vases.

2 Apollodorus 2.4.2.

3 Hesiod, *Theogony* 275–279.

4 Lowe (2015), 101–2.

5 Beard (2017), 73–9.

6 Chapter 3, p. 54, describes Harryhausen's creative process. Medusae in the fifth edition of *Dungeons & Dragons* are depicted with legs, but this probably arises from their origins as cursed elves (Duffy 2018).

7 Harryhausen abandoned a boob tube he experimented with in early conceptual drawings as he felt it looked vulgar (Harryhausen and Dalton, 2009: 272).

8 A *Clash of the Titans* video game was released in 2010 on PlayStation 3 and Xbox 360 and advertised before the film in cinemas.

9 See also Chapter 4, p. 70.

10 In film publicity posters, Medusa's portrait begins mid-calf, maintaining visual ambiguity about her lower half.

11 See, for instance, Weinlich (2015) on different approaches children's picture books take to retelling particular myths. Examples of the retelling of the Perseus myth include *Perseus and the Gorgon Medusa* by Geraldine McCaughrean (1998), Kate McMullan's *Say Cheese, Medusa!* (2003) and Paul Storrie and Thomas Yeates' *Perseus: The Hunt for Medusa's Head* (2008).

12 Powers (2015), 68.

13 Ibid., 178.

14 Ibid., 270.

15 Ibid., 152–3.

16 Ibid., 196–7.

17 Ibid., 348.

18 Masello (2011), 349.

19 Ibid., 353.

20 Ibid., 391.

21 Ibid., 399.

22 Ibid., 299.

23 The construction of what makes a child and what makes an adult is constantly redefined; see Immel (2009).

24 Suzanne Collins has often spoken about the importance of the Theseus myth to the *Hunger Games*, see, e.g., Collins (n.d.).

25 Keaton (2011), 2–3.

26 Ibid., 3–5.

27 Jernigan and Austin (2011) outline the conventions of the paranormal romance.

28 Ibid., 229–34.

29 Ibid., 232.

30 Ibid., 196.

31 Lyons (2015).

32 Ibid. (2014), 45.

33 Ibid., 247.

34 This story is included in Clarke (2002).

35 Certain groups of jellyfish are classified under the subphylum Medusozoa, presumably because of their long tentacles and dangerous stings.

36 Baxter and Reynolds (2016), 109.

37 Ibid., 110–11.

38 Ibid., 10.

39 Ibid., 57.

40 Brown (2008) appraises the relationship between classics and science fiction (SF).

41 Baxter and Reynolds (2016), 291.

42 Condé Nast declined permission to reproduce the cover, although it is easily accessible via an internet search.

43 Holmes (2007) provides a sensitive biography of Baartman, including the repatriation of her remains to South Africa in 2002.

44 Gilroy (2004), 21–2.

45 Ovid's refers to drops of Medusa's blood turning into snakes as Perseus flew over the Libyan Desert with her head (*Metamorphoses* 4.610–20).

46 Heaf (2013).

47 A star's image consists of 'not just his or her films, but the promotion of those films and of the star through pin-ups, public appearances, studio hand-outs and so on, as well as interviews, biographies and coverage in the press of the star's doings and "private" life' (Dyer, 1986: 2–3). This image creates 'a certain aura of expectations' around the star (Carlson, 2001: 67), which Rihanna uses to her advantage.

48 Young (2017).

49 Goodman (1996), 200–1.

50 This discussion is deeply indebted to Byrd and Tharps (2002). While both Rihanna and Smartt come from Barbados, similar racist pressures arising from the island's history as a British sugar colony and transatlantic trading hub for enslaved people have created a hair culture where 'straight' is good and 'nappy' is bad.

51 Butler (2007), 69.

52 Gray (2017).

53 Fleetwood (2012) analyses the links Rihanna and her publicists created between erotic violence and black female desire.

54 Ibid., 432.

Chapter 8

1 Ovid, *Metamorphoses* 8.152–182, *Heroides* 4; Apollodorus 3.1.3–4, 3.15.7–*Epitome* 1.10.

2 Hyginus *Fabulae* 40.

3 I thank Deborah Roberts for her paper, 'Picturing duality: The Minotaur as beast and human in illustrated myth collections for children', given at the Chasing Mythical . . .

The Reception of Creatures from Graeco-Roman Mythology in Children's & Young Adults' Culture as a Transformation Marker International Conference, Warsaw, 3 May 2016.

4 Storey (2014), 27–8.
5 Gaiman (1996 [2001]), 310.
6 Ibid., 314.
7 Elber-Aviram (2013).
8 Douglass (2002 [2004]), 11.
9 Ibid., 489.
10 Fletcher (2006 [2007]), 372.
11 Ibid., 424.
12 Ibid., 432.
13 Ibid., 416, 420, 427, 444.
14 Ibid., 426.
15 Fletcher (2009), 126.
16 Douglass (2002 [2004]), 10.
17 Sherrill (2003 [2004]), 162.
18 Ibid., 229.
19 Ibid., 234.
20 Ibid., 1.
21 Ibid., 84–5.
22 Ibid., 84.
23 Ibid., 36.
24 Ibid., 283.
25 Ibid., 100.
26 Ibid., 176.
27 Ibid., 190–1.
28 Ibid., 201.
29 See Chapter 2, pp. 27–8.
30 Sherrill (2003 [2004]), 211.
31 Ibid., 243.
32 Ibid., 280.
33 Ibid., 281.
34 Ibid., 283.
35 Ibid., 311.
36 Ibid., 232.
37 Sherrill partly answered this in the sequel, *The Minotaur Takes His Own Sweet Time* (2016).
38 Gibbons (2000 [2006]), 52.
39 Middle Grade fiction, targeting readers aged between 7 and 14, adds further confusion.

40 Traweek (2014) explores the nature of the novel as an exploration of remembering and retelling.
41 Pelevin (2006), 25.
42 Ibid., 160.
43 Ibid., 162.
44 Haraway (1991), 152.
45 Womack (2016), 20.
46 Ibid., 40–1.
47 Ibid., 239.
48 Vine (2005 [2006]), 74.
49 Ibid., 156.
50 Ibid., 157.
51 Ibid., 161.
52 Ibid., 180.
53 Ibid., 105–6.
54 Ibid., 127.

Epilogue

1 Video available at: http://thenakedtruthproject.com/jason (accessed 19 July 2018).
2 Hassig (1996), 104–14, explores the evolution of the siren through the medieval bestiary tradition, which is probably responsible for the eventual fusion between siren and mermaid.

Filmography

Feature films

King Kong, dir. Merian C. Cooper and Ernest B. Schoedsack, RKO Radio Pictures (1933).
Godzilla (*Gojira*), dir. Ishirô Honda, Toho Company (1954).
Earth vs. the Flying Saucers, dir. Fred F. Sears, Columbia Pictures (1956).
Hercules (*Le fatiche di Ercole*), dir. Pietro Francisci, Lux Film (1958).
The 7th Voyage of Sinbad, dir. Nathan Juran, Columbia Pictures Corporation (1958).
Ben-Hur, dir. William Wyler, Metro-Goldwyn-Mayer (1959).
Spartacus, dir. Stanley Kubrick. Universal Pictures (1960).
Jason and the Argonauts, dir. Don Chaffey, Columbia Pictures Corporation (1963).
The Golden Voyage of Sinbad, dir. Gordon Hessler, Columbia Pictures Corporation (1973).
Sinbad and the Eye of the Tiger, dir. Sam Wanamaker, Columbia Pictures Corporation (1977).
Clash of the Titans, dir. Desmond Davis, Metro-Goldwyn-Mayer (1981).
Hercules, dir. Ron Clements and John Musker, Buena Vista Pictures (1997).
O Brother, Where Art Thou?, dir. Joel Coen, Buena Vista Pictures (2000).
Sin City, dir. Frank Miller and Robert Rodriguez, Dimension Films (2005).
300, dir. Zac Snyder, Warner Bros. (2006).
El Laberinto del Fauno (*Pan's Labyrinth*), dir. Guillermo del Toro. Warner Bros. (2006).
Percy Jackson & the Olympians: The Lightning Thief, dir. Chris Columbus, Twentieth Century Fox (2010).
Clash of the Titans, dir. Louis Leterrier, Warner Bros. (2010).
Wrath of the Titans, dir. Jonathan Liebesman, Warner Bros. (2012).
Hercules, dir. Brett Ratner, Paramount Pictures (2014).

Television series

Doctor Who: The Myth Makers, BBC (1965).
Doctor Who: The Mind Robber, BBC (1968).
Doctor Who: The Time Monster, BBC (1972).
Doctor Who: Underworld, BBC (1978).
Doctor Who: The Horns of Nimon, BBC (1979–80).

Ellen, American Broadcasting Company (1994–8).

Friends, National Broadcasting Company (1994–2004).

Hercules: The Legendary Journeys, Universal Television (1995–9).

Xena: Warrior Princess, WB Television Network (1995–2001).

Buffy the Vampire Slayer, WB Television Network (1997–2001), United Paramount
   Network (2002–2003).

Hercules: The Animated Series, American Broadcasting Company (1998–9).

Queer as Folk, Showtime Networks (2000–2005).

Doctor Who, season six, BBC (2011).

Bibliography

Adams, Douglas (1986) *The Hitchhiker's Guide to the Galaxy: A Trilogy in Four Parts*, London: Heinemann.

Asma, Stephen (2009) *On Monsters: An Unnatural History of Our Worst Fears*, Oxford: Oxford University Press.

Attebery, Brian (2014) *Stories about Stories: Fantasy and the Remaking of Myth*, Oxford: Oxford University Press.

Augoustakis, Antony and Stacie Raucci (eds) (2018) *Epic Heroes on Screen*, Edinburgh: Edinburgh University Press.

Barton, Carlin A. (1993) *The Sorrows of the Ancient Romans: The Gladiator and the Monster*, Princeton, NJ: Princeton University Press.

Baudrillard, Jean (1994) *Simulacra and Simulation*, trans. Sheila Faria Glaser, Ann Arbor, MI: University of Michigan Press.

Baxter, Stephen and Alastair Reynolds (2016) *The Medusa Chronicles*, London: Gollancz.

Beard, Mary (1980) 'The sexual status of Vestal Virgins', *Journal of Roman Studies*, 70: 12–27.

Beard, Mary (1995) 'Re-reading (Vestal) virginity', in R. Hawley and B. M. Levick (eds), *Women in Antiquity: New Assessments*, 166–77, London: Routledge.

Beard, Mary (2017) *Women & Power: A Manifesto*, London: Profile Books.

Benjamin, Walter (2008) 'The work of art in the age of its technological reproducibility: Second version', in Michael W. Jennings, Brigid Dohert and Thomas Y. Levin (eds), *The Work of Art in the Age of Its Technological Reproducibility, and Other Writings on Media*, trans. Edmund Jephcott et al., 19–55, Cambridge, MA: Belknap.

Benshoff, Harry M. (1997) *Monsters in the Closet: Homosexuality and the Horror Film*, Manchester and New York: Manchester University Press.

Berman, Ruth (1988) 'Sirens', in M. South (ed.), *Mythical and Fabulous Creatures: A Source Book and Research Guide*, 147–53, New York: Bedrick.

Blanshard, Alastair J. L. and Kim Shahabudin (2011) *Classics on Screen: Ancient Greece and Rome on Film*, Bristol: Bristol Classical Press.

Booker, Keith (2001) *Monsters, Mushroom Clouds, and the Cold War: American Science Fiction and the Roots of Postmodernism*, Westport, CT, and London: Greenwood Press.

Boyden, Joseph (2005) *Three Day Road*, Toronto and New York: Viking.

Braidotti, Rosi (2002) *Metamorphoses: Towards a Materialist Theory of Becoming*, Cambridge: Polity Press.

Brown, Sarah Annes (2008) '"Plato's Stepchildren": SF and the classics', in Lorna Hardwick and Christopher Stray (eds), *A Companion to Classical Receptions*, 415–27, Oxford: Blackwell.

Buckingham, David and Julian Sefton-Green (2004) 'Structure, agency and pedagogy in children's media culture', in Tobin and Acereda (eds), *Pikachu's Global Adventure*, 12–33.

Butler, Anthea (2007) *Women in the Church of God in Christ: Making a Sanctified World*, Chapel Hill, NC: University of North Carolina Press.

Byrd, Ayana D. and Lori L. Tharps (2002) *Hair Story: Untangling the Roots of Black Hair in America*, New York: St. Martin's Press and Godalming: Melia.

Campbell, Joseph (1949) *The Hero with a Thousand Faces*, [USA]: Bollingen Foundation.

Carlson, Marvin (2001) *The Haunted Stage: The Theatre as Memory Machine*, Ann Arbor, MI: University of Michigan Press.

Carroll, Noël (1990) *The Philosophy of Horror or Paradoxes of the Heart*, New York: Routledge.

Caudill, Helen (2003) 'Tall, dark and dangerous: Xena, the quest, and the wielding of sexual violence in *Xena* on-line fan fiction', in Early and Kennedy (eds), *Athena's Daughters*, 27–39.

Clarke, Arthur C. (2002) *The Collected Stories*, London: Gollancz.

Click, Melissa A., Hyunji Lee and Holly Willson Holladay (2013) 'Making monsters: Lady Gaga, fan identification, and social media', *Popular Music and Society* 36 (3): 360–79.

Coen, Ethan and Joel Coen (2000) *O Brother, Where Art Thou?* London: Faber and Faber.

Cohen, Jeffrey Jerome (1997) 'Monster culture (seven theses)', in J. J. Cohen (ed.), *Monster Theory: Reading Culture*, 3–25, Minneapolis, MN: University of Minnesota Press.

Collins, Suzanne (n.d.) 'Interview with Suzanne Collins'. Available at: https://clubs-kids.scholastic.co.uk/clubs_content/18829 (accessed 19 July 2018).

Coonts, Stephen (1989 [2002]) *The Minotaur*, London: Orion Books.

Courcoux, Charles-Antoine (2009) 'From here to antiquity: Mythical settings and modern sufferings in contemporary Hollywood's historical epics', *Film & History*, 39 (2): 29–38.

Cyrino, Monica S. and Meredith E. Safran (2015a) 'Cinemyths: Classical myth on screen', in Cyrino and Safran (eds), *Classical Myth on Screen*, 1–11.

Cyrino, Monica S. and Meredith E. Safran (eds) (2015b) *Classical Myth on Screen*, New York: Palgrave Macmillan.

Davies, Ann, Deborah Shaw and Dolores Tierney (2014) 'Introduction', in Ann Davies, Deborah Shaw and Dolores Tierney (eds), *The Transnational Fantasies of Guillermo del Toro*, 1–10, New York: Palgrave Macmillan.

de Lauretis, Teresa (1984) *Alice Doesn't: Feminism, Semiotics, Cinema*, Bloomington, IN: Indiana University Press.

Diak, Nicholas (2018) 'Introduction', in *The New Peplum: Essays on Sword and Sandal Films and Television Programs Since the 1990s*, 4–19, Jefferson, NC: McFarland & Company.

Douglas, Mary (1966) *Purity and Danger: An Analysis of Concepts of Pollution and Taboo*, London: Routledge and Keegan Paul.

Douglass, Sara (2002 [2004]) *Hades' Daughter*, Adelaide: Griffin Press.

duBois, Page (1982) *Centaurs and Amazons: Women and the Pre-History of the Great Chain of Being*, Ann Arbor, MI: University of Michigan Press.

Duffy, William S. (2018) '20-sided monsters: The adaptation of Greek mythology to Dungeons and Dragons', unpublished conference paper, 114th Annual Meeting of the Classical Association of the Middle West and South, Albuquerque, NM, 11–14 April.

Dyer, Richard (1986) *Heavenly Bodies: Film Stars and Society*, London: Macmillan Education.

Early, Frances and Kathleen Kennedy (2003a) 'Introduction: Athena's daughters', in Early and Kennedy (eds), *Athena's Daughters*, 1–10.

Early, Frances and Kathleen Kennedy (eds) (2003b) *Athena's Daughters: Television's New Women Warriors*, Syracuse, NY: Syracuse University Press.

Elber-Aviram, H. (2013) '"The past is below us": Urban fantasy, urban archaeology, and the recovery of suppressed history', *Papers from the Institute of Archaeology*, 23 (1): p.Art. 7. Available at: https://pia-journal.co.uk/articles/10.5334/pia.426/# (accessed 19 July 2018).

Faludi, Susan (1993) *Backlash: The Undeclared War Against Women*, London: Vintage.

Felton, D. (2012) 'Rejecting and embracing the monstrous in ancient Greece and Rome', in Mittman (ed.) with Dendle, *Ashgate Research Companion*, 103–31.

Fleetwood, Nicole R. (2012) 'The case of Rihanna: Erotic violence and black female desire', *African American Review*, 45 (3): 419–36.

Fletcher, Charlie (2006 [2007]) *Stoneheart*, St Ives: Clays Ltd.

Fletcher, Charlie (2007) *Ironhand*, St Ives: Clays Ltd.

Fletcher, Charlie (2009) *Silvertongue*, St Ives: Clays Ltd.

Foucault, Michel (2003) *Abnormal: Lectures at the Collège de France, 1974–75*, trans. Graham Burchell, New York: Picador.

Freud, Sigmund (1919 [2003]) 'The Uncanny', in *The Uncanny*, trans. David McLintock, 123–62, London: Penguin.

Gaiman, Neil (1996 [2001]) *Neverwhere*, New York: HarperTorch.

Gibbons, Alan (2000 [2006]) *Shadow of the Minotaur*, St Ives: Clays Ltd.

Gilroy, Paul (2004) *Between Camps: Nations, Cultures and the Allure of Race*, new edn, London: Routledge.

Gloyn, Liz (2013) '"The Dragon-green, the Luminous, the Dark, the Serpent-haunted Sea": Monsters, landscape and gender in *Clash of the Titans* (1981 and 2010)', *New Voices in Classical Reception Studies*, Conference Proceedings Volume One: 64–75.

Goodman, Lizbeth (1996) 'Who's looking at who(m)? Re-viewing Medusa', *Modern Drama*, 39 (1): 190–210.

Gray, Danielle (2017) 'This woman made a video game to tackle people touching black women's hair without permission'. Available at: https://www.allure.com/story/hair-nah-stop-touching-black-womens-hair-video-game (accessed 19 July 2018).

Green, C. M. C. (2007) *Roman Religion and the Cult of Diana at Aricia*, Cambridge: Cambridge University Press.

Halberstam, Judith (1995) *Skin Shows: Gothic Horror and the Technology of Monsters*, Durham, NC: Duke University Press.

Haraway, Donna (1988) 'Situated knowledges: The science question in feminism and the privilege of partial perspective', *Feminist Studies*, 14 (3): 575–99.

Haraway, Donna (1991) 'A Cyborg manifesto: Science, technology and socialist-feminism in the late twentieth century', in *Simians, Cyborgs and Women: The Reinvention of Nature*, 149–81, New York: Routledge.

Haraway, Donna (1992) 'The promises of monsters: A regenerative politics for inappropriate/d others', in Lawrence Grossberg, Cary Nelson, Paula Treichler (eds), *Cultural Studies*, 295–337, New York: Routledge.

Hardwick, Lorna (2003) *Reception Studies*, Oxford: Oxford University Press.

Harrisson, Juliette (2017) '*I, Claudius* and ancient Rome as televised period drama', in Pomeroy (ed.), *A Companion*, 271–92.

Harryhausen, Ray and Tony Dalton (2009) *Ray Harryhausen: An Animated Life*, London: Aurum Press.

Harryhausen, Ray and Tony Dalton (2011) *Ray Harryhausen's Fantasy Scrapbook: Models, Artwork and Memories from 65 Years of Filmmaking*, London: Aurum Press.

Hassig, Debra (1996) *Medieval Bestiaries: Text, Image, Ideology*, Cambridge: Cambridge University Press.

Heaf, Jonathan (2013) '*GQ*'s 25th anniversary cover star: Rihanna by Damien Hirst'. Available at: https://www.gq-magazine.co.uk/article/rihanna-damien-hirst-gq-cover-pictures (accessed 19 July 2018).

Hills, Matt (2002) *Fan Cultures*, London and New York: Routledge.

Hobden, Fiona (2017) 'Ancient world documentaries', in Pomeroy (ed.), *A Companion*, 491–514.

Holmes, Rachel (2007) *African Queen: The Real Life of the Hottentot Venus*, New York: Random House.

Hughes, Howard (2011) *Cinema Italiano – The Complete Guide from Classics to Cult*, London: I.B. Tauris.

Immel, Andrea (2009) 'Children's books and constructions of childhood', in M. O. Grenby and Andrea Immel (eds), *The Cambridge Companion to Children's Literature*, 19–34, Cambridge: Cambridge University Press.

James, Paula (2011) *Ovid's Myth of Pygmalion on Screen: In Pursuit of the Perfect Woman*, London: Bloomsbury Academic.

Jernigan, Jessica and Beth Austin (2011) 'Sealing the deal: The wet and wild world of selkie romance novels', *Bitch Media*. Available at: https://www.bitchmedia.org/article/sealing-the-deal (accessed 26 July 2018).

Johnson, Catherine (2005) *Telefantasy*, London: British Film Institute (BFI).

Jones, Sara Gwenllian (2000) 'Starring Lucy Lawless?', *Continuum: Journal of Media & Cultural Studies*, 14 (1): 9–22.

Keaton, Kelly (2011) *Darkness Becomes Her*, New York: Simon & Schuster Children's.

Keaton, Kelly (2012) *A Beautiful Evil*, New York: Simon & Schuster Children's.

Keen, Antony (2010) 'It's about tempus: Greece and Rome in "classic" *Doctor Who*', in David C. Wright, Jr. and Allan W. Austin (eds), *Space and Time: Essays on Visions of History in Science Fiction and Fantasy Television*, 100–15, Jefferson, NC: McFarland & Company.

Keen, Antony (2013) 'Greek elements in the Sinbad Movies of Ray Harryhausen: A lesson in reception', *New Voices in Classical Reception Studies*, Conference Proceedings Volume One: 29–40.

Keen, Antony (2015) 'An alternative model for looking at classical movies'. Available at: http://tonykeen.blogspot.com/2015/09/an-alternative-model-for-looking-at.html (accessed 19 July 2018).

Kennedy, Kathleen (2003) 'Love is the battlefield: The making and unmaking of the just warrior in *Xena: Warrior Princess*', in Early and Kennedy (eds), *Athena's Daughters*, 40–52.

Kermode, Mark and Guillermo del Toro (2006) '*Guardian* interviews at the BFI: Guillermo del Toro'. Available at: https://www.theguardian.com/film/2006/nov/21/guardianinterviewsatbfisouthbank (accessed 19 July 2018).

Köster, Isabel (2014) 'Feasting centaurs and destructive consuls in Cicero's *In Pisonem*', *Illinois Classical Studies*, 39: 63–79.

Kristeva, Julia (1982) *Powers of Horror: An Essay on Abjection*, trans. Leon S. Roudiez, New York: Columbia University Press.

Lacey, Liam (2012) 'Wrath of the Titans: By Zeus, there's a video game in this!' Available at: https://www.theglobeandmail.com/arts/film/wrath-of-the-titans-by-zeus-theres-a-video-game-in-this/article4097000/ (accessed 19 July 2018).

LaSalle, Nick (2012) '*Wrath of Titans* review: Futility of fake effects'. Available at: https://www.sfgate.com/movies/article/Wrath-of-Titans-review-Futility-of-fake-effects-3444858.php (accessed 19 July 2018).

Lees, Dominic (2016) 'Cinema and authenticity: Anxieties in the making of historical film', *Journal of Media Practice*, 17 (2–3): 199–212.

Levina, Marina and Diem-My T. Bui (eds) (2013) *Monster Culture in the 21st Century: A Reader*, New York: Bloomsbury Academic.

Lindsay, Richard (2016) 'Menstruation as heroine's journey in *Pan's Labyrinth*', in J. W. Morehead (ed.), *The Supernatural Cinema of Guillermo del Toro*, 182–200, Jefferson, NC: McFarland & Company.

Lowe, Dunstan (2015) *Monsters and Monstrosity in Augustan Poetry*, Ann Arbor, MI: University of Michigan Press.

Lowe, Dunstan and Kim Shahabudin (eds) (2009) *Classics for All: Reworking Antiquity in Mass Culture*, Newcastle upon Tyne: Cambridge Scholars Publishing.

Lyons, Heather (2014) *The Deep End of the Sea*, [USA]: Cerulean Books.

Lyons, Heather (2015) 'FAQ'. Available at: http://heatherlyons.net/faq/ (accessed 19 July 2018).

Marshall, C. W. (2018) 'Classical reception and the Half-elf Cleric', in Brett M. Rogers and Benjamin E. Stevens (eds), *Once and Future Antiquities in Science Fiction and Fantasy*, 149–71, New York: Bloomsbury Academic.

Masello, Robert (2011) *The Medusa Amulet*, London: Vintage Books.

Maurice, Lisa (2015a) 'From Chiron to Foaly: The centaur in classical mythology and fantasy literature', in Maurice (ed.), *The Reception*, 139–68.

Maurice, Lisa (ed.) (2015b) *The Reception of Ancient Greece and Rome in Children's Literature: Heroes and Eagles*, Leiden: Brill.

Mayor, Adrienne (2000) *The First Fossil Hunters: Paleontology in Greek and Roman Times*, Princeton, NJ: Princeton University Press.

McCaughrean, Geraldine (1998) *Perseus and the Gorgon Medusa*, London: Orchard Books.

McMaster, Aven and Mark Sundaram (2017) '"O tempora, o mores": Class(ics) and education in *Doctor Who*', in Carey Fleiner and Dene October (eds), Doctor Who *and History: Critical Essays on Imagining the Past*, 35–46, Jefferson, NC: McFarland & Company.

McMullan, Kate (2003) *Say Cheese, Medusa!*, New York: Scholastic.

Michelakis, Pantelis and Maria Wyke (eds) (2013) *The Ancient World in Silent Cinema*, Cambridge: Cambridge University Press.

Mittman, Asa Simon (2012) 'Introduction: The impact of monsters and monster studies', in Mittman (ed.) with Dendle, *Ashgate Research Companion*, 1–14.

Mittman, Asa Simon (ed.) with Peter J. Dendle (2012) *The Ashgate Research Companion to Monsters and the Monstrous*, Burlington, VT: Ashgate.

Murnaghan, Sheila and Deborah H. Roberts (2017) 'Myth collections for children', in Zajko and Hoyle (eds), *A Handbook*, 87–103.

Neumaier, Joe (2012) 'Sam Worthington is back as Perseus to handle troublesome gods in "Wrath of the Titans"'. Available at: http://www.nydailynews.com/entertainment/movies/sam-worthington-back-perseus-handle-troublesome-gods-wrath-titans-article-1.1052748?localLinksEnabled=false (accessed 2 February 2018).

Newby, Zahra (2012) 'The aesthetics of violence: Myth and danger in Roman domestic landscapes', *Classical Antiquity*, 31 (2): 349–89.

Nisbet, Gideon (2006) *Ancient Greece in Film and Popular Culture*, Exeter: Bristol Phoenix Press.

Nisbet, Gideon (2011) 'An ancient Greek graphic novel: *P.Oxy.* XXII 2331', in George Kovacs and C. W. Marshall (eds), *Classics and Comics*, 27–42, Oxford: Oxford University Press.

Ogden, Daniel (2013) *Drakōn: Dragon Myth and Serpent Cult in the Greek and Roman Worlds*, Oxford and New York: Oxford University Press.

OKell, Eleanor (2013) 'The look of Harryhausen's Cyclops: Human v. monster in the eye of the beholder', *New Voices in Classical Reception Studies*, Conference Proceedings Volume One: 42–63.

Pache, Corinne Ondine (2011) *A Moment's Ornament: The Poetics of Nympholepsy in Ancient Greece*, Oxford and New York: Oxford University Press.

Pallant, Chris (2011) 'Developments in peplum filmmaking: Disney's *Hercules*', in M. G. Cornelius (ed.), *Of Muscles and Men: Essays on the Sword and Sandal Film*, 175–86, Jefferson, NC: McFarland & Company.

Pelevin, Victor (2006) *The Helmet of Horror*, trans. Andrew Bromfield, Edinburgh: Canongate Books.

Pomeroy, Arthur J. (2017a) 'The peplum era', in Pomeroy (ed.), *A Companion*, 145–60.

Pomeroy, Arthur J. (ed.) (2017b) *A Companion to Ancient Greece and Rome on Screen*, Malden, MA: Wiley-Blackwell.

Potter, Amanda (2018) 'Greek myth in the Whoniverse', in Fiona Hobden and Amanda Wrigley (eds), *Ancient Greece on British Television*, 168–86, Oxford: Oxford University Press.

Powers, Tim (2015) *Medusa's Web*, London: Corvus.

Prince, Stephen (2004) 'Dread, taboo and The Thing: Towards a social theory of the horror film', in Stephen Prince (ed.), *The Horror Film*, 118–30, New Brunswick, NJ: Rutgers University Press.

Radford, Fiona (2017) 'Hollywood ascendant: *Ben-Hur* and *Spartacus*', in Pomeroy (ed.), *A Companion*, 119–44.

Raucci, Stacie (2015) 'Of marketing and men: Making the cinematic Greek hero', in Cyrino and Safran (eds), *Classical Myth on Screen*, 161–71.

Riordan, Rick (2013) *Percy Jackson and the Lightning Thief*, New York: Hyperion Books for Children.

Roberts, Deborah (2016) 'Picturing duality: The Minotaur as beast and human in illustrated myth collections for children', paper given at the Chasing Mythical ... The Reception of Creatures from Graeco-Roman Mythology in Children's & Young Adults' Culture as a Transformation Marker International Conference, Warsaw, 3 May.

Rose, Carol (2000) *Giants, Monsters, and Dragons: An Encyclopedia of Folklore, Legend and Myth,* Santa Barbara, CA: ABC-CLIO.

Rowland, Richard (2016) *Killing Hercules: Deianira and the Politics of Domestic Violence, from Sophocles to the War on Terror*, London: Routledge.

Rushing, Robert A. (2016) *Descended from Hercules: Biopolitics and the Muscled Male Body on Screen*, Bloomington, IN: Indiana University Press.

Ryfle, Steve (1998) *Japan's Favorite Mon-Star: The Unauthorised Biography of 'The Big G'*, Toronto: ECW Press.

Salzman-Mitchell, Patricia and Jean Alvares (2017) *Classical Myth and Film in the New Millennium*, Oxford: Oxford University Press.

Sedgwick, Eve Kosofsky (1990) *Epistemology of the Closet*, Berkeley and Los Angeles, CA: University of California Press.

Sheldrick, Giles (2011) 'Doctor Who: Who's scariest foe ... aliens in suits'. Available at: https://www.express.co.uk/news/uk/239945/Doctor-Who-Who-s-scariest-foe-aliens-in-suits (accessed 20 July 2018).

Sherrill, Steven (2003 [2004]) *The Minotaur Takes a Cigarette Break*, Edinburgh: Canongate Books.

Sherrill, Steven (2016) *The Minotaur Takes His Own Sweet Time*, Winston-Salem, NC: John F. Blair.

Simpson, Audra (2014) *Mohawk Interruptus: Political Life Across the Borders of Settler States*, Durham, NC: Duke University Press.

Solomon, Jon (2001) *The Ancient World in the Cinema*, revised and expanded edn. New Haven, CT, and London: Yale University Press.

Sorbo, Kevin (2011) *True Strength: My Journey from Hercules to Mere Mortal and How Nearly Dying Saved My Life*, Philadelphia, PA: Da Capo Press.

Stafford, Emma (2012) *Herakles*, London: Routledge.

Stoichita, Victor I. (2008) *The Pygmalion Effect: From Ovid to Hitchcock*, trans. Alison Anderson, London and Chicago, IL: University of Chicago Press.

Storey, John (2014) *From Popular Culture to Everyday Life*, London: Routledge.

Storrie, Paul and Thomas Yeates (2008) *Perseus: The Hunt for Medusa's Head*, Minneapolis, MN: Graphic Universe.

Strauss Clay, Jenny (1993) 'The generation of monsters in Hesiod', *Classical Philology*, 88: 105–16.

Tobin, Joseph and Alberto Acereda (eds) (2004) *Pikachu's Global Adventure: The Rise and Fall of Pokémon*, Durham, NC: Duke University Press.

Topper, Kathryn (2007) 'Perseus, the maiden Medusa, and the imagery of abduction', *Hesperia*, 76 (1): 73–105.

Torjussen, Stian Sundell (2016) '"Release the Kraken!" – The recontextualization of the Kraken in popular culture, from *Clash of the Titans* to *Magic: The Gathering*', *New Voices in Classical Reception*, 11: 73–85.

Traweek, Alison (2014) 'Theseus loses his way: Viktor Pelevin's *Helmet of Horror* and the old labyrinth for the new world', *Dialogue: The Interdisciplinary Journal of Popular Culture and Pedagogy*, 1 (1). Available at: http://journaldialogue.org/issues/issue-1/theseus-loses-his-way-viktor-pelevins-helmet-of-horror-and-the-old-labyrinth-for-the-new-world/ (accessed 20 July 2018).

Vine, Barbara (2005 [2006]) *The Minotaur*, London: Penguin Books.

von Stackelberg, Katharine T. (2009) *The Roman Garden: Space, Sense and Society*, London: Routledge.

Weinlich, Barbara (2015) 'The metanarrative of picture books: "Reading" Greek myth for (and to) children', in Maurice (ed.), *The Reception*, 85–104.

Weinstock, Jeffrey Andrew (2012) 'Invisible monsters: Vision, horror, and contemporary culture', in Mittman (ed.) with Dendle, *Ashgate Research Companion*, 275–89.

Weisbrot, Robert (1998) *Hercules, The Legendary Journeys: The Official Companion*, New York: Doubleday.

Western, Bruce and Becky Pettit (2010) 'Incarceration & social inequality', *Daedalus*. Available at: https://www.amacad.org/content/publications/pubContent.aspx?d=808 (accessed 20 July 2018).

Whelehan, Imelda (2013) 'Aging appropriately: Postfeminist discourses of ageing in contemporary Hollywood', in Joel Gwynne and Nadine Muller (eds), *Postfeminism and Contemporary Cinema*, 78–95, New York: Palgrave Macmillan.

Whitty, Stephen (2011) '"Immortals" review: A version of Greek myth for fans of "300"'. Available at: https://www.nj.com/entertainment/movies/index.ssf/2011/11/immortals_review_a_version_of_greek_myth_for_fans_of_300.html (accessed 20 July 2018).

Willis, Ika (2017) 'Contemporary mythography: In the time of ancient gods, warlords, and kings', in Zajko and Hoyle (eds), *A Handbook*, 105–20.

Womack, Philip (2016) *The Double Axe*, Richmond: Alma Books.

Wood, Robin (1984) 'An introduction to the American horror film', in Barry Keith Grant (ed.), *Planks of Reason: Essays on the Horror Film*, 164–200, Metuchen, NJ: Scarecrow Press.

Wyke, Maria (1997) *Projecting the Past: Ancient Rome, Cinema and History*, New York: Routledge.

Young, Cate (2017) 'Black Venus rising: The symbolism of Beyoncé's pregnancy photos'. Available at: https://www.bitchmedia.org/article/black-venus-rising/symbolism-beyoncés-pregnancy-photos (accessed 20 July 2018).

Zajko, Vanda and Helena Hoyle (eds) (2017) *A Handbook to the Reception of Classical Mythology*, Malden, MA: Wiley-Blackwell.

Index

Note: Page numbers in *italics* refer to figures.